**ADULT EDUCATION AS
THEORY, PRACTICE AND RESEARCH**

RADICAL FORUM ON ADULT EDUCATION SERIES
Edited by Jo Campling, Series Consultant: Colin Griffin

Curriculum Theory in Adult Lifelong Education
Colin Griffin

Learning Liberation — Women's Response to Men's Education
Jane L. Thompson

Adult Education and Community Action
Tom Lovett, Chris Clarke and Avila Kimurray

Mutual Aid Universities
Edited by Eric Midwinter

Post-education Society
Norman Evans

*University Adult Education in England and the USA:
A Reappraisal of the Liberal Tradition*
Richard Taylor, Kathleen Rockhill and Roger Fieldhouse

Adult Education and Socialist Pedagogy
Frank Youngman

Adult Education and the Working Class
Kevin Ward and Richard Taylor

Educational Responses to Adult Unemployment
Barbara Senior and John Naylor

Class, Ideology and Community Education
Will Cowburn

Radical Approaches to Adult Education
Tom Lovett

Learning for Life: Politics and Progress in Recurrent Education
Edited by F. Molyneux, G. Low and G. Fowler

Women in Distance Education: International Perspectives
Edited by Karlene Faith

Adult Education as Theory, Practice and Research

THE CAPTIVE TRIANGLE

ROBIN USHER AND IAN BRYANT

ROUTLEDGE
London & New York

First published 1989
by Routledge
11 New Fetter Lane, London EC4P 4EE
29 West 35th Street, New York, NY 10001

© 1989 R. Usher and I. Bryant

Printed and bound in Great Britain by
Biddles Ltd, Guildford and King's Lynn

All rights reserved. No part of this book may be reprinted or
reproduced or utilized in any form or by any electronic, mechanical or
other means, now known or hereafter invented, including photocopying
and recording, or in any information storage or retrieval system, without
permission in writing from the publishers.

British Library Cataloguing in Publication Data
Usher, Robin. 1944–
   Adult education as theory, practice and research:
   the captive triangle. — (Radical forum on adult
   education series).
   1. Adult education.
   I. Title. II. Bryant, Ian. 1946– III. Series.
   374
   ISBN 0-415-02359-9
        0-415-03624-0 pbk

CONTENTS

1. Exploring the Triangle
   - Concerns and Content — 1
   - The 'Captive Triangle' — 4
   - Structure of the Book — 6
   - Reading the Text — 8

2. Critique of Traditional Models of Research
   - The Natural Science Paradigm — 10
   - The Post-empiricist Critique — 14
   - The Interpretive Paradigm — 23
   - The Interpretive Paradigm and Hermeneutic Understanding — 28

3. The Problem of 'Foundation' Disciplines
   - Introduction: Disciplines as Foundations — 41
   - Psychology as a Foundation Discipline — 43
   - Sociology as a Foundation Discipline — 54
   - The Problem of Foundations — 63

4. Reconceptualizing Theory and Practice
   - Theoretical and Practical Knowledge — 71
   - The Critique of Technical-Rationality — 74
   - Theoretical Knowledge and Values in Education — 77
   - Reconsidering the Nature of Practice — 79
   - The Limitations of Informal Theory — 83
   - The Implications for Educational Theory — 88

5. The Practice of Adult Education Research in Context
   - Introduction — 97
   - Conventional Representations of Research — 98
   - The Foundational and Institutional Language of Research — 100
   - Some Recent Research into Adult Education Participation — 104
   - The Formal and the Informal in Research and Practice — 111

6. The Logic and Problems of Action Research
   - Introduction — 116
   - The Impetus to Action Research and its Promise — 118
   - Action Research as Conventionally Understood — 119
   - Towards an Educational Understanding of Action Research — 124
   - Action Research as Reflective Practice — 130
   - Some Action Research in Practice — 141
   - The Requirements for Adult Education Action Research — 144

7. The Self in Research and Reflective Practice
   - Introduction — 148
   - The Self in the Research Arena — 150
   - The Self in Discourse — 154
   - Critical Thinking and Research as Engagement — 157
   - The Promise of 'New Paradigm' Research — 160
   - The Validity Issue — 165

8. Learning about Research: Curriculum Implications
   - Introduction — 169
   - 'Theory' in Adult Education as a Field of Study — 172
   - The Nature of Practical Knowledge — 179
   - Re-defining Theory in Adult Education — 184
   - Implications for Curriculum Design and Teaching — 188
   - Teaching and Experiencing Research — 192

Bibliography — 199
Index — 207

Chapter One

EXPLORING THE TRIANGLE

CONCERNS AND CONTENT

The overall purpose of this book is to examine the relationship between theory, practice, and research in adult education. The authors are themselves practitioners <u>within</u>, and theorists and researchers <u>of</u>, adult education. Our underlying assumptions are that there is a <u>unity</u> between theory, practice, and research, and that the need to constantly improve and enhance practice is best fulfilled by recognizing that unity and being aware of the consequences. The book is therefore concerned with these themes.

We take the view that improving and enhancing practice is a matter of its enrichment through <u>critical reflection</u>. This, however, inevitably involves an examination of both 'theory' and the place of research within practice. Research has been a recent growth phenomenon in adult and continuing education, and one of the problems is that we are trapped in inappropriate models and assumptions about the nature and purposes of research, the place of theory, and the relationship between these and practice. Our task, therefore, is to subject the models, assumptions, and conventional paradigms to critical scrutiny, and to suggest a more appropriate and helpful alternative.

In broad terms, our thesis is that adult education as a <u>field of study</u> (in which we include theorizing and researching) should be appropriately located in adult education as a <u>field of practice</u>. The latter, however, is notoriously difficult to write about because, in the main, it is something which we simply just go and 'do'. It is literally there and the practising adult educator invariably takes it as a given. Consequently, we see our task as one of examining the nature of practice, both in general terms and, more specifically, in terms of adult education. We have concentrated on two main themes. First, the 'situatedness' of practice and, second, the nature of the knowledge contained in practice. These themes are connected, since practical knowledge is always situational.

The context within which we write is that of adult education as an expanding field of practice which, nevertheless, urgently needs to understand its own situatedness or grounding. We would argue that adult education has its own integrity but that this is rarely understood reflexively. We therefore believe that without this understanding it will become increasingly difficult to defend and maintain the integrity of the field.

The most obvious characteristic of the expansion is its diversity. Adult education as a field of practice now manifests an almost bewildering variety of forms - staff development, professional updating, continuing vocational education, counselling, personal 'growth', adult basic education, in-house training, and community education. Potentially, the list is endless. Each of these areas is evolving its own particular practices, theories, and research procedures. Our concern, however, is to examine the relationship of practice, theory, and research against this background of growth and diversity in the field. Furthermore, we want to make the point that by examining the relationship we may be able to improve adult education as a field of study. In our view this is sorely needed.

Since the field of practice is extensive, it embraces many different types of practitioner. Although we do not intend to produce a practice or practitioner typology, one way of distinguishing between the latter is in terms of the consciousness of having an educational role in working with adults. At one end of the spectrum is the full-time 'professional' educator of adults, and at the other the individual whose vocational and non-vocational activities have repercussions for adult learning.

Our general conception of the situatedness of practice as such acknowledges that there are differences between practitioners' roles and, consequently, the specific 'meanings' of their practice as understood by themselves and others. These are matters for empirical investigation that are not considered here. However, we do anticipate that our arguments concerning the relationships between the theory and practice of adult education will provide different kinds of practitioner (and, hopefully, those who do not naturally see themselves as 'adult educators') with an opportunity to re-examine their own roles.

Given our concern for maintaining the integrity of adult education in all its diversity, we would not want this to be construed as a defence of the 'uniqueness' of adult education. Rather, we would stress that adult education is very much part of the world of education generally. In many significant respects, adult education is, of course, different from schooling - although, with the increasing institutionalization of adult education and the growth of forms of state-led and state-controlled provision, perhaps the differences are not as great as they were. None the less, a recognition of differences does not imply an acceptance of 'uniqueness'.

We would argue that the emphasis on uniqueness has not served adult education well. On the contrary, one could say that an essentialist defence of adult education has, in fact, contributed to its marginalization. This position is now changing, although whether the increased centrality of adult education is in an entirely benevolent direction is another matter. Perhaps because of this it is even more important for adult education to both see itself and be seen as part of the world of education. Accordingly, in our analysis of practice, theory, and research, we refer to education generically; only referring specifically to adult education on those occasions when a significant difference needs a distinctive emphasis.

There is, however, another aspect of 'uniqueness' which is perhaps less obvious but equally in need of critical analysis. In adult education as a field of study there has been an emphasis on the 'uniqueness' of the adult, particularly in relation to learning. It is maintained that the adult as learner has unique characteristics and that these should therefore be the basis upon which the field of study is constructed. In effect, and we examine this point in some detail during the course of the book, adult education is conflated to the psychology of learning and the sociology of the learner.

We recognize that psychology and sociology have a necessary place within the field of study. There is also a place, and an equal place, for other kinds of formal knowledge. It is important to recognize, however, that the appropriate place for any kind of formal knowledge is itself problematic. We would argue that such a problematization reveals that it is highly questionable to base adult education as a field of study on so-called 'foundation' disciplines.

Accordingly, our approach is not based on any particular discipline. Our analysis is not psychological or sociological. We are certainly not concerned to establish any psychological or sociological 'truths', although we are concerned to locate these and the practice of the disciplines within their enabling paradigms. If there is an approach, it is essentially 'philosophical' (although we would want to emphasize that we are not assuming philosophy to be a foundation discipline). Furthermore, although our approach is philosophical, the conceptual or linguistic analysis beloved of the Anglo-American empirical-analytical tradition will not be found here. Instead, the approach is essentially pragmatic and 'practical' in its concern for furthering critical reflection by exemplifying it.

An important theme in the book is the implication of practice with understanding and interpretation; the texts which have helped us most and to which we make extensive reference have therefore been those which have concerned themselves with these matters. We emphasize this not only to provide the reader with a background for our own understanding, but to explain why the 'standard' texts on adult education theory are not our reference point.

THE 'CAPTIVE TRIANGLE'

The sub-title of the book is intended to suggest an exploratory metaphor for understanding the relationship between practice, theory, and research. The metaphor is offered in order to depict the way in which each of these three elements of the triangle are conventionally represented in relation to each other and to (adult) education. One of the things we are trying to say is that we are 'captured' within a conventional and restricted understanding of the triangular relationship.

The idea of the 'triangle' represents what we wish to subject to critical and demystifying scrutiny, namely that theory and research are a foundation or base, with practice as superstructure or apex. This foundationalism implies that the relationship of theory and research to practice is always one where the former are applied to the latter. We are, therefore, 'captive' to application and ultimately foundationalism and we can only free ourselves from this if we first recognize the nature of our captivity.

Our rationale for the book as a whole is that we want readers to be able to use it as a vehicle for re-thinking and hopefully improving their practice, whether it be theorizing, researching, teaching, or any other form of practice. Our purpose, therefore, is to promote a new way of thinking about the three elements of the 'triangle' that does not privilege any one at the expense of the other(s). The idea is to help release the practitioner from the 'captivity' of the triangle. The metaphor also suggests that there is a 'captivation' about our conventional understandings, in so far as they offer a misleading and inappropriate promise that 'good' practice can be guaranteed by getting the theory 'right' or doing the 'right' kind of research.

Essentially, we are making certain kinds of general claims about the triangular relationship between practice, theory, and research; claims which, we believe, have implications for interpreting and thus 'opening-up' the varieties of practice. To do this it is necessary to 'open up' the triangle although this does not mean that we can ever dispense with it entirely. The elements of practice, theory, and research will always be there, and will always be in some relationship to one another. The important thing is not to privilege any one element by treating it as foundational. This also suggests a further consideration that, since the elements are always situated, we can never entirely escape from being 'captive'. This does not necessarily mean, however, that we can never improve our practice or increase our understanding; or, indeed, that we are stuck in a relativistic trap, triangular or otherwise! It simply means that we have to <u>recognize</u> our situatedness, and be prepared to engage in dialogue with our situation (with ourselves, and others) and with knowledge (in its variety of forms).

The title of the book refers to adult education as theory, practice, and research. The implication is that adult education as a field of study is constituted by (and therefore in) theory, practice, and research. Consequently, we have seen our task as one of deconstructing these three components for an enhanced understanding of the 'practical' in adult education. We have tried to 'open up' and recast the relationship because we believe that this is <u>educational in itself</u>. It is designed to bring about a 'better' understanding, in a pragmatic sense, of what adult education practice could be and very often is. The hope is, therefore, that the 'opening-up' on behalf of adult education will help serve the idea and 'ideal' of reflective, critical practice.

There are two particular aspects of this which we would stress. The first is that, given our emphasis on reflective, critical practice, we would wish to encourage a 'coming-together' of practitioner and researcher, and of research and practice. Equally, this book helps to sensitize the would-be practitioner/researcher to what is actually involved in undertaking such an activity. Second, we hope that any practitioner involved in teaching adults will, through the 'opening-up', undertake reflective research on their own practice and thus be better able to evaluate critically the nature of their own and fellow practitioners' knowledge claims.

STRUCTURE OF THE BOOK

The following is a brief summary of each chapter, offered as a guide to what the reader can expect. We would emphasize that the book can be read as a continuous narrative or as a series of discrete chapters. The book has been consciously written this way to provide the reader with maximum flexibility. Each chapter has a distinctive theme which can 'stand alone' but which has links to other chapters and to the overall theme of the book.

Chapter 2 is a critical examination of traditional models of research. In particular, we focus on the 'natural science' model which takes research as a linear and applicative process where the findings of research become part of an accumulating stock of formal knowledge. We show how contemporary critiques have undermined this model and introduce the notion of research as a social practice guided by paradigms. This is a key interpretive concept which we use throughout the book. The critique of the 'natural science' model suggests an alternative interpretive model which places practice, theory, and research in social contexts and stresses the importance of hermeneutic understanding.

Chapter 3 looks at two disciplines, psychology and sociology, which feature prominently in adult education as 'foundation' disciplines. In the case of psychology we undertake an exercise in 'deconstruction' designed to show that, given the nature of the formal knowledge of 'scientific' psychology, there is an incompatibility with all forms of educational practice. This means, therefore, that it is inappropriate to see psychology as a 'foundation' or 'base' to be <u>applied</u> to education. Within this general theme we argue that <u>sociology</u> cannot be specifically applied to adult education, and we highlight the way in which the discourse of sociologists and practitioners may appear to have the same reference points but, in reality, do not. This then leads on to a critique of foundations in general and a questioning of whether foundations are required in any case.

<u>Chapter 4</u> is concerned with the long-standing problem of the nature of the relationship between theory and practice. We attempt to 're-present' the relationship in a way compatible with the nature of adult education. This involves a problematization of both 'theory' and practice, leading to the introduction of the idea of 'informal' practitioner-based theory and the claim that, because of the existence of this form of theory, practice should not be seen merely as a routine, 'mindless' activity.

<u>Chapter 5</u> considers the claim commonly made that research as an activity provides the link between theory and practice. This chapter is concerned with examining some key pieces of adult education research. First, an example of formal survey research is analysed to show how the foundational and institutional language of research <u>constitutes</u> the objects it purports to discover. An example of research using a grounded theory approach is then considered, to show how this mode of inquiry actually does identify an important dimension to adult learning, one which is neglected by other approaches. These issues are finally considered in relation to the formal and informal dimensions of knowledge production through both research and practice.

<u>Chapter 6</u> looks at 'action research' as a preferred mode of inquiry in adult education and the reasons for this. An examination of some of the justifications offered by its proponents are found wanting because they do not necessarily lead to the development of reflective practice by practitioners. The problem of 'distorted communication' in relation to dialogue is considered and the potential contribution of 'critical theory' to an educational understanding and justification of action research is discussed. Some of the real problems in conducting action research are exemplified through setting out the requirements for adult education as a reflective practice.

<u>Chapter 7</u> considers the 'self' in the research process as

conventionally understood from an interactionist perspective. This has helped in appreciating the totality of research as a practice in terms of the management of (potential) role conflict. The 'self' is considered as a sense-making, interpreting participant and knowledge-claimant within the research process. It is argued that a recognition of the situatedness of all understanding in research and practice is a pre-condition for fulfilling the promise of so-called 'new paradigm' research for adult education.

Chapter 8 has two main themes. The first is concerned to argue that adult education as a field of study must be located in the 'practical'. The second is a critical examination of current 'theory' in adult education. The two themes are related to the idea that teaching and learning about research must start with practitioner-based theory but must also include a critical dimension in the light of the constitutive power of ideology. The implications for curriculum design and implementation within the professional formation of adult educators is considered, with particular reference to the appropriate place of 'formal' theory.

READING THE TEXT

It might seem odd, perhaps, to be offering advice on how to read this text. However, we do so both in order to ensure that there is no misunderstanding as to exactly what this book is about and because of the nature of the arguments we are putting forward within it.

First, we would emphasize that this book is not about research methods nor is it a manual on 'how to do' research. We are not offering preferred versions of theory or research methods but a means for thinking about and 're-visualising' practice through a fresh and critical examination of its theoretical and procedural groundings. In effect, we are offering conceptual resources which adult educators can draw upon and adapt to their own purposes. We are inviting readers to 'think along' with us and use what we say pragmatically.

Second, we argue for an interpretive understanding which can facilitate reflective practice and thus, hopefully, refine and improve that practice. As a consequence, we cannot offer final and definitive arguments and conclusive, firmly established 'truths'. Instead, we would like the reader to examine our arguments from the point of view of their own situatedness as 'doers' of practice, theory, and research.

We continually advocate the need for dialogue. Equally, our text is an <u>invitation</u> to dialogue. We would expect readers to recognize their own situatedness, just as we have tried to recognize ours as adult educators within the academy. Given this, it is impossible for us to be definitive and to provide a secure foundation, since it is precisely this that we have sought to criticize. However, what we can hope for through this dialogue is to bring about a 'fusion of horizons' which can enhance both understanding and practice.

In this way, adult educators can put themselves in touch with the 'captive triangle'; they can explore its parameters and situate themselves within it. As readers and interpreters of this text, adult educators can also 'step out' of the immediate concerns of practice in the many forms it takes - theory building, teaching, conducting research, programme planning, policy making, etc. A general and holistic perspective on practice can be adopted which helps develop an understanding of the details and specifics of practice that is informed by a view of the whole - the hermeneutic circle in action! In effect, we return to a point made earlier concerning the need to open up the 'captive triangle', to look at it from new perspectives and return to practice in all its forms with a new sense of possibility. Then, perhaps, the 'triangle' will not be quite so 'captive' after all!

Chapter Two

CRITIQUE OF TRADITIONAL MODELS OF RESEARCH

THE NATURAL SCIENCE PARADIGM

Research is conventionally thought to be the means of systematically discovering truths about the world. Its characteristics are that it is conducted in a systematic and controlled way, that it is empirical in the sense that its results must be experientially validated, and thus continually open to refutation or modification (Cohen and Manion, 1985). This conventional portrayal, which defines the nature of research in the natural sciences, is a very powerful one. It has tended to be seen as the norm to which all research, including educational research, should aspire. We will characterize it as the natural science paradigm.

This paradigm contains a number of core assumptions, one of which is that there is a real world external to and independent of individuals. Knowledge of this world can be discovered empirically using proper methods and procedures. Knowledge, although potentially accessible to individuals, is 'objective' and 'out there'. The conditions for obtaining knowledge are essentially concerned with eliminating bias and value-commitment, indeed subjectivity of any kind. This is to allow knowledge of the world to be distinguished from mere belief or opinion and to thus be warranted or well-founded because it truly 'mirrors' the reality of the world.

These assumptions have certain implications for research. First, the purpose of research is to produce theory as a generalized explanation of the world. Theory is universal in scope and not contextually bound. Although the researcher works with particulars, the aim is to arrive at generalizations consisting of statements of law-like regularities which describe and, more importantly, explain the world. This is clearly illustrated in the use of the hypothetico-deductive method of inquiry where hypotheses are formulated in general terms from which particular inferences (deductions) are drawn. These can then be judged in terms of their correspondence with observational and experimental outcomes. The process, therefore, is one which consists of generalizations tested against observed outcomes (the 'facts' of what actually happened).

Second, the research process consists of formulating hypotheses and validating them in terms of whether they do or do not fit the facts (gathered through neutral and disinterested observation). If the hypothesis fits the facts, it is plausible and can be reasonably held; if not, then it is decisively refuted, and no reasonable grounds can exist for entertaining it. Research therefore consists of establishing knowledge about the world which is empirically validated. In this scheme there is no room for goals, purposes, and values, other than the disinterested pursuit of truth! As Popkewitz puts it: 'the statements of science are believed to be independent of the goals and values which people may express within a situation' (Popkewitz, 1984:37). The purpose of research is to accumulate knowledge about the world as it is, not as it ought to be. Furthermore, in finding out about the world, researchers must put aside their own feelings and values. They must concentrate on what they find, regardless of what they think or believe about their inquiry and its outcomes. The impersonality of science and its universalistic explanations can only be guaranteed by the impersonality and value neutrality of the researcher. Method, approach, and attitude are therefore inseparable.

Natural science seeks not only to describe but also to explain the world and does so by using a 'deductive-nomological' mode of explanation. A feature of the world (let us call it X) can be explained by showing how X necessarily follows from the combination of statements of a universal law and certain particular conditions. Essentially, therefore, to explain X is to bring it under a universal law; hence the explanation is nomological. The explanation can be deduced (i.e. it follows logically) from the law and the statement of conditions. So long as the conditions are present, then X (since it is a sub-species of a universal regularity) must be explainable by the latter.

This mode of explanation contains a number of further assumptions and implications. One is that the universal law is itself empirically validated and truly universal so that it is, in effect, a statement of necessary connections between experiential phenomena. To explain, therefore, is to refer to causes; if the situation described by the conditions exists, then it will 'cause' X. It is part of a 'necessary connection' in the world described by the universal law. The deductive-nomological mode of explanation clearly implies, therefore, that the world is causally patterned and thus events and phenomena can be explained. This is vital to the natural science paradigm since it implies that the external world can be uncovered. As the world is not random and arbitrary, it can be understood. Knowledge of the regularity and patterning can be accumulated in the form of universal laws through research.

This also provides the means to predict the world. To explain why something happens is to also predict that it will happen, since prediction requires no additional knowledge. Indeed, it would make no sense to say that one could explain but was unable to predict. The deductive-nomological mode can both explain retrospectively and predict prospectively (Anderson et al., 1986). The ability to predict is enormously important because it makes possible the ability to control. Again, the same knowledge involved in explanation and prediction enables control; if Y can be explained in terms of X then it is possible to predict and control Y because one knows when Y will occur and under what conditions. Research, therefore, through enabling prediction and control is a vital tool in decision-making and policy. As Fay (1987) points out, causal knowledge of the world enables successful intervention in the world. It leads to an instrumentalist conception of knowledge and of the theory-practice relationship which will be examined in later chapters.

However, although 'lawful', the world is none the less complex, and the researcher cannot proceed without simplifying this complexity to render it manageable for inquiry. The 'variable' as the operational unit in research facilitates manageability; variables are taken to be distinct from one another, each having invariant meaning. Research proceeds by postulating 'dependent' and 'independent' variables and showing how one influences the other. Those variables which constitute the focus of inquiry can be manipulated, whilst others which might bias the results are held 'constant' so that their influence can be assessed and therefore discounted.

Quantification allows variables to be measured.

However, the emphasis on quantification is not just a matter of making research more systematic through eliminating ambiguities and facilitating empirical testing. It is an essential part of the 'lawful' matrix which constitutes the world view of the natural science paradigm. If the world as postulated is essentially a mechanistic one, then quantification is not only a procedure for understanding but also reflects the objectivity and exactness of that world, hence providing a <u>warrant</u> for the veracity of explanations.

The main purpose of research, therefore, is through the use of appropriate methods, to construct an edifice of systematic knowledge comprising statements of universal laws which have been empirically derived and tested. This systematic knowledge is 'theory'. Theory can be seen as grouped concepts which provide a systematic view of the world through a postulated relationship between certain variables, and thus designed to explain that world (Kerlinger, 1970).

Theory is a means of organizing and making sense of the external world and, most important, a dynamic source of further research. Theory, therefore enables at one and the same time explanation, prediction, control, and the self-correction of research through new inquiry and new discoveries. It is both the vehicle for accumulating secure knowledge and yet, because of its provisional status, is also the means by which knowledge can be continuously changed.

This provisionality follows from the empirical assumptions of the natural science paradigm. Any universal law must be capable of inferences testable by appeal to the objective world. This means therefore that, in principle, every theory supposedly contains within itself the means of its disconfirmation. The hypotheses generated by theory must be able to withstand the test of disconfirmation; if they cannot, they are then invalid and the theory must be rejected. Even if hypotheses continually withstand disconfirmation, the status of theory is still provisional, since a theory could never encompass <u>all</u> that can <u>ever</u> be known about even a small part of the external world. It is a feature of the dynamic of research and the never-ending accumulation of knowledge that, in principle, theories are continually in the process of being replaced - not because they have been proved wrong but because alternative theories are formulated which are more sophisticated in their scope and/or more elegant in their formulations. Such alternatives are able to explain that part of the world they purport to investigate, encompassing more of the facts within a more generalized and often more simplified structure.

The natural science paradigm runs into serious problems both as an explanatory paradigm of the nature of natural science and its adequacy as a model for social, including educational, inquiry. Before examining this more closely it is worth emphasizing a feature which many working within the natural science paradigm have drawn attention to. Kerlinger refers to research as a 'controlled, rational process of reflective inquiry'. We would not question this but merely make the point that it is reflection of a particular kind which takes place in certain conditions and with a very specific purpose. We should not, therefore, see it as universally appropriate although it is the case that this is the way it is seen by those working within the natural science paradigm.

THE POST-EMPIRICIST CRITIQUE

Within the natural science paradigm, the predominant image of science is that of an evolutionary, cumulative, and linear construction of theoretical knowledge. Through research, new universal laws are discovered, new facts brought to light, and new theories formulated. Every discovery builds on what has gone before and the stock of knowledge grows progressively over time. As we have noted earlier, this image of science is linked to a conception of the researcher as objective and value-neutral, pursuing the truth using rational procedures and committed only to the discovery of valid knowledge. However, this image of science has been subjected to a root-and-branch critique from which it has never fully recovered. Although it cannot be solely attributed to Kuhn (1970), the post-empiricist critique (as it became known) is, in a sense, exemplified by his work and, in what follows, we shall draw extensively from it. We shall also refer to the inevitable counter-critique which has emerged.

Kuhn's purpose was to show that the natural science paradigm was limited and unrealistic in its image of science and in its depiction of the process of scientific inquiry. Scientists, he claimed, work within paradigms which provide a framework for understanding the world and rules and methods for conducting inquiry. Consequently, a paradigm defines its own conception of the world and thus the range and kinds of problems which require investigation. In essence, it defines the boundaries of investigation. Kuhn characterized the situation where such a stable paradigm exists, as 'normal science'. In conducting 'normal science', however, 'anomalies' increasingly emerge which resist solution. As more and more 'anomalies' emerge, a 'crisis' is precipitated and the dominant paradigm is increasingly brought into question. Eventually a rival paradigm is proposed and a struggle commences between the proponents of the new paradigm and the established paradigm which is now no longer stable. The struggle may end with a scientific 'revolution' or paradigm 'shift' where the established paradigm is overthrown.

This view of the nature of scientific inquiry has a number of important implications. First, a paradigm is, in a sense, 'all embracing'. It generates a particular view of the world, such that any theory formulated through 'normal science' is both a response to the problems that are defined by the paradigm and must comprise knowledge compatible with the paradigm's view of the world. Second, it functions as a 'disciplinary matrix' (Anderson et al., 1986), defining the kind of work carried out within a science or discipline. Third, a paradigm constitutes an exemplar. This is the idea of 'paradigm as achievement', where a paradigm shift is associated with some 'exemplary success in solving an old problem in a completely new way using new concepts' (Hacking, 1983:10). This then becomes a model or exemplar for the new paradigm.

Within a scientific revolution, the struggle between rival paradigms is not conducted at the level of universal logic or reason. Kuhn compares scientific to political revolutions, emphasizing that the choice between paradigms is not ultimately decided by 'proving' that one paradigm is logically superior to another or that it 'explains' the evidence better. Rather, the process is compared to a 'gestalt switch'. Paradigms are 'incommensurable' and literally 'slice up' the world differently; their interpretations of reality are different, so that, after a paradigm shift, the same world is seen differently.

Paradigms are located within communities of research practitioners who accept a paradigm as their own and adopt its framework of understanding and rules of investigation. Equally, a scientific revolution is presaged by the formation of a new community of practitioners, united in their dissatisfaction with the established paradigm and its failure to resolve anomalies. This implies, therefore, that all paradigms (including the natural science paradigm) and their associated frameworks, rules, and methods are socially located and products of particular social and historical contexts.

A crucial consequence of Kuhn's socio-historical approach, which Carr and Kemmis (1986) emphasize, is that research as a social practice takes place in a community of research practitioners, which in most cases will be institutionally organized and where paradigm acceptance occurs through initiation and socialization. The dominant paradigm will define certain beliefs, values and attitudes and generate sets of expectations, all of which will guide the thoughts and actions of members of the research community. Researchers are not isolated individuals, disinterestedly pursuing the 'truth'. Rather they pursue a 'truth' which is commensurate with a dominant paradigm's framework of understanding and within a context of expectations and values prescribed by that framework. This relates to the point made earlier about reflective inquiry. This does occur, but in 'normal' times will be related only to the specific 'problems' identified by the exemplars, not to questioning the paradigm and its assumptions or the validity of work done. As Dreyfus and Rabinow point out, 'normal' science is concerned with the accumulation of knowledge 'where knowledge means accuracy of prediction, number of different problems solved ... not truths about how things are in themselves' (Dreyfus and Rabinow, 1982:198).

Since paradigms are socially located and produced, then so also will be the knowledge generated. When a paradigm 'shift' occurs, the process, as we have seen, is one of 'conversion' where the world is seen differently. Kuhn refers to 'incompatible modes of community life' and points out that paradigms are defended with arguments <u>from</u> the paradigm.

Choosing between paradigms is a matter of altering fundamental beliefs and values and thus switching allegiance from one community of practitioners to another. Doing research, therefore, is always value-laden - it is never merely the value-neutral process of 'scientific method'. It presupposes a commitment to a particular view of the world which in the end is justified by a set of values, and not by an appeal to the facts or to experience. Clearly, therefore, this calls into question the very foundations of the natural science paradigm with its emphasis on objective knowledge and value-neutral research, and thus its claimed superiority as a model of research.

Hanson (1958) had claimed, even before Kuhn, that observation (the basis of empirical validation) was paradigm-dependent. This is supported by Kuhn's argument that observations are made in the context of a paradigm's framework of understanding. The natural science paradigm postulates that our knowledge of the world is direct and unmediated - our experience gives us access to the world, and knowledge (constructed from experience) is therefore discovered.

If observation is theory-laden then there is no secure theory-neutral grounding for knowledge. To investigate something in the world we need to have a theory about what that something is and how we are to go about investigating it. The 'facts' that emerge from investigation do not constitute neutral descriptions of the world as it is - rather, 'facts' are constituted by the prior theory which make observation possible. As we have already seen, theories (in the sense of frameworks of understanding) can change, as paradigms change. Since paradigm shifts involve fundamental changes in frameworks, and thus in 'new' theories, then these shifts can lead to new observations. In order to see things in new ways we do not therefore need new observations but new theories which are, however, always paradigm-dependent.

Theory is unproblematic if it is implicitly accepted that observation is unproblematic. This leads to the seeming paradox that every advance in knowledge reinforces the underlying framework. The natural science paradigm has inherently conservative tendencies, in the sense that knowledge is always taken as something outside social practices whose validity is never a matter of social consensus but of correspondence with the truth and an accurate mirroring of reality. However, these tendencies extend beyond its epistemology and methodology. By never examining locating social contexts, it takes research and the nature of the world which is the object of that research as a given:

> the results it produces simply reinforce and legitimise its presuppositions, namely that certain social conditions and relations are given and natural.
> (Harris, 1979:17)

It is this aspect which has led to the claim that the natural science paradigm portrays an image of science as ideology. Certainly, the process of induction into a paradigm, with its emphasis on faith rather than reason and the shifting of paradigms being more a matter of 'conversion' than of logic, would strongly support this. At the same time, since the natural science paradigm is both epistemologically and socially conservative in its implications and consequences yet conceals this through emphasizing universality, objectivity, value-neutrality, and rationality, the case would appear to be strong. At the least, it seems incontrovertible that research within the natural science paradigm is always conducted within a framework of values whose nature and consequences are never explicitly acknowledged.

Naturally, the post-empiricist critique has not itself been without critics. An important element has been the claim that post-empiricism leads directly and inexorably to a relativistic morass, and in so doing reflexively dissolves itself in common with all relativistic positions. Critics have maintained that, although knowledge is not based on the security of neutral observation, we must distinguish between how knowledge is originated and how it is justified. In terms of the latter, the theory-ladenness of observation, it is claimed, does not affect the status of knowledge. As D.C. Phillips puts it, 'in order to test or validate a theory one must use that theory's way of seeing the world' (Phillips, 1987:10). As an example, he gives Freudian theory, which would be tested through its own categories rather than say those of Skinnerian theory. Furthermore, the objective testing of a theory is still possible because, even if we see the world through observation in a way constrained by theory, it does not follow that 'the world is thereby bound to confirm that theory' (Phillips, 1987:10).

This raises an important point about testing which places the argument distinguishing origination from justification on somewhat shaky ground. As we have seen, values are at the very foundation of research. Being a member of a research community demands commitment to the value positions of the paradigm and its framework of understanding. These therefore influence not only the way in which knowledge is originated through observation but also the way in which it is justified. The selection of problems is determined by the paradigm, and anomalies are normally accommodated either through ignoring them or, if they persist, through adjusting the paradigm. Even the way in which knowledge is justified is not therefore value-neutral and objective. D.C. Phillips recognizes this when he says:

> A theory that does not necessitate a precise set of observational consequences can never be decisively probed by any test for there must always been some leeway or looseness that would allow the scientist to argue that the theory was somehow compatible with the test results.
> (Phillips, 1987:11)

In other words, no test can be 'absolutely authoritative'.

If there are different frameworks of understanding, and thus different frameworks for constituting the facts of the world as 'facts', then what is found in the world is open to a variety of interpretations. As Harris puts it, 'instances or phenomena can be picked out by many theories (even competing and conflicting ones)' (Harris, 1979:39). In research terms, this means that:

> theories are underdetermined by evidence. Whatever evidence is available a variety of theories can exist that are compatible with it; furthermore as new evidence accumulates there are a variety of ways in which everyone of these competing theories could be adjusted in order to take account of new material.
> (Phillips, 1987:12)

Changes in theory are not compelled by changes in facts or evidence and no theory can therefore be conclusively proved or refuted by appeal to the facts alone. This seems ultimately to question whether knowledge has any rational warrant at all. The stock response to this has always been that knowledge is justified when it is based on 'good arguments, relevant observations, and solid experimental results' (Phillips, 1987:18). Unfortunately, the criteria upon which arguments can be judged as 'good', observations 'relevant', etc. are themselves not objective and value-neutral.

This 'best available' response does not really provide an answer. If investigation of the world is through frameworks of understanding that describe categories, then the 'best available' is itself the product of certain social-historical contexts within which these frameworks and theories are located. There would appear to be nothing outside of this to which we could appeal in judging what is the 'best available'.

This is related to Kuhn's notion of the incommensurability of paradigms. The most common interpretation is that no rational communication, and hence no rational resolution of disagreements, is possible across paradigms. Consequently, there are no criteria which exist outwith a framework that would allow disagreements as to what is the 'best available' to be resolved - in other words, there is no impartial and final court of appeal. The 'best available' is only the best relative to a particular paradigm.

This seems to point incontrovertibly to relativism. All knowledge appears to be relative to particular frameworks of understanding which are contingent and contextual. Concepts such as rationality, truth and reality 'must be understood as relative to a specific conceptual scheme, theoretical framework, paradigm, form of life, society or culture' (Bernstein, 1985:8).

If rationality is relative to paradigms, then it would appear that there is no such thing as a final rational justification. In that case, the same argument could apply to the post-empiricist position and we would, therefore, have no rational grounds for accepting this position. We may accept it as a matter of faith but we could not accept it on the grounds that it was true. This argument against relativism, that it reflexively undermines itself, is a familiar one in philosophy. A relativist would presumably wish his argument to be taken as true, yet if truth is relative it could also be false. As Bernstein points out 'relativistic arguments could be both true and false simultaneously - clearly an impossible situation' (Bernstein, 1985:9). On the face of it, therefore, there would appear to be both an absence of certainty and secure grounds for knowledge, and also no overarching criteria for rationality; yet, on the other hand, acceptance of such a position appears to be not only impossible but unrealistic.

A post-empiricist position need not inevitably lead to this kind of relativism. Whilst knowledge, for example, is in a significant sense created and not merely discovered, it does not follow that anything goes! Whilst theories may well be underdetermined by the evidence, this does not mean that all theories are either equally acceptable or equally problematic. There are theories which have successfully withstood challenge over a long period of time and there are many observations which, although they may, in principle, be open to question, are not actually in that position at this point in time and may never be so. Acceptance, therefore, is rational, although the criteria for this may not be those defined by the natural science paradigm.

We can exemplify this argument through Kuhn's incommensurability thesis. Is it really the case that Kuhn is saying that practitioners with different paradigms <u>literally</u> cannot understand one another, that they have no way of conducting a rational discussion? This seems an extreme position which has been rightly criticized. Although paradigms will differ in important respects, there will be other and equally important ways where they will overlap. Alternative paradigms can be discussed and, although there will be failure to <u>agree</u>, it does not follow that there will be failure to <u>understand</u>.

According to Bernstein, Kuhn is challenging the notion that we can know in advance a 'set of rules' which will rationally decide any disagreement and which is essential to research and enquiry. Even though there is overlap between paradigms, this does not require the prior assumption of a 'something' (the set of rules?) which permanently exists and which allows comparisons between paradigms to be made. So he denies the existence of a universal 'framework' which stands over and above all other frameworks thus providing the standard of commensuration.

Bernstein concludes from this that Kuhn is not saying that 'science is irrational but rather that something is fundamentally wrong with the idea that commensurability is the essence of scientific rationality' (Bernstein, 1985:86). In other words, Kuhn's target is a <u>particular variety of rationality</u> and <u>a particular view of action</u>. Bernstein puts it this way:

> in the modern world the only concept of reason that seems to make sense is one in which we think of reason as an instrument for determining the most efficient and effective means to a determinate end and ... the only concept of activity that seems viable is one of technical application, manipulation and control
> (Bernstein, 1985:46)

Kuhn is suggesting that there is another kind of rationality, another kind of reasoning which is appropriate not only in the 'human' or social sciences but in the natural sciences also. This alternative rationality is <u>practical</u>

reasoning, which is concerned with right action in particular contexts. It is about making choices in a context where ends are not 'determinate' and value conflicts exist about both ends and means. In practical reasoning there is no master set of rules which are simply applied to situations and which unequivocally determine what action is to be taken in those situations. Where general rules do exist they must be mediated through human interpretation. Judgement is therefore crucial and disagreement inevitable. However, the resolution of disagreement is intrinsic to practical reason but does not involve 'an appeal to precisely formulated determinate rules' (Bernstein, 1985:55). The process is different but not irrational, since reasons must be given to <u>support</u> (not to <u>prove</u>) judgements. The reasons, however, are needed to make a <u>good case</u> rather than establish unassailable foundations. What is a 'good case' will depend on the context rather than a set of universal rules.

Incommensurability does not mean that those who hold opposing paradigms cannot communicate with one another or that their commitment to their paradigm is essentially irrational, in the sense of an arbitrary, personal preference. Disagreement between holders of rival paradigms cannot be settled by appeal to a set of universal 'master' rules but they can be discussed and sometimes resolved. The process involved utilizes practical reasoning and pragmatic criteria. This means that the relativistic morass can be avoided. According to Bernstein, 'the "truth" of the incommensurability thesis is not closure but <u>open-ness</u>' (Bernstein, 1985:91). Practical reasoning is concerned with interpretation, understanding, and <u>justification</u> - through communication and dialogue. It must assume openness. As soon as we attempt to justify our positions and our choices, as soon as we try to settle differences pragmatically, we are moving <u>outside</u> our relativistic frameworks.

In the final analysis, the issue of incommensurability is not confined simply to paradigm shifts since how we see this has profound implications not only for our understanding of natural science but for our understanding of the nature of research and its relationship to practice. Earlier we referred to the natural science paradigm as a species of ideology which posited a particular view of scientific method, valid knowledge and 'proper' research. The debate over incommensurability demonstrates this even more clearly. The claim is to universal scope, sure access to knowledge and truth, and an exclusive legitimacy for its mode of rationality. By conjuring up the fear of subjectivity, irrationality, and relativism as the only alternative, it could also be seen as an oppressive ideology which imprisons research in a constraining positivistic straitjacket of spurious 'scientific' respectability - 'spurious' because it is questionable as an accurate portrayal of what natural scientists actually do in conducting research and constructing knowledge.

THE INTERPRETIVE PARADIGM

The natural science paradigm has not remained unchallenged. With the development of the social sciences, the main thrust of the challenge has come from within an interpretive paradigm which questions the appropriateness of the natural sciences as a model for the social sciences. This usually involves a rejection of the view that explanation and 'scientific method' in the social sciences takes the same form as in the natural sciences.

The attack has concentrated on the positivist features of the natural science paradigm, as revealed in the degeneration of research into a naive empiricism concerned only with hypothetico-deductive processes and supportive data collection. This reveals a naivety in terms of what counts as data and inquiry (Anyon, 1982) and is part of the wider critique of a positivism emphasizing the supremacy of the methods and modes of explanation of empiricist natural science.

The natural science paradigm has been criticized for its underlying model of man, in particular the failure to recognize the capacity of human beings not only to experience the world but also to interpret it, to impose meanings on it, by representing the world through the medium of symbolic systems such as language. This itself presupposes the existence of a social order and social interaction. Society can, therefore, be seen as being 'created in and through meanings' (Hughes, 1980:123). The interpretive paradigm portrays the individual as part of a social world, quite unlike the isolated asocial individual of the natural science paradigm. Individuals 'create' society through their practices and the meanings or understandings that they give them.

The possession of consciousness differentiates human beings, from other objects in nature. They are capable of reflecting on that consciousness and changing it as a result. This has important implications for research. At the very least, it implies that human beings cannot be experimented on as if they were inanimate objects. It is not just simply a matter of ethics, for the existence of consciousness throws the validity of the results of experimentation into serious doubt. Consciousness and its effects are a 'variable' which the experimenter can never hope to control or eliminate from consideration. This in itself has implications for the claims made by psychology to be a 'science'.

The interpretive paradigm is concerned with 'interpretation' and 'understanding' as against 'explanation'. It is not concerned with uncovering law-like regularities but with understanding social life 'as created and sustained through symbolic interactions and patterns of conduct' (Popkewitz, 1984:40). The emphasis is on interpreting the 'rules' and meanings which are both produced by and at the same time regulate social life.

An important aspect is the emphasis on 'action' and 'interaction'. Action is distinguished from behaviour because it always has a subjective meaning attached to it which requires interpretation. This involves understanding the <u>intention</u> of the individual in performing the action. Actions are embedded in a social context, they are neither random nor private but have a social character and can only be identified as a particular kind of action within the context of a set of social rules which define that action. Since actions are performative they must be located in 'ways of living' or 'forms of life'. In other words, a social order provides the norms or criteria for judging the rightness or adequacy of actions (Heaton, 1979).

Actions have subjective meanings but these are socially located. Interpretation therefore involves not only elucidating <u>intentions</u> but also the social rules, norms and language which constitute the pre-given frameworks of understanding and structure - the intentions of individuals. <u>The subjective can only be understood in terms of its location within a social context.</u>

The meaning attached to action by individuals takes account of the actions of others; action is therefore reciprocal and meanings are interactive. Meaning attribution is a dynamic process where negotiation is the norm. In any social situation the sets of rules which define actions are both maintained and modified as people within those situations interact and therefore continually and

Critique of Traditional Models

reciprocally modify their expectations about each other's actions.

In the interpretive paradigm, therefore, the concern is to understand the subjective world of human experience, particularly the generation of subjective meanings. For example, humanistic psychology attempts to understand the subjective world of active, goal-oriented human beings in all its dimensions. The social rules that structure the experiences and actions of human beings, and through which they make sense of the world, are the subject of research. The aim is therefore not to generate 'causal explanations of human life but to deepen and extend our knowledge of why social life is perceived and experienced in the way it is' (Carr and Kemmis, 1986:90).

A different notion of causation is used which stresses the centrality of intention. As Popkewitz points out, 'cause' is used in the 'in order to' sense rather than the 'because of' sense of the natural science paradigm. An action is performed 'in order to' bring something about - in other words it was 'caused' by the intention rather than any temporal antecedent event or object. Objectivity is redefined in terms of intersubjective agreement. The rules generated through social life are consensual norms which allow for things to be defined in intersubjective ways and the consensus defines 'objectivity'. This raises two important points. The first is the conventionality of concepts such as 'objectivity'. A procedure or method is 'objective' not because it adheres to some universal and external criteria but because it is conventionally so defined by social consensus. Implicitly, this leaves open the possibility that at some point it may cease to be so or, at the least, that a particular kind of objectivity is not part of the natural order. The second is the link between intersubjective agreement and social consensus and our earlier discussion about practical reasoning as an alternative mode of rationality, emphasizing communication and dialogue.

If the purpose of theory is to understand socially located meanings then this has certain implications for research. First, since deductive-nomological modes of explanation are avoided, research does not consist of starting with a theory (a universal law) and then trying to find evidence to support it. Instead, the idea is to ground theory in social interaction; it thus emerges from research rather than precedes it. Second, research is directed towards the generation of theory which seeks to elucidate and understand specific forms of social life; as such, its methods tend toward the qualitative rather than the quantitative. Third, the validity of the theory generated by qualitative research is not to be judged in terms of external and consensual criteria of rationality but in terms of its coherence, consistency, interpretive power, and whether it makes sense to those whom it is researching. As a consequence, therefore, theory can help people to understand themselves better and, through this, to change themselves. Finally, since research is not concerned with finding universal laws but rather with an understanding of sets of rules contextually located, then the approach is essentially ideographic, emphasizing the particular and the specific. There is no one theory but many which 'are likely to be as diverse as the sets of human meanings and understandings which they are to explain' (Cohen and Manion, 1985:40).

A key criticism of the interpretive paradigm is the emphasis on 'subjective meanings' and 'interactions' which, it is felt, neglects the influence of social structure. The latter may actually inhibit the way in which social reality is constructed through interaction and limit the range of meanings which individuals can give to their actions. It is not enough, therefore, merely to look at interactions and the meanings they produce. Individuals not only give meanings they also take them. According to Bernstein, the meanings of situations may well be negotiated but this presupposes a structure of meanings outside the negotiation. For instance, within social situations, some individuals may have the power to impose their meanings on others, either directly or indirectly. However, there may be more to understanding social life than understanding the meanings which individuals give to it.

In focusing on the meanings given to actions, and the negotiated definitions of the meanings of social situations, there is an implicit assumption that the descriptions which individuals give of their actions always 'mesh' with the actions themselves. If this is not the case, however, then these 'understandings and explanations may be no more than rationalisations that obscure the true nature of their situation and mask reality in some important way' (Carr and Kemmis, 1986:96). Furthermore, the need for theory to make sense to those whom it purports to understand may simply result in accounts that merely describe people's habits, prejudices, and common-sense understandings.

Research methods which rely heavily on the use of verbal accounts to elucidate meanings can be criticized on these grounds.

Finally, it has been said that the interpretive paradigm still has one major point of similarity with the natural science paradigm (despite all their differences), in that both do not use knowledge of the world to change the world. Both see theory as essentially formal and neutral. As Popkewitz puts it 'interpretive theories are not thought of as a necessary catalyst within which the social complex of life is confronted' (Popkewitz, 1984:43). Theory is contemplative, it is designed to facilitate reflection and communication, and its relationship to change is indirect. Through the interpretive understanding provided by theory, individuals may initiate change. But this is a value commitment, or preference, on their part which is in no way prescribed by theory. In principle, therefore, theory can change consciousness but may not provide the means for changing the social reality in which that consciousness is located. There is no mutually interactive link between theory, consciousness, and social reality.

If theory is limited to understanding the meanings given by interacting individuals, then it seems unable to account for the effect of ideology. This seems a serious constraint, given the power of ideology to shape meanings in ways in which the individual is not always aware. Consciousness may be changed but people may cling to their meanings. There is a paradox here, in the sense that the natural science paradigm is an ideology which cannot recognize itself as such. However, it does account for ideology in terms of subjective and irrational 'distortion'. The interpretive paradigm, on the other hand, is not an ideology since it is capable of self-reference; yet it cannot account for ideology!

The failure to locate theory in an historical and social matrix (and the consequent inherent conservatism of theory) is a failure shared, to a lesser or greater degree, by both the paradigms examined. This affects the way in which they conceptualize education and educational research. In the case of the natural science paradigm, the relationship of research to practice is solely one of manipulation. With the interpretive paradigm, research is located in practitioners but the influence of power and ideology is not considered. In both cases, therefore, the involvement of research in forms of educational practice, which are both reflective and critical, is problematic. In different ways, both can project an image of research which is passive and divorced from the situatedness of practice.

THE INTERPRETIVE PARADIGM AND HERMENEUTIC UNDERSTANDING

In contrasting the interpretive and natural science paradigms, the obvious implication was that the former is more appropriate to the social sciences and, by extension, to education. However, this would not command universal assent. Some would still retain a commitment to the natural science paradigm as appropriate to the social sciences. They would take a positivist view that, ultimately, our claims to knowledge of the social sciences must be based on empirical investigation of an external social world. So long as methods are rigorous and value-free ('scientific') then the claim to know is based on a privileged and legitimate access to truth. As Hughes points out, 'this conception spawned what are today the orthodox research methods of social science' (Hughes, 1980:122). Any doubts concerning the efficacy of these methods is countered with the claim that, given time, they will be perfected, and match those in the natural sciences.

The opposition to modelling the social on the natural sciences is not a contemporary phenomenon. Dilthey for example, distinguished the social sciences from the natural in terms of the concerns of the former with 'meanings' and the latter with causal explanation. He took the position that the objects of study of the social sciences were symbolically structured. The structure of explanation in focusing on meanings was thus different to that in the natural sciences, although Dilthey was also concerned to emphasize that the social sciences were still sciences whose aim, in common with the natural sciences, was to discover objective knowledge (Rickman, 1976). Essentially, therefore, Dilthey saw the social sciences as interpretive, in terms of their structure of explanation, but using rigorous scientific method and thus making legitimate claims to knowledge.

It is important to note the emphasis on 'objective' knowledge. By accepting this as a shared aim, the way is always left open for positivist attacks on the interpretive paradigm. Unless the natural science paradigm is itself deconstructed, it inevitably constitutes a model for attaining objective knowledge, against which interpretive approaches will always be judged to be inferior. The problem is that the natural science paradigm takes itself to be ahistorical and asocial. It takes a 'God's eye' view in providing an appropriate standard for all times, all places, and all modes of endeavour. But the notion of paradigms has itself undermined the acceptability of this view.

At this point we would like to introduce the notion of hermeneutic understanding which will play a central part in our analysis. By origin, hermeneutics is the study of ancient texts in order to interpret their underlying and often obscure meaning. Texts were seen as products of human practices embedded in cultures no longer directly knowable to the interpreter. Interpretive study, therefore, had to be historical and had to attempt to uncover the meanings, practices, and culture of those who produced the texts. A hermeneutic approach rather than a 'scientific' method was seen as more appropriate:

> Heremeneutics came to refer not just to the study of historical texts and the problems of translation, comprehension and contextualising associated with them, but to a broader endeavour; that of discovering or uncovering the meanings of all human artifacts and actions
>
> (Anderson et al., 1986:65)

It is for this reason that the hermeneutic approach is of interest to us. Human practices are akin to texts and can be similarly studied. Like texts, the meanings which underly practices are not always clear, hence one task of research is to elucidate these underlying meanings. Most importantly, however, practices only have meaning for those participating in the 'form of life' within which they are embedded; although, as we have already seen, meanings are structured and can thus be communicated and shared.

Traditionally, hermeneutics has been about understanding the past 'from the standpoint of the present' (Anderson et al., 1986:68). Our interest is more in terms of how we understand and cope with the familiar, the puzzling, and the problematic, from the standpoint of our normal practice. We consequently use hermeneutics in the understandings and concerns which underly those practices and the situations within which they are located.

Our appropriation of hermeneutics is not primarily in

terms of its method. Rather we follow Gadamer (1975) in his claim that hermeneutic understanding is not a question of method but <u>central</u> to any human practice. Furthermore, it is in practice that we can come to understand one another. All understanding must start from one's own situationally-located standpoint rather than from a God-like 'objectivity' which anyhow is itself situated. The natural sciences are located within a historical tradition and standards of objectivity are the 'prejudices' of that tradition.

This has a number of implications. To expect the social sciences to have the same standards is inappropriate because they (the natural sciences) are 'constituted within a certain tradition appropriate, perhaps, for certain purposes but not at all one that can be absolutised as a general demand' (Warnke, 1987:3). Furthermore, there is no ahistorical and acontextual model of scientific method which guarantees objective knowledge. All models involve prejudices or prejudgements which are the products of a historical tradition that cannot be transcended through taking a 'God's eye' position. In general, all forms of understanding are influenced by what Gadamer calls 'effective history', in other words they are historically and socially grounded. The form of understanding to be found in the natural sciences is no exception.

Gadamer (1975) claims that understanding has two characteristics - first, it is <u>ontological</u> in the sense that understanding is a primary mode of our existence as human beings and, second, it is <u>universal</u> because it is present in <u>all</u> our activities (Bernstein, 1986). Simply through living, human beings <u>must</u> be involved in the process of understanding and this is not something which we <u>choose</u> to do. 'Viewed from this perspective, understanding is not primarily a scientific understanding of entities but rather a practical understanding of one's life and possibilities' (Warnke, 1987:40). Furthermore, as Bernstein (1986) points out, understanding is not a psychological or mental activity essentially subjective in nature, but an 'objective' characteristic of human living and thus universal in scope.

At this point we should note the emphasis upon interpretation within hermeneutic understanding, which clearly locates it generally within an interpretive paradigm. But the claim is that meanings exist in the world and, like ancient texts, they require interpretation. It is through this that understanding emerges and it is thus indissolubly linked to interpretation. Furthermore, interpretation always goes

Critique of Traditional Models

beyond the 'facts' as given. Our interpretations are located in our own situation, since we interpret from a particular context and perspective. 'Understanding is only possible because of the prejudices and prejudgements that are constitutive of what we are - our own historicity' (Bernstein, 1986:98). We are located in history and our interpretations are always <u>from our present historical location</u>, which itself is influenced by our historical past or 'tradition'. Finally, meanings cannot simply be 'read off' from the text; they are often obscure, elusive, and difficult to articulate. This leaves the way clear for taking account of the possible distorting effect of ideology.

Prejudices and tradition play a central role in understanding. We cannot abolish our 'prejudices' by an act of will - stand 'outside' them as it were - since such an understanding would itself be a prejudice. Gadamer's emphasis on the inescapability of prejudice and tradition flies directly in the face of the dominant trend in the scientific-technological culture and ideology of the West which takes the diametrically opposed view that it is precisely through rejecting 'prejudice' and 'tradition' that proper claims to knowledge can be made and access to the truth guaranteed. The 'revolution' which founded the natural sciences enthroned reason and scientific method at the expense of prejudice and tradition, and led to the belief that one could stand 'outside' one's historical location through an act of will. Yet, Gadamer says that this is impossible, that this scientific-technological project is historically located, and is itself a tradition built on a prejudice of standing outside one's historicity.

Prejudices, therefore, are the starting-point for understanding the past and, within the present, the unfamiliar and problematic. This raises the twin issues of whether a distinction can be made between 'blind' and 'enabling' prejudices and whether because of the influence of prejudice and tradition we are thereby imprisoned by them.

In arguing for the rehabilitation of 'prejudices', Gadamer makes the point that they 'constitute the initial directedness of our whole ability to experience' and that 'they are the conditions whereby we experience something - whereby what we enounter says something to us' (Gadamer, 1975:239). He is claiming that prejudices are literally a condition of understanding and knowledge, but that some prejudices are 'blind' whilst others are 'productive of knowledge' (Gadamer, 1975:247). But how are we to

31

distinguish?

To distinguish between these two types of prejudice it is important to emphasize that Gadamer sees all prejudices as located within a tradition. Our prejudices are not arbitrary or simply a matter of personal eccentricity. As Warnke puts it, 'the issues we bring to the process of interpretation are not our preoccupation alone but rather refer to the issues and concerns that have developed within the historical tradition to which we belong' (Warnke, 1987:78). Prejudices, therefore, because they are located in a tradition, both allow us to interpret the familiar and to provide the foundation to interpret the unfamiliar:

> Gadamer tells us that it is only through the dialogical encounter with what is at once alien to us, makes a claim upon us and has an affinity with what we are that we can open ourselves to risking and testing our prejudices.
>
> (Bernstein, 1985:128)

Tradition, therefore, is always operative in our lives. It is an 'effective history', such that in the very act of rejecting tradition we implicitly endorse its presence. In one sense, therefore, we cannot 'escape' from it. In a more positive sense, however, it provides a set of parameters orienting us towards that which is 'worth knowing'.

Bernstein (1986) in commenting on Gadamer's thesis, claims that prejudices have three characteristics. First, they are located in tradition but at the same time shape us in the present. Second, our 'affinity' with tradition (noted in the quoted extract above) is due to this location. However, at the same time, prejudices are not simply residues of the past, they also orient us toward the future. One consequence of this future orientation is that prejudices are not imprisoning walls but things that are always open to 'risking and testing'. They are, as Gadamer puts it, 'biases of an openness to the world'.

Understanding something involves projecting meaning through prejudices located in tradition. All understanding involves interpretation and vice versa (Bernstein, 1985:138). Equally, understanding is never complete, since an initial projection of meaning is constantly being revised. It is to this process which the hermeneutic circle refers:

> The anticipation of the global meaning of an action, a

> form of life ... etc. becomes articulated through a dialectical process in which the meaning of the parts or components is determined by the foreknowledge of the 'whole', whereas our knowledge of the 'whole' is continuously corrected and deepened by our increase in knowledge of the components
>
> (Kockelmans, 1975:85)

The hermeneutic circle is a process whereby the parts are understood through an understanding of the whole and the whole is understood through an understanding of the parts.

The operation of the hermeneutic circle can be seen in the simple example of asking a question. When we do so we always have *some* idea of what the answer is likely to be, since if we did not we would neither be able to formulate the question in the first place nor identify any answer *as* an answer. Whilst this shows the dependence of the question on the answer, it is equally the case that an answer can only be understood in terms of the question that occasioned it. There is, therefore, a mutually constitutive link between the question (the part) and the answer (the whole).

Understanding is thus a circular relationship between whole and parts, the known and the unknown the object and its context (Rowan and Reason, 1981). Hermeneutic understanding consists of interpretations that seek to give meaning to the parts whilst integrating them into a consistent whole (Warnke, 1987).

In the hermeneutic circle of understanding, first, there is the object to be understood (the whole), which Gadamer calls the 'things themselves'. This could be, for example, the puzzling or the problematic in practice. He tells us that we must open ourselves to what the 'things themselves' are trying to tell us, and we do so by assuming that they are both coherent and that they make claims to truth. This is the initial assumption we must make if we are to 'break' into the hermeneutic circle although in proceeding around it we come to revise these assumptions.

Second, we can only understand the object (the things themselves) through our prejudices. Gadamer talks of the interplay of our prejudices with the 'things themselves' which opens up the possibility of new understandings. In this way we can distinguish between 'blind' and 'productive' prejudices. Prejudices are the basis of our understanding of the 'things themselves' but, in attempting to understand, these prejudices can themselves change.

The standard objection to the hermeneutic circle is that it is, in effect, a vicious circle. It is claimed that, in understanding the parts in terms of the meaning of the whole, it is impossible to understand the latter through the former and vice versa. It is clear that the hermeneutic circle, in so far as it appears to be based on circular arguments, would be unacceptable in conventional logic. Equally, an empiricist would object on the grounds that the circle of interpretations must at some point be broken out of and grounded in empirical verification.

This presupposes that the hermeneutic circle is something we can choose to avoid or reject. As we have seen, however, Gadamer's argument is that 'we are essentially beings constituted by and engaged in interpretive understanding', and that meanings of things themselves can 'only be grasped through the circle of understanding, a circle that presupposes the forestructures that enable us to understand' (Bernstein, 1985:137). So the question of choosing the hermeneutic circle as the model of understanding does not really arise - the only choice is how well we operate it, as a closed or open system of understanding.

This is a point made by Rowan and Reason (1981) who describe the hermeneutic circle more specifically. When we investigate an object (things themselves) we have provisional ideas about its meaning. As the parts are studied, the meaning of these become partially clear. Understanding can then be deepened by relating the meaning of the parts to each other and to the whole. By so doing, the meaning of the whole can be re-assessed and this in turn can lead to a deepening of the understanding of the parts. As Geertz puts it, 'Hopping back and forth between the whole conceived through the parts which actualise it and the parts conceived through the whole which motivates them we seek to turn them into explications of one another' (Geertz, 1975:53). Rorty claims that 'coming to understand (through the hermeneutic circle) is more like getting acquainted with a person than like following a demonstration' (Rorty, 1980:319).

A possibly more serious objection is that the hermeneutic circle enshrines subjectivism and relativism. Understanding appears to be subjectively arbitrary interpretation. In the same way as we need to discriminate between 'blind' and 'productive' prejudices, so do we need to discriminate between understanding and misunderstanding.

Otherwise, we could be left in a position where 'anything goes'. The problem is exacerbated because the underlying theme of Gadamer's work is that there is no ahistorical and acontextual 'foundation' which 'guarantees' understanding. The essence of hermeneutic understanding is its situatedness. Not only does all understanding involve interpretation but all interpretation involves application. Interpretations are meanings for myself in my particular situation. As Gadamer puts it, we cannot 'look away' from ourselves and our concrete situation.

On the other hand, Gadamer denies that this necessarily implies subjectivism and relativism. First, hermeneutic understanding is located in a tradition of interpretation, in other words, we do not just decide arbitrarily how we are going to interpret. Second, in understanding, we must accept the truth of what we are trying to understand, initially at least. In effect, therefore, 'our interpretations are not our interpretations alone but have historical roots; moreover, we can test their adequacy by comparing them to the truth of the object with which we are concerned' (Warnke, 1987:90).

We are always shaped by 'effective history' even though we may not be aware of it. It influences both the objects we seek to understand and how we go about understanding them. Effective history is 'already operative in the choice of the right question to ask' (Gadamer, 1975:268). Even scientists cannot escape from this. Effective history constitutes a limit to our understanding but it is a limit which is always open and changing.

This is an important point because it counters another criticism often made of the hermeneutic circle - that in order to avoid relativism we become prisoners of the past in the form of 'effective history' and tradition. Although understanding is always situated and therefore limited, the limits are not perpetually closed but always open to the possibility of change. They constitute a starting-point but not an end-point of understanding.

Gadamer argues that, in trying to understand something, we engage in a process which he terms the 'fusion of horizons'. This consists of bringing together our own 'horizon', limits, and situatedness with the 'horizon', of that which we seek to understand. We assume that something has a truth and 'apply' it to our situation; in so doing we enlarge our understanding, both of it and of our own situation, through the 'fusion of horizons'. In other words, we start off by assuming the truth of something but end up by modifying our understanding of it. Through applying its truths to our situation, we change both it and ourselves. The 'fusion of horizons' therefore allows us to enlarge our own horizons through testing and modifying our prejudices (Bernstein, 1986). This dialectical interplay between self and the object through which the understanding of both is changed is perhaps the most important and not immediately obvious aspect of the hermeneutic circle.

There is another aspect to the 'fusion of horizons' worth noting. It refers to the outcome of intersubjective agreement where different and conflicting interpretations have been harmonized. In sharing a common historical location, by comparing and contrasting 'our various interpretations, in this historical context, we can achieve a fusion of horizons despite our differences' (Solomon, 1988:170). This intersubjective agreement constitutes an alternative standard of objectivity.

The implication is that there is, on the one hand, nothing which cannot be potentially understood and, on the other, that our understanding of anything is never closed. The essential condition of understanding is an awareness that one does not know everything and that one is always learning. Hermeneutic understanding, therefore, is a learning experience which involves a dialogue between ourselves and the object of understanding. It is a dialogue because that is what the 'fusion of horizons' is, in the final analysis. Just as dialogue results in consensus, even if it is agreement to disagree, so hermeneutic understanding is equivalent to dialogic consensus involving a 'kind of mediation between past and present or between the alien and familiar that is part of any sincere attempt to understand' (Warnke, 1987:103). The consensus that emerges represents something new, in the sense that both ourselves and the object of understanding have been transformed.

At this stage we can return to our starting-point, which was concerned with the paradigms appropriate to the natural and social sciences. The argument we wish to make is that inquiry based on hermeneutic understanding is not too many miles apart from the nature of inquiry suggested by the post-empiricist critique. In other words, we are pointing to a recognition that the natural as well as the social sciences are based on hermeneutic understanding. This claim has been put forward by a number of contemporary scholars. For example, Bernstein talks of

Critique of Traditional Models

'recovering the hermeneutical dimension of science through the critique of naive empiricism, the underdetermination of theory by facts and the recognition of the theory-ladenness of observation' (Bernstein, 1985:31). Rorty (1980) has sought to show that scientific knowledge is not a reflection or 'mirror' of reality and that science is not legitimated simply because it tells us what the world 'really' is. In the natural <u>and</u> the social sciences what counts as 'objective' <u>knowledge depends</u> on historically located norms and conventions. Rorty takes all forms of inquiry as being in the end pragmatically-based. The sciences are an '"effective vocabulary for coping" which in the case of the natural sciences are bound to prevail over other vocabularies in the game of prediction' (Bernstein, 1986:86). That does not necessarily mean, however, that they are a <u>privileged</u> vocabulary, even less that they are a model for other forms of discourse and practice.

Furthermore, according to Rorty (1980), it means that we should give up the fruitless quest for 'justification' or foundational grounding of our understanding and knowledge. Since science is not the 'mirror' of nature, it does not need justifying in those terms. All our knowledge is historically located and situated, all understanding is interpretation. When we try to understand the world we are, says Rorty, finding ways of coping and of 'self-creation' (a point echoed by Gadamer's 'fusion of horizons').

As Bernstein puts it:

> Science must be understood as a historically dynamic process in which there are conflicting and competing paradigm theories, research programmes and research traditions ... it is necessary to see that reasons and arguments employed by the community of scientists are grounded in social practices and that there is an essential open-ness in the very criteria and norms that guide scientific activity
>
> (Bernstein, 1985:171-2)

This is not a nihilistic attack upon the status or existence of science, or scientific knowledge. Rather the attempt is to 'conventionalise' science, to see that it is one 'language game' among many. What is being questioned is the positivistic notion of a <u>foundation</u> of science which exists outside history and outside society. If there is an attack it is an attack upon what both Rorty (1980) and Derrida (1978) call 'the metaphysics of presence' - i.e. the notion that there are 'real' foundations of knowledge, objectivity, and truth, which stand outside human discourse and practice. Gadamer claims that we make ourselves <u>through practice</u> which we share with others. It enables us to understand, communicate, and act, but this itself is not universal or foundationally-grounded.

The natural sciences therefore, it is claimed, are themselves hermeneutic. They are situated, and involve understanding and interpretation. Prejudice and tradition are vital, since questions (research) and answers ('facts') are shaped by these. There are alternative and competing theories, since theories are not simply based on facts. As Habermas (1972) has pointed out, all scientific knowledge is constituted by tradition or interests, and paradigms are another way of talking about these.

If the natural sciences are hermeneutic, then this is even more the case with the social sciences. The latter, it has been said, are characterized by a 'double hermeneutic' (Giddens, 1976). If social science is concerned with meanings, then so too are the objects of the social scientist's gaze. The social sciences and their field of study are both located within symbolically structured discourses and practices. According to Bernstein:

> the hermeneutical dimension is even more important in the social disciplines than in the natural sciences since they are concerned with human beings who are always engaged in the social construction and deconstruction of their world.
>
> (Bernstein, 1985:173)

Hughes concludes that the existence of the double hermeneutic means that 'social science cannot help but be engaged in a discourse with its own subject matter' (Hughes, 1980:126). Adopting a positivistic model of inquiry is therefore doomed to failure, since it floats theory in a situationless vacuum, detaches the 'stuff' of study from its locating 'paradigms', and thus must always be partial in its understanding.

Finally, the existence of the double hermeneutic reinforces an important point touched upon earlier. This is that hermeneutic understanding is not a special esoteric kind of understanding engaged in only by scientists and theoreticians. Rather, it describes <u>ordinary everyday</u>

understanding and interpretive method. This is to say, the hermeneutic circle 'is just one example of an everyday process through which persons make sense of their world' (Rowan and Reason, 1981:132). Hermeneutic understanding is, to echo Gadamer, our primary mode of being in the world. If this is so, then the 'hermeneutic phenomenon' is a 'fact about people'; in other words, people practice hermeneutics (Rorty, 1980:358).

REFERENCES

Anderson, R.J., Hughes, J.A., and Sharrock, W.W. (1986) Philosophy and the Social Sciences, London: Croom Helm.
Anyon, J. (1982) 'Adequate social science, curriculum investigations and theory', Theory into Practice, 21 (1), 34-7.
Bernstein, R.J. (1985) Beyond Objectivism and Relativism, Oxford: Blackwell.
---- (1986) Philosophical Profiles, Oxford: Polity Press.
Carr, W. and Kemmis, S. (1986) Becoming Critical, Lewes, Sussex: Falmer Press.
Cohen, L. and Manion, L. (1985) Research Methods in Education (2nd edn), London: Croom Helm.
Derrida, J. (1978) Writing and Difference, tr. by Alan Bass, Chicago: University of Chicago Press.
Dreyfus, H.L. and Rabinow, P. (1982) Michel Foucault: Beyond Structuralism and Hermeneutics, Brighton, Sussex: Harvester Press.
Fay, B. (1987) Critical Social Science, Oxford: Polity Press.
Gadamer, H.G. (1975) Truth and Method, London: Sheed and Ward.
Geertz, C. (1975) 'On the nature of anthropological understanding', American Scientist, 63, 47-53.
Giddens, A. (1976) New Rules of Sociological Method, London: Hutchinson.
Habermas, J. (1972) Knowledge and Human Interests, tr. by J.J. Shapiro, London: Heinemann.
---- (1974) Theory and Practice, tr. by J. Viertel, London: Heinemann.
Hacking, I. (1983) Representing and Intervening, Cambridge: Cambridge University Press.
Hanson, N.R. (1958) Patterns of Discovery, Cambridge: Cambridge University Press.

Harris, K. (1979) *Education and Knowledge*, London: Routledge & Kegan Paul.
Heaton, J.M. (1979) 'Theory in psychotherapy', in N. Bolton (ed.) *Philosophical Problems in Psychology*, London: Methuen.
Hughes, J. (1980) *The Philosophy of Social Research*, London: Longman.
Kerlinger, F.N. (1970) *Foundations of Behavioural Research*, New York: Holt, Rinehart & Winston.
Kockelmans, J. (1975) 'Towards an interpretive or hermeneutic social science', *Graduate Faculty Philosophy Journal*, 5(1), 73-96.
Kuhn, T.S. (1970) *The Structure of Scientific Revolutions* (2nd edn), Chicago: University of Chicago Press.
Phillips, D.C. (1987) *Philosophy, Science and Social Inquiry*, Oxford: Pergamon.
Popkewitz, T.S. (1984) *Paradigm and Ideology in Educational Research*, Lewes, Sussex: Falmer Press.
Rickman, H.P. (ed.) (1976) *Dilthey, Selected Writings*, Cambridge: Cambridge University Press.
Rorty, R. (1980) *Philosophy and the Mirror of Nature*, Oxford: Blackwell.
Rowan, J. and Reason, P. (1981) 'On making sense', in P. Reason and J. Rowan (eds), *Human Inquiry: A Sourcebook of New Paradigm Research*, London: Wiley and Sons.
Solomon, R.C. (1988) *Continental Philosophy Since 1750*, Oxford: Oxford University Press.
Warnke, G. (1987) *Gadamer: Hermeneutics, Tradition and Reason*, Oxford: Polity Press.

Chapter Three

THE PROBLEM OF 'FOUNDATION' DISCIPLINES

INTRODUCTION: DISCIPLINES AS FOUNDATIONS

The term 'foundation' disciplines is used in two different but related senses. In the first, disciplines constitute a 'base' or 'source' of knowledge that has a clear supporting connection with a superstructure of practice. Since disciplines are a foundation, this implies that the knowledge base is secure and reliable as a consistent evidential feature. Medicine and engineering are often used as examples: the former based on disciplines such as anatomy and biochemistry, the latter on physics and mathematics. These disciplines are seen as having a demonstrable relationship to the practice of medicine and engineering, providing explanations and descriptions of the world upon which practice must be based if patients are not to die and bridges fall down!

In this sense, therefore, foundation disciplines are a necessary part of the relationship between 'theory' and 'practice', constituting one leg of the relationship. The second sense of 'foundation' disciplines refers to their place within a 'field of knowledge'. This is a composite of disciplines integrated around a particular theoretical or practical orientation (Hirst, 1974). Medicine and engineering are examples of a practical field of knowledge. Adult education, in common with education generally, is difficult to categorize and uncertain of its status. It has tried to become a <u>theoretical</u> field of knowledge but whether it is that or a <u>practical</u> field or neither is a matter of contention.

A field of knowledge is normally taken to have three main characteristics (Bright, 1985). First, the body of knowledge within the field originates from outside the field in its foundation disciplines. Second, a field of knowledge may be composed of more than one discipline. Third, the constituent disciplines are organized and integrated in a way appropriate to the nature of the field; in particular, according to its theoretical or practical orientation. In a practical field of knowledge, for example, knowledge is geared to practical use and is organized around the need for application.

Here, therefore, foundation disciplines refer to the constituents of a field of knowledge. However, the two senses of the term are related. A relationship exists between, on the one hand, foundation disciplines as the theory of a practice and, on the other, foundation disciplines as components of a field of knowledge. A practical field of knowledge is constituted by its disciplines, and organized to facilitate the practical application of the knowledge contained in those disciplines.

Adult education, on the face of it, would appear to be a field of knowledge. It is clearly a branch of education and, as education is normally considered to be a field of knowledge, then adult education must be too. However, this is not just a matter of logic, since adult education independently conceputalizes itself as such. Whether it is or should be, however, is problematic, and we shall need to consider this later. Assuming, for the moment, that adult education's own conceptualization is accepted, the question then becomes whether it is a theoretical or practical field of knowledge. Bright (1985) cogently argues that it cannot be the former but, because it does conceptualize itself in this way, it is prevented from being the latter. The main problem, as he sees it, is that, in trying to be a theoretical field of knowledge, adult education bases itself upon the knowledge contained in theoretical disciplines such as psychology and sociology but lacks a theory of its own which would integrate this knowledge into a coherent interdisciplinary composite appropriate to the particular purposes of adult education as a theoretical field of knowledge. In so doing, however, it also fails to be a practical field of knowledge since an appropriate theory is also needed if the theoretical knowledge of the disciplines is to be applied to a practical activity.

Bright's case is based partly on an analysis of the logical implications of the term 'field of knowledge' and partly on observation and personal experience in designing and teaching courses of adult education studies. The case which we argue is also based on the latter but not on the former, although we take account of it. Instead, our concern is to examine the appropriateness of disciplines providing a basis or foundation of knowledge for a practical activity such as adult education. By looking at the nature of the disciplines of psychology and sociology we challenge the conventional notion of a 'foundation', and thus the assumption that it is possible in any sense to 'apply' the knowledge contained in such disciplines to educational practice.

We hope in this way to show that conceptualizing adult education as a field of knowledge, of either the theoretical or practical variety, is both inappropriate and unhelpful. It will be evident that the issues discussed are much more complex than they might appear - none the less, we will attempt an alternative conceptualization. Finally, we would wish to emphasize the point made in Chapter 1 - that adult education is a branch of education. It follows that what we have to say applies equally, in the main, to the former as it does to the latter. For the sake of convenience we will use the terms 'education/educational' as referring also to adult education, unless there are clear and pertinent differences which need to be specified.

PSYCHOLOGY AS A FOUNDATION DISCIPLINE

Our starting point is the example mentioned earlier of the relationship of the doctor and engineer to their foundation disciplines. Now, unlike these cases, it is difficult to argue that there is an equivalent and demonstrable relationship between psychological knowledge ('theory') and educational practice as there is, for example, between a knowledge of mechanics and the building of bridges. The practice of teaching is not based on theoretical knowledge, since it is not an applied science. The nature of psychology as a theoretical activity and of education as a practical activity are equally relevant considerations.

Doctors and engineers apply theories whose status is both reasonably secure and relatively uncontentious; where the operative paradigms, content, and methodological procedures of foundation disciplines command (at least during periods of 'normal science') a large measure of consensual agreement. The same, however, could not be said of psychology. The descriptions and explanations which psychology provides of the world, and the security of its claim to 'truth', are problematic and contentious issues within the discipline. Of course, it must be emphasized that to talk of psychology as if there were one psychology which is a unified discipline is very far from being the case - this, in itself, is also part of the problem. We simply point to the existence of many psychologies each with its own, often radically different, paradigm where the only point of commonality is that each claims to have secure access to the 'truth'. At this stage we are confining ourselves to what is conventionally known as 'scientific' or 'mainstream' psychology.

Its proponents would claim that their discipline is still in its scientific infancy and is therefore still refining and elaborating its concepts, procedures, and knowledge base, and that, given time, doubts about its security will disappear. Others, however, claim that it is the very assumption that psychology is a scientific discipline which is at the root of the problem.

The main criticism made against scientific psychology is really about its location in a positivistic, natural science paradigm which, it is maintained, is not only naive and outmoded in comparison with the model way the natural sciences operate (Harre, 1980), but has led to theories whose nature militates against their application to education. As Egan (1984) points out, the stress on experimentation and quantification has resulted in 'phenomena insensitivity'. Salmon (1985) succinctly formulates the problem:

> Psychology as a discipline has seen itself as distinctive insofar as it entails the application of 'scientific' methodology to questions of human conduct and human experience. That methodology is set up for the investigation of universal laws. It presupposes generality: cause-effect relationships which apply regardless of particular contexts. It is tailored to quantification and measurement.
>
> (Salmon, 1985: 39-40)

The consequence of this is that the phenomena studied are narrowed to the point that any theory seems to have little explanatory value outside the experimental situation and is thus of little use in accounting for 'real life' human beings and human action (Louch, 1966). This failure of 'ecological validity' is a serious one because it is precisely these kinds of explanations which education would appear to require.

Related to this is a problem about psychology's description of the world. Is the description one which comprises empirical necessities about the world which the emphasis on 'universal laws' would seem to indicate? Or is it the case, in reality, that these descriptions, far from being universally valid, are subject to cultural contingency and local variation? The fact is that even the most positivistically inclined would be hard pressed to quote a single instance of such a universal law. More significantly, however, the question shows how psychology is left between a rock and a hard place. If psychology is describing empirical necessities about, for example, the way in which thinking develops in human beings, then there is little that education can do in the face of these 'necessities' - a problem, for example, which Piagetian educationalists face. But if the descriptions are culturally - and contextually - contingent, then they are no longer 'theory' in the way in which the natural science paradigm would understand theory, although it is precisely these contingencies and variations that education is most interested in. However, if psychology does not describe 'necessities' then there is nothing in psychology that need constrain education. In this sense, psychology does not have the equivalent status of mechanics in engineering, which does appear to be a useful way of describing universal empirical 'necessities' and therefore would appear to be relevant to engineering and must be taken account of in practice.

What this seems to point to is that 'psychology and education are enterprises guided by radically different ground rules' (Swann, 1985:35). As we have already noted, one aspect of this is the emphasis on <u>generalization</u> and the elimination of individual differences, particularly through the use of statistical techniques (Mittler, 1982). Richardson et al. (1987), in commenting on the applicability of research in cognitive psychology to educational settings, make the point that it has tended to concentrate on processes 'common' to individuals, rather than individual differences. Education, on the other hand, is crucially concerned with such differences, adult education particularly so. As Salmon points out, psychology's generalizations fail to take account of 'biography, personal relationships or the social context of the learner' (Salmon, 1980:6). Such considerations are vital for education, with its emphasis on the <u>content</u> of learning

by <u>particular</u> individuals in particular <u>contexts</u>.
A related aspect of this is psychology's emphasis on the <u>impersonal</u>. In terms of the development of learning theory, this has resulted in a concentration upon the behavioural and the cognitive to the neglect of the affective dimension in human learning - an emphasis which ultimately led to a reaction in the form of humanistic psychology's emphasis on the 'whole person'. In the main, 'scientific' psychology has tended to operate with a very narrow conception of the 'individual'. The connection with experimentation, quantification and generalization is clear. As Saljo remarks, 'research subjects became ahistorical and asocial beings whose ways of interpreting the world were consciously put aside' (Saljo, 1987:103). They have been 'put aside' because of the supposed dictates of scientific method, particularly the need for 'objectivity' and the consequent rejection of anything that appeared to leave room for the subjective. In the process, as we have already noted, the kind of descriptions and explanations produced seemed to have little relevance for the kinds of issues and problems which educators had to deal with in their practice.

Parallel with the neglect of the subjective is the neglect of the <u>social</u> dimension. Saljo's comment above points to the failure to recognize that the 'individual' of psychology is an abstract, depersonalized entity without history, society, or culture. This relates to the point made earlier about psychology's failure to take account of biography (history) and contextual factors. Their influence on learning, for example, can be clearly seen in the way in which knowledge is socially constructed. This is related to the general failure to take account of the <u>content</u> of knowledge. Essentially, the social aspect is simply regarded as one pole of the 'individual-society' dichotomy. Even humanistic psychology, despite its critique of psychology's 'scientific' enterprise and positivistic gaze still shares the emphasis on the individuated subject (Henriques <u>et al.</u>, 1984). On the other hand, education cannot but be concerned with the social dimension, since its practice is bound by social contexts and is located in a socio-cultural structure.

Enough has been said, therefore, to indicate that the kind of 'theory' which prevails in psychology is one which would appear to be largely irrelevant to educational practice and which it would be inappropriate to 'apply' to that practice. The claim that education is a practical field of knowledge, within which psychology is a foundation discipline, appears to be unsupportable and, therefore, the assumption that psychology could be the basis and guide for educational practice is misconceived. To put it simply, psychologists cannot tell educators what they must do, since scientific psychology cannot, by its very nature, address the concerns of education.

Having said this, however, it is necessary to account for the fact that psychology has been seen as something that is appropriately applicable to education. Despite the critique we have outlined, it still retains a powerful hold. At a fairly obvious level, there are concepts which appear to be common to both psychology and education - the concept of 'learning', for example. This seems to indicate that perhaps psychology and education do, after all, have common concerns. However, anyone who has been involved in the teaching and training of educational practitioners would undoubtedly agree that what the latter mean by 'learning' is not the same as what psychologists mean.

In Chapter 2 we pointed to the existence of paradigms and 'prejudices' which all practitioners have, whether they be theorists, researchers, or 'in the field' which structures the experience of practice. Educational activities such as teaching and research consist of informed actions which are explainable and thus comprehensible to the practitioner. Paradigms both make practice intelligible and point practitioners in certain directions. They are inevitable in defining what can be done and what ought to be done - the very heart of decision-making in practice. They constitute a standpoint for the practitioner and a way of thinking and doing. Now, although psychology is a theoretical activity, it is clear that, like education, it too involves practice. In other words, for psychologists, the production of theory is through a practice which is also guided by paradigms. These are similar to the educational practitioner's, in the sense that they also constitute a standpoint, orient the psychologist in certain directions, define what can and ought to be done, and incorporate a set of concepts, assumptions, and methods of working.

In both cases, paradigms exist because the activities of both the theorist and the practitioner are consciously intentional and can only be understood by reference to such paradigms. Equally clearly, however, the content of these frameworks will be different, because the educational practitioner is concerned with a practical activity whilst the psychologist is concerned with a theoretical activity. In other words, because their activity is concerned with different purposes, so also will differ the paradigms which guide their activity.

Looked at in this way, therefore, it is clear why the concepts used by educational practitioners do not mean the same as those used by psychologists. Despite the verbal similarity, they emanate from different paradigms. It is also clear why the kinds of assumptions made and the methodological procedures used in psychology appear neither appliable to nor fruitful for education. They, too, emanate from different paradigms and, while they may be appropriate in terms of their own paradigm and its purpose, they are not appropriate to a paradigm guiding a different activity with a different purpose. This becomes even more apparent when psychology is located within a natural science paradigm.

As we have pointed out earlier, there is no such thing as a theory in psychology. Within psychology there are differing and conflicting paradigms and, while it would be inappropriate to examine these closely, what needs to be stressed is that some have a greater relative affinity and pragmatic force for educational paradigms than others. Psychotherapeutic paradigms are a good example. Many diverse figures in psychotherapy have made significant contributions, not only to the body of knowledge in their own field but simultaneously to educational theory and practice - for example, Rogers (1961, 1969) and Kelly (1963). Stevens (1983) sees psychoanalytic therapy as akin to educational practice, recalling, no doubt, Freud's comparison of the analyst with the educator in terms of their common concern with stimulating insight, awareness, and understanding.

Of course, in making this point there is again a danger of oversimplification, giving that there are many different, conflicting, paradigms even within psychotherapy. To lump the Rogerian and the psychoanalytic together would strike many as ludicrous. However, there is an area of commonality in these paradigms which differentiate them from the 'scientific' psychology paradigm because, unlike the latter, they are explicitly prescriptive, value-laden, and action oriented. Psychotherapy, like education, is a practical activity. Psychotherapeutic paradigms assume the whole person not just a particular aspect (for example, cognition). They are ideographic rather than nomothetic and their approach is hermeneutic in that they seek to interpret and understand rather than explain and predict. Therapeutic practice like educational practice is contextually-located and problems in both are resolved by taking proper action within particular contexts. Finally, they recognize the existence of human consciousness and thus the reflexive character of their own knowledge.

Smail describes therapy as a situation where 'the therapist cannot change the patient through the application of technical rules read off from some kind of diagnostic manual' (Smail, 1980:181). This could well describe education if 'teacher' were substituted for 'therapist' and 'student' for 'patient'. Within psychotherapy there is a recognition that practice is not a mere application of 'theory'. However, Smail does point out that such an approach is conditional on rejecting a scientistic framework with its emphasis on objectivity and value-neutrality. In other words, psychotherapy has an affinity and force for education because it recognizes and clarifies the values implicit within its own locating paradigms.

This is an important point, since one of the problems with scientific psychology is precisely its refusal to acknowledge this. As we saw in Chapter 2, this is a feature of the natural science, positivist paradigm. As a mode of understanding, scientific psychology originates within particular socio-cultural contexts (it, too, has a history), and is bound to be saturated by the values intrinsic to those contexts. For the scientific psychologist, the values are those of positivistic natural science but are not acknowledged as such. The result has been the kind of assumptions which have already been mentioned - abstracted individualism, the felt need for impersonal and 'objective' procedures, and a rejection of the social aspects. These are characteristics of the scientific technological culture of the West - a culture with values which are unacknowledged, indeed are reified as objective, eternal 'truths'. Scientific psychology denies both its own value commitments and its status as a construct located in a particular culture.

One consequence of this is the 'high premium placed on knowledge that is technically exploitable, knowledge that can be used to change, control, manipulate, and order both nature and society. Psychology has itself shown a strong inclination to develop into the technology of human behaviour' (Emler and Heather, 1980:135). An example of this is the way in which the concept of intelligence has been

49

formulated and used. 'Scientific' forms of thinking became the 'model for human intelligence', and, in the Piagetian concept of formal operational thinking, are taken as an intrinsic human disposition, the summit of achievement from which no further progression could be made. The values of the scientific technological culture thus became the objective standard against which the quality of people's thinking, reasoning, and cognitive capacities generally were judged. Through the use of quantitative measures, such as IQ, not only was one way of being intelligent alone accorded worth but this particular way became an important weapon in the arsenal of differentiation, selection, and the determination of life chances and social position.

The tendency of psychology to develop into a technology of human behaviour is therefore very marked. We can also detect its influence through behaviourism in the objective approach to curriculum planning and, indeed, in the whole notion of 'instruction'. The powerful appeal of such developments should not be underestimated, since they appear to provide a more rational and efficient approach to educational activity than is apparently warranted by the 'truth' and 'objectivity' of science.

Psychology, therefore, is a cultural construction which, in common with all the human 'sciences', operates through a set of coherent culturally-located values defining the paradigm or theoretical framework of the discipline. Yet these values are not in the main acknowledged; psychology sees itself as making claims to 'truths' which are universal, and even humanistic psychology, whilst rejecting a positivistic methodology, would still wish to lay claim to the 'truth'. There seems to be an apparent contradiction here which needs further investigation; in the process, it will also be possible to throw further light on why it is that despite seemingly good grounds for rejecting the 'application' thesis, it none the less still retains a powerful hold on the minds of educational practitioners.

Psychology can be seen not simply as a body of abstract, theoretical knowledge but as centrally implicated in educational practices. Walkerdine (1984, 1985) suggests that psychology is 'everywhere' and that 'schooling and psychology have developed hand-in-hand'. She points out that schools, for example, are not places where psychology has been applied but where 'certain truths about children are continually produced'. These provide the 'objective' basis for legitimizing certain kinds of pedagogic practice (for example, discovery learning). At the same time, these practices define the content of student behaviour; so that, for example, transmittal practices are associated with certain kinds of behaviour which will be different from those associated with participatory practices. The behaviour is itself the 'evidence' upon which teachers base their judgements and conduct their practice. But the behaviour has been <u>created</u> by a particular practice and the evidence is therefore <u>relative</u> to that practice. Ultimately, it is relative to the 'truths' about the nature of the child; truths which themselves are not objective descriptions of 'reality' or discoveries in the world, but constructs relative to a particular kind of culture and paradigm embodying particular values and implicated within these regulatory practices.

Psychology plays a complex role in these processes. First, through its practices, 'scientific' knowledge is produced which claims to embody truths about a number of phenomena with which education is concerned. Second, by contributing to the defining and shaping of pedagogic practices, the 'truths' of psychology are embodied in those practices. They are incorporated into the paradigms of practitioners and become part of their stock of common-sense knowledge. It is in this sense that psychology does not have to be applied to practice because it is already there!

This could well account for the powerful hold of the application thesis, although it is clear the process involved is not one of application. Psychological theory does not exist in a vacuum; it exists in practices of various kinds where the aim of social regulation has been implicit, if not always acknowledged, from the very birth of modern psychology as a 'scientific' discipline. Psychology's 'objective' and universalistic claims are not simply descriptions of the world but 'creations' relative to those practices. However, the more scientifically respectable psychology became, the more its claims to 'truth' were accepted, then the more it came to be taken for granted by educational practitioners and seen as common-sense knowledge.

Psychology's claim to scientific status, is therefore not merely a misguided attempt to attain respectability but vital to the very production of psychology itself. Scientific psychology is closely implicated in the rise and expansion of certain kinds of modern social practices of a regulatory kind; for example, those of schooling, the modern corporation, public administration and health. Psychology needed to be located within a natural science paradigm because otherwise it could not claim to be describing the 'real' and to be grounded in the 'facts'. Without this, it would appear to have no warrant in a scientific-technological culture. However, by possessing this warrant, psychology could legitimate certain kinds of educational practice and provide the working concepts, methods, and frameworks of assessment appropriate to those practices.

This analysis can also be used with reference to the relationship between adult education and psychology. Adult developmental psychology, for example, relates to certain educational and administrative practices and to an 'andragogical' discourse centred on conceptions of the 'adult' constituted in a particular way by those practices and discourse. In considering current theories of adult cognitive development, we should look not simply to their internal coherence or to whether they are 'true' but to what it is that enables this particular theory at this particular time. In other words, if we see theory as a socio-cultural construct we need to understand what makes the construct possible. In saying this, however, one is not making a case for socio-cultural determinism but attempting to analyse the various practices - theory-building, research, and field practice - which make possible new theoretical formulations.

This does not necessarily imply that there is no independently pre-given object, the adult, about which psychology makes 'discoveries'. Rather, it is to say that in certain important respects the 'developing adult' is actually constituted by psychology. The adult with certain characteristics becomes the object of theorizing and the object of educational and administrative practices and is therefore 'given' within these practices. The current characterization of the 'developing adult', for instance, is in terms of domain-specific knowledge and post-formal styles of thinking (Rybash et al., 1984). Yet it was not so long ago that the 'developing adult' was characterized quite differently in terms of 'the socially persistent stereotype of inevitable and irreversible decline' in cognitive abilities (Allman, 1983).

The characterization of the adult in terms of 'decline' was located within a maturational paradigm. We can now see this not merely as stating 'facts' or somehow mirroring 'reality' but as part of a network of practices in psychology, education, and the wider society which privileged children and 'front-end' schooling. Thus, adults and the provision of educational opportunities were marginalized. The marginalization was itself the product of a socio-economic situation where no powerful regulatory motive existed for extending educational opportunities and provision beyond a certain age. Whatever regulation of adults was needed could be achieved in sites and through practice other than the educational.

Maturational theory took central processes and componential abilities as objects of its enquiry and psychometric testing as its preferred mode of research. Empiricist models of either a behaviourist or information-processing type provided the explanatory framework. The role of biography and context was either ignored or downgraded. The consequence was that educational intervention was seen as potentially limited in its effectiveness.

However, once the theoretical framework changed, a different picture emerges. Cognitive decline is now no longer inevitable and uniform but is significantly dependent on the nature and quality of interaction with contexts. Componential abilities are no longer seen as crucial for cognitive effectiveness in the 'real' world. Situational or contextual theory is constructed, laboratory experimentation and psychometric testing is replaced by naturalistic and ethnographic research as being more 'authentic' ways of finding out about adults and their cognitive capabilities. The 'new' theory therefore constitutes the 'developing adult' in a new way, now according him or her a capacity for life-long development and thus affording scope for educational intervention.

This theory is now part of a discursive practice which eschews general abilities and displaces formal reasoning from the cognitive apex. What adults know and how they think are modelled on 'real life'. They are conceptualized as 'expert systems' with domain-specific knowledge, who can think and reason post-formally. We see, therefore, how the 'discoveries' are relative to the discursive frameworks, objects of inquiry, and modes of research.

At the same time, we have also witnessed developments in certain practices involving the formation of adults, in those skills and attitudes perceived as functional to the needs of the contemporary socio-economic structure. The adult has now joined the child in being the object of psychological research and theory, and simultaneously of certain practices (of which education and training are perhaps the most important) whose purpose is essentially regulatory. Therefore, we find once again that adult psychology, in so far as it is recognized as giving access to the 'truth', is part of the process of legitimating certain kinds of adult education practice through defining the assumptions and criteria of curriculum design, pedagogy, and assessment.

SOCIOLOGY AS A FOUNDATION DISCIPLINE

We now switch our focus to the specific consideration of what sort of foundation sociology is for the adult educator. Again, it is important to emphasize that there are a plethora of different 'sociologies' and no constructions seem 'safe' from attack by theoretical alternatives. The argumentative character of the discipline appears to be due to its paradigms, themselves products of the social world and its realm of contested values. As Walsh (1972) points out, sociological constructs are of a 'second order', in that they are constructs of a world that is itself composed of the different meanings that are given to it by participating actors. This is the 'double hermeneutic' referred to in the previous chapter.

The sociological is inescapably a domain of the social. Many of sociology's analytical concepts are carefully considered and refined. As such, they are less likely to be unconsciously intuited than those we routinely employ commonsensically in finding our way around the world. But this does not mean that they are any the less contestible as representations of social structures and processes.

The so-called 'foundation disciplines' of any practice must integrate concepts (representations) with theories (explanations), relating each in some way to the practice itself (interventions). The question of the usefulness of sociology to adult educators is therefore one which can be broken down into several parts. Contestibility is evident at the conceptual level, both in terms of the thing which is being represented and its qualities which justify a sociological rendering.

It is at this point that one can reasonably ask what is actually meant by 'adult education'. There might well be some agreement that adult education has a plurality of purposes and forms. But it is questionable whether an agreement at so general a level is of much practical worth.

Foundation Disciplines

Many standard adult education texts portray a diversity of practices, purposes, and constituencies. There are elaborate taxonomies differentiating sub-divisions of the field by various social and philosophical criteria. Whilst all this may be valuable in providing an appreciation of the complexities of the field as a whole, a proviso is needed (but not always supplied) that all the demarcations are artificial and fluid.

One way of putting the conceptual problematic of any sociology of adult education is to say that the theorist is dealing, at a representational level, with the inherent permeability of system boundaries. This is less troublesome for the sociologist of pre-adult education, where institutional demarcations are more settled and there is less institutional incoherence about what is to count as an instance of 'education' of a particular type. It is for this reason, perhaps, that many readers would agree with Ruddock that 'adult education ... will never be at home within the philosophical, sociological, psychological and pedagogical systems based on school education' (Ruddock, 1972). Whilst agreeing with this up to a point, we would not wish to characterize adult education as 'unique' either in theoretical or practial terms.

To illustrate some of the difficulties involved when an attempt is made to bring sociological insights to bear upon the practice of adult education, we can consider the question of 'participation' and the issues arising from the viewpoint of the practitioner.

1. The salience of participation as an 'issue'
For whom is this an issue (practitioners, policy-makers, individual members of the public, particular social groups, society as a whole)?
What form do these concerns take (difficulty in recruitment, inability to attend, lack of provision, occupational skill shortages, low literacy levels, etc.)?

2. The meaning of 'participation'
What is meant by participation and how is this to be measured (e.g. by a comparatively simple enumeration of attendance or by more complex indices of involvement which measure different levels/types of learner responsiveness)?

3. The characteristics of participants and non-participants
What personal and social features do these groups exhibit and how are they related to the forms and extent of involvement?

Under what circumstances do non-participants become participants and vice-versa?
4. The motives for participation
Are these recreational, intellectual, instrumental, 'social'?
Is there a mixture of motives and can they change?
How are motives related to expectations?
5. The control of participation
What choices do participants have in terms of subject matter and learning styles?
How should these be managed?
What institutional controls are placed upon the content, siting, timing, and sequencing of events?
What forms of guidance and counselling are appropriate?
6. The experience of participation
What aspects of participation are, or should be, judged and by whom?
How are evaluations made?
How do learning experiences relate to other elements of personal biography, social, and cultural location?
7. The consequences of participation
What are the concurrent and subsequent effects of adult learning for individuals, communities, and society as a whole?
How can these be assessed in terms of personal and social changes?

This list does not exhaust all the questions that could be asked about just one aspect of adult education, but it is sufficient to give an appreciation of the diversity of the practitioner's field of action and inquiry. The questions are interrelated in various ways, and adult educators will be concerned at different levels with the complex interplay of policy matters, marketing, organizing provision, teaching, learner support, and evaluation. The general issue of 'participation' will touch on each of these concerns at some point, raising sub-categories of questions whose representation in turn will vary within and between practices. Although the number of questions that could be asked is potentially infinite, as a general principle the framing of these questions will be practitioner-dependent. This involves the adoption of institutional and organizational vocabularies of purpose and procedure, interpreted in each case through the personal experience of practice itself and within particular practitioner paradigms.

The participation questions that practitioners raise will

have social dimensions that are also the province of the sociologist. However, in developing social theories of participation and in seeking supporting evidence, sociologists will frame their questions differently. Like the psychologist, they will operate with different paradigms to those of the practitioner. The sociologist's practices are to do with the theory-construction and testing considered necessary for the status of sociology as a discipline and requiring a formalized approach. Concepts and measurements, as with psychology, have to meet impersonal criteria of validity and reliability. The technical vocabulary of the sociologist, although deemed an analytical necessity of the discipline, is not the situated vocabulary of the adult educator.

It is a requirement of any formal theory that the concepts it employs retain the same meaning throughout. Any particular representation of selected aspects of 'participation' must therefore be internally consistent, even though the definition and use of sociological concepts will differ between theories and when other aspects are considered. The 'logic' of formal theory-construction and the sociologist's analytic framing has a transcendental, ahistorical quality that cannot be mapped directly on to practice. We find that, as in psychology, the discourse of the theorist and the practitioner are not equivalent (even where some of the same terms are being used by both). Consequently, the value of the former for the latter is not self-evident. This will be the case no matter what kind of sociological theory is on offer. Essentially, the sociologist and the psychologist, although pursuing different disciplines, work within theoretical paradigms and, as we have noted earlier, these have a different purpose to the paradigms of the educational practitioner.

From a sociological viewpoint, therefore, the kinds of practitioner concerns described above will be regarded quite differently. This can be shown by giving examples of the sorts of questions that sociologists might raise, and the types of theory and method that may be brought to their understanding of the different dimensions of 'participation'.

1. The salience of participation as an 'issue'
How do particular events and social trends become 'issues'? What roles are played by the media, pressure groups, and 'key' individuals?
Direct observations and documentary analysis of the micro

and macro politics of agenda-setting.
Conflict and pluralist theories of differential and relative valuation.

2. The meaning of 'participation'

How can one understand the types and extent of engagement in group activities?
Are there minimum criteria for 'participation' in given circumstances?
What variations are evident in the role-taking of participants?
Sociometric studies of active/passive group membership.
Network theories of individual/group affiliations.
Collectivist and individualist accounts of involvement.

3. The characteristics of participants and non-participants

In developing theories of social representation, how are the ascriptive and achieved criteria of economic, social and cultural location to be understood?
In what ways do they determine participation?
How can class, stratification, gender, and 'life cycle' theories of differential participation draw on comparative and longitudinal survey material, interviews, and biographical accounts of involvement?

4. The motives for participation

What distinctions can be drawn between intrinsic and extrinsic motivation?
How do the internal components of selfhood and external social factors shape particular choices?
What are the relationships between personal motivation, institutional values, general belief systems, and social activity?
How can these be modelled in theories of identity-maintenance or transformation, or in interest theories of group motivation?

5. The control of participation

What models are available to represent the distribution of apparent and real power in institutions?
How is power retained or relinquished?
What are the relative merits of models of coercion and legitimation?
Theories of formal organizations and their authority structures.
Systems accounts of means-ends relationships and status dependencies.
Structural, centre-periphery models of relative influence.

6. The experience of participation
What factors are involved in the signification of meaning and the making of judgements in relation to individual, community, institutional and social policy purposes?
What criteria can be used in the auditing of experience and how is one to assess their interpretive validity?
The comparative value of 'insider' and 'outsider', formative and summative accounts.
7. The consequences of participation
What analytical distinctions can be made between the manifest and latent functions, and the intended and unintended consequences, of purposive activity?
On what terms does participation lead to a reinforcement or transformation of structures and values?
How does the evidence of (non-)participation support theories of empowerment or subordination?
Over what period of time can effects be detected and attributed to identifiable causes?

One of the problems that adult educators are faced with, in their own professional formation and development, is deciding what sorts of sociological theories to accept and which formal questions are relevant to their own substantive ones. Different theories (each with their own conceptual representations, analytical structures, and value implications) may invite inter-theory comparisons but often only at formal or polemical levels, rather than in substantive or situational terms. The dilemma for the adult educator, either as student or practitioner, is that theories contained in disciplines are presented as if they were of fundamental importance, yet it is difficult to discern which are of substantive relevance or indeed whether any of them have such relevance at all.

Knowles (1984) attempts to list the options open to the adult educator in this situation. First, one can claim to ignore theories, on the grounds that they are too abstract or obtuse to be of any value in one's practice. This overlooks the fact that it is impossible to be without theory even if it is only informal theory. In any event, as we noted earlier, formal theory is always already present even if unacknowledged. Second, one can choose and stick to one theory, either because it squares with one's personal values or because it is organizationally acceptable. These are inappropriate criteria for choosing, however, since 'personal preference' may be simply 'routine' and 'official theory' is no better than any other (and may be a lot worse), merely because it has institutional credibility. Third, one can pick different theories for different operational domains. This ignores any contradictions by employing the convenience of segregation. The problem here is that this may be questionably opportunistic and invite discursive confusion when it becomes difficult to distinguish between domains. Fourth, one can be eclectic by incorporating plausible ideas from different types of theory without accepting them uncritically or in toto. This is the option that we favour and which we argue for throughout. We would favour this option for reasons which we will present in detail in later chapters but will only touch on briefly here.

If, in one circumstance, participation is taken to refer to a 'propensity to attend', then a social-class theory of differential enrolment (using occupational categories as class identifiers) might be appropriate; if, in another circumstance, the reference is to 'quality of involvement in the classroom', then an interactionist or group dynamics approach would perhaps be more pertinent. In suggesting that it is the operational concerns of the practitioner which should guide the choice of theory, the difficulties of giving effect to this principle should not be minimized. Ideally, however, the test of any theory about its usefulness in practice is that it should facilitate understanding and deal with matters of explicit concern to the practitioner.

It is unnecessary and indeed impossible to get the theory 'right' as a prerequisite to tackling the problems of practice. In the absence of a disciplinary consensus in sociology, what or who would be the arbiter of 'correct' theory? What is needed is a different appreciation of the way in which theory can be used - one which is consciously detached from the stylistic and explanatory allegiances of particular paradigms and schools (positivism, Marxism, functionalism, symbolic interactionism, ethnomethodology, etc.). An alternative understanding requires a reconsideration of the relationship between sociology (taken as an informative and analytical foundation discipline) and the technology of educational practice. To achieve this, it is necessary to problematize some of the ideas encompassed in the 'foundation metaphor' and its associated 'applicability thesis' of the theory-practice connection, and to do this with specific reference to sociology.

As we have already seen, in our analysis of psychology a foundation implies something that is both fundamental and secure - the former in the sense that it is the basic thing upon which other things depend, the latter in the sense that it can be relied upon as a consistent evidential feature. The metaphor also embodies the notion of precedence in its temporal sense - the idea that 'good practice' follows in the wake of 'correct theory' which shows the way. This begs the question of what practitioners are to do in the meantime (presumably, muddle along as best they can) until the theorists get it right. To take the theoretical or foundation disciplines as having these kinds of epistemological priority over practice is to require that adult educators <u>be dependent upon</u> sociologists, psychologists, and philosophers. But if the priorities are claimed without providing convincing assurances of good theory leading to better practice, or of the latter standing more firmly upon the former as implied by the metaphor, then practitioners are justified in questioning any of the explicit or tacit promises of academic disciplines. In any case, the exigencies of practice will require all adult educators, even 'professionals' (more often than not) to act rather than to pursue an unattainable surety for the grounding of their actions in formal theory. Thus, the strong claims for sociology and psychology being the foundation disciplines of (adult) education, in the sense that they are indispensible to its practice, must be rejected.

An alternative to the assertion that sociological theory provides a necessary basis for practice is the more modest, yet more realistic, claim that <u>it allows practice to be viewed in different contexts and from different explanatory perspectives</u>. 'Real life' contains a repertoire of interpretive frames (Goffman, 1974). This notion can be extended to the sociology of adult education. As a discipline, sociology incorporates many different paradigms or frames, each of which can identify and illuminate particular aspects of adult education that remain hidden in others. This 'optical metaphor' is more flexible; it acknowledges the inherent variety of social theories and educational practices, and also the transactional qualities of a visionary process relating theory to practice in an interdependent way. The metaphor can be extended to locate either possibilities for a greater breadth or depth of understanding by making use of theories as multiple or magnifying frames, or the dangers of confusion or 'masking' through an inappropriate overlay of contradictory explanations.

Recently, 'contextualist' explorations of the possible

relationships between various social theories and adult education's multiple purposes and practices have been undertaken by Jarvis (1985) and Elsey (1986). Although they proceed in different ways, both are concerned to identify and compare the key features of distinct sociological perspectives so that they may be juxtaposed with different ideological and structural forms of adult education. In each case, this positioning is accomplished by placing theoretical analysis in terms of levels and concepts alongside different kinds of educational purposes and processes (see, for example, Jarvis, 1985, p. 12 and Ch. 4, passim; Elsey, 1986, p. 120). The intention is to draw together some general affinities between the ways in which society has been comprehended by the main schools of sociological thought (none of which has paid any particular attention to adult education as a substantive field of concern) and the ways in which practitioners (few of whom could be described as acting from considered sociological principles) have intervened in society as educational agents.

There is a limit to the heuristic value of such context-setting: Elsey recognizes this when he states at the outset that 'theory should relate to practice if only because it provides scope for intelligent discussion about purposes, efficiency and effectiveness in the delivery of adult education' (Elsey, 1986:1). He further acknowledges that it is an 'open question' whether the knowledge organized in various social theories actually does improve policy-making and practice. Practitioners who simply want a broader appreciation of the social contexts of adult education through being able to select from an extended repertoire for sociological understandings may be satisfied with such a prospect. But we suggest that they are likely to require more from social theory than this.

Adult educators frequently express disappointment or cynicism after exposure to general sociological theory and philosophies of purpose. They find it difficult to locate with any confidence their own practice, characterized invariably by a high degree of contingency, within a broad explanatory, substantive, or purposive spectrum. Put another way, the situational relevance of macro-theories (such as functionalism or Marxism) to different forms of provision is not self-evident. It is therefore impossible to take these ideas directly into practice, even in supportive circumstances, and to expect that they will automatically give a firmer grounding to that practice. This does not mean that general sociological theories of generalized educational forms are unimportant. Rather, their generality does not in itself provide an appropriate theoretical focus that can be brought to bear on the specific conditions of practice and help practitioners decide how to act. To do this, sociological theories must have instantial relevance if they are to be of operational benefit. The problem then, as with psychological theories, is whether they would any longer be formally considered as 'theory'.

Within the particular circumstances of practice, adult educators are bound to ask about the ways in which theory enables a greater understanding of their situation. From this basic question further questions will be generated concerning the role of theory and action, particularly in terms of the likely consequences of alternative courses of action. Furthermore, these kinds of questions will be considered in terms of the way in the situation and circumstance of practice itself changes as action is taken and new understandings develop. In effect, this is an iterative process of questioning whereby the practitioner develops a deeper understanding, both of the (changing) conditions of practice and of the (changing) relevance of different theories to these conditions. It is hardly surprising, therefore, that when theories in foundation disciplines do not facilitate such analytical and experiential interchanges, practitioners consider them to be of little value.

THE PROBLEM OF FOUNDATIONS

It is clear from our discussion of psychology and sociology that these disciplines are not merely bodies of neutral knowledge located in some abstract theoretical vacuum. On the contrary, we have seen that they are located in social practices of a theoretical and practical kind. This feature of disciplines necessarily leads to a questioning of the very notion of 'foundations'. It is not simply a questioning of whether disciplines such as psychology and sociology are legitimately foundations of education but the foundations of disciplines themselves in certain conceptions of knowledge, truth, and rationality. The use of the metaphor of 'foundations', which we noted in the relationship of disciplines to education, also pervades our understanding of the foundations of foundations and may be equally misleading. Formulating these ultimate foundations has traditionally been recognized as the task of philosophy, specifically of epistemology. The latter is therefore not so much a foundation discipline but more the arbiter of what would count as such - the discipline of disciplines.

All disciplines are ultimately founded on an epistemology or theory of knowledge. The latter, certainly in Western philosophy, can be characterized as a search for those foundations which guarantee knowledge as sure and certain. The concern is with how beliefs are to be justified and how competing interpretations can be judged. For a belief to be accepted as knowledge and an interpretation to be judged as valid there must, it is thought, be some ultimate foundation which itself does not need justification. Such a foundation supposedly provides universal criteria against which all claims and interpretations can be judged.

A great deal of contemporary philosophy can be seen as a critique of this foundationalism. It would be beyond the scope of the book to examine this in depth. However, much of what has been already said is informed by this critique - for example, the discussion of post-empiricism in the natural sciences and the argument that all understanding is hermeneutic.

What we would emphasize here is that in so far as disciplines consist of systematically organized knowledge about the world, they are based on certain assumptions about the nature of knowledge, truth, and rationality which have been shown to be increasingly problematic by recent philosophical thinking. If for example, we recall the analysis presented in Chapter 2 concerning the nature of hermeneutic understanding, the clear message was that understanding always involved interpretation and appropriation (application).

This has profound implications for the conception of knowledge and truth which underlie disciplines. Knowledge is only deemed to be knowledge (as against belief) if it is true. What is true is that which corresponds with the way the world really is. But if we follow Gadamer's argument we never know the world as it really is, since to know it is to understand it and in the act of understanding we have already interpreted and appropriated it. We always interpret in one particular way because of our situatedness - a situatedness which is an interplay between our prejudices and our traditions and ultimately located in our society and culture. The critique here is that knowledge somehow 'mirrors' reality - a position which, as was earlier noted, has been given a hard knock by philosophers such as Rorty (1980). If knowledge does not mirror or 'represent' reality, then its foundational character and the notion of foundations generally is undermined.

The emphasis now, therefore, has switched to one which places context and history at the centre of the stage. The situations in which we live and work as part of larger communities with associated 'language games', norms and conventions, or 'paradigms', are the essential framework within which conceptions of knowledge, truth, and rationality are located. This is an emphasis which privileges social practices and human construction. At the same time, however, as Warnke points out it also emphasizes our 'finitude' and 'the utterly contingent character of our efforts to understand' (Warnke, 1987:1). The reference to 'finitude' reminds us that, as individuals, our situatedness is one which both precedes and 'post-dates' us. We cannot, as it were, decide to step out of it, although we can try to change it.

But what is the significance of saying that our efforts to understand are always contingent? Bernstein makes the point that 'there can never be absolute knowledge (and) finality in understanding' (Bernstein, 1986:63). Gadamer reminds us that our situatedness defines our 'horizons', which are not limits but the possibility of a continual process of openness to experience and thus the very conditions of learning.

Rorty (1980) maintains that, since knowledge does not mirror reality, it is not therefore concerned with a pursuit of truth which unequivocally and finally settles claims to knowledge. Rather, claims to knowledge are settled conventionally within socially located paradigms. Their justification is pragmatic, not foundational. In other words, do they allow us to cope more effectively with the world and do they allow us to understand and change? Rorty describes this as a process of edification.

Edification is concerned with knowledge in terms of coping and personal development. The arena in which it takes place is dialogue rather than experimentation and the application of scientific method. Since the concern is with understanding rather than 'finding out', with development rather than certainty, and since validation is pragmatic rather than foundational, then edification must emphasize the 'contingent' character of our understanding and knowledge.

Edification also has implications for what we take

rationality to be. In Chapter 2 we presented a critique of the notion that there is only one universal mode of rationality. Rationality, at least since the Enlightenment, has been seen as a mode of justifying arguments and claims which was a priori not itself in need of justification, was universal in scope, and invariant in character. However, we are saying that what counts as rational is conventional in the sense of being located in paradigms and 'forms of life'. It is important at this point to emphasize that this is not an attack on the <u>existence</u> of rationality nor to say that there are no <u>standards</u>, or that <u>any</u> standard will do for validating claims and justifying beliefs. Rather, the standards themselves are conventional - they do not stand <u>outside</u> of history and social practices and we must, therefore, have a concept of rationality which is implicated <u>within</u> society and practices. The same argument can be used in terms of the notion of 'scientific method' - its existence is not being challenged nor the fact that it has proved successful in facilitating the endeavours of natural science (although as we have seen it is not what some philosophers of science have conventionally thought it to be). However, it is not eternal and universal and again therefore has to be seen as conventional.

An alternative to this a priori conception of rationality is the idea of <u>dialogical</u> rationality. This rejects foundations and instead sees claims and beliefs as being justified through dialogue involving interpretation, deliberation, and choice. In rejecting foundations, the idea of some universal and invariant standard is also rejected and replaced by the idea that standards are located in dialogue. So we argue for or against a belief but we do so not in terms of whether it has a secure foundation in a universal rationality but pragmatically in terms of the concrete advantages and disadvantages of the belief. So, too, we can see 'objectivity' as an expression of consensus (Rorty, 1980), and truth as that which can be dialogically validated by those 'who share the same world at a given time in history' (Rowan and Reason, 1981:133).

It follows from this that dialogue may reach a temporary end-point but by its nature is never permanently terminated. This links to the earlier point about the contingency of knowledge. It will be recalled that Gadamer's notion of the 'fusion of horizons' left open the possibility of simultaneously changing one's prejudices and deepening understanding of the unfamiliar and the problematic. The same is the case for standards of rationality. Warnke makes the point that rationality is 'a willingness to admit the existence of better options'; even though knowledge may be contingent this 'is not a basis for suspending confidence in the idea of reason but rather represents the very possibility of rational progress' (Warnke, 1987:173).

There is another aspect to this which is of the greatest importance. To talk of the place of dialogue is to recognize that our existing beliefs, claims, and practices can be seen to be inadequate only through being confronted by <u>other</u> beliefs, claims, and practices. The 'foundation' disciplines may, in certain circumstances, fulfil the role of this 'other'. However, they can only do so if they are genuinely <u>part of</u> the dialogue - in other words if they ceased to be seen as <u>foundations</u>.

We would claim that it is unnecessary to see disciplines as foundations of anything. The very notion of 'foundations' is part of philosophy's obsessive search for a counter to the 'Cartesian Anxiety' which Bernstein describes in the following way: 'either there is some basic foundational constraint or we are confronted with intellectual and moral chaos' (Bernstein, 1986:42). But is 'chaos' the only alternative?

The fear of 'chaos' springs from the fear of scepticism and relativism - a fear which, as we have seen, is also thought to exist in accepting the hermeneutic circle. Traditionally, scepticism argues that no claim to knowledge can ever be justified while relativism argues that there is no way of deciding between the true and the false. We, however, are not adopting such a stance towards disciplines and their knowledge claims. We are certainly not saying that the latter can never be justified or that we cannot decide between the true and the false. Rather, we are saying that we accept the view taken by contemporary critics of foundationalism, that in evaluating claims to knowledge and in deciding the true from the false we cannot, as it were, 'step out' of ourselves, our history, and our socio-cultural practices.

This certainly implies that there are no <u>universal</u> and <u>invariant</u> foundations and criteria for deciding. In his reading of Rorty, Bernstein interprets him to be saying that 'there is no other way to justify knowledge claims or claims to truth than by appealing to those social practices which have been hammered out in the course of human history' (Bernstein, 1986:41). The way in which we inquire, the way in which we build knowledge are themselves social practices and it is within these that standards and evaluative frameworks are formed. If this is so, then forms of knowledge (disciplines) are conventions whose justification is not dependent on the universal and ahistorical criteria of truth and rationality. Instead, they can only be justified pragmatically within the arena of dialogue. The alternative to 'chaos', therefore, is dialogue (in the sense of edification), which from the viewpoint of the relation between education and the disciplines is a good deal more appropriate and useful than all the arguing about whether or not disciplines are foundations.

On the other hand, just as forms of knowledge and standards are situated, so too are we situated within 'prejudices' and 'traditions'. We have already noted that dialogue may not be genuine and unconstrained, that openness to learning may be limited by ideology and that knowledge is always co-implicated with power. We will explore these issues in greater depth in later chapters. For the moment we would emphasize that disciplines are not just neutral bodies of knowledge but have constitutive and regulative features. For educational practitioners, disciplines and the notion of foundations are inevitably part of their prejudices and traditions. At the same time, however, these are not fixed and immune to change. Although we cannot 'step out' of prejudices generally we can 'step out' of particular prejudices.

Our interpretive horizons change as our understandings change. The significance of the hermeneutic circle is that understandings start from ourselves but, as we change, so things which had an apparently fixed and unchanging meaning no longer do so. If we are able to surface our prejudices and thus reveal the influence of tradition and the nature of our situatedness, this critical process of self- and situational-awareness can enable us to transcend the limitations and constraints of ideology and power. In later chapters we will consider how educational intervention in the form of teaching and research can facilitate this critical process. In the next chapter we go on to consider more specifically the part that foundation disciplines, as formal theory, have within practice.

REFERENCES

Allman, P. (1983) 'The nature and process of adult development' in M. Tight (ed.) Adult Learning and Education, London: Croom Helm.
Bernstein, R.J. (1986) Philosophical Profiles, Oxford: Polity Press.
Bright, B.P. (1985) 'The content-method relationship in the study of adult education', Studies in the Education of Adults, 17 (2) 168-83.
Egan, K. (1984) Education and Psychology, London: Methuen.
Elsey, B. (1986) Social Theory Perspectives on Adult Education, Nottingham.
Emler, N.P. and Heather, N. (1980) 'Intelligence: an ideological bias of conventional psychology' in P. Salmon (ed.) Coming to Know, London: Routledge & Kegan Paul.
Gadamer, H.G. (1975) Truth and Method, London: Sheed & Ward.
Goffman, E. (1974) Frame Analysis Harmondsworth: Penguin.
Harre, R. (1980) 'Man as rhetorician', in A.J. Chapman and D.M. Jones (eds), Models of Man, Leicester: British Psychological Society.
Henriques, J. et al. (1984) Changing the Subject, London: Methuen.
Hirst, P.H. (1974) Knowledge and the Curriculum, London: Routledge & Kegan Paul.
Jarvis, P. (1985) The Sociology of Adult and Continuing Education, London: Croom Helm.
Kelly, G.A. (1963) A Theory of Personality: The Psychology of Personal Constructs, New York: Norton.
Knowles, M. (1984) The Adult Learner: A Neglected Species, (3rd edn), Houston.
Louch, A.R. (1966) Explanation and Human Action, Oxford: Blackwell.
Mittler, P.J. (1982) 'Applying developmental psychology', Educational Psychology, 2 (1), 1-5.
Richardson, J.T.E. et al. (1987) Student Learning, Milton Keynes: Open University Press.
Rogers, C.R. (1961) On Becoming a Person, Boston: Houghton Mifflin.
---- (1969) Freedom to Learn, Columbus, Ohio: Merrill.
Rorty, R. (1980) Philosophy and the Mirror of Nature,

Oxford: Blackwell.

Rowan, J. and Reason, P. (1981) 'On making sense', in P. Reason and Rowan, J. (eds) *Human Inquiry: A Sourcebook of New Paradigm Research*, London: Wiley & Sons.

Ruddock, R. (1972) *Sociological Perspectives on Adult Education*, Manchester, Monograph 2.

Rybash, J.M., Hoyer, W.J. and Roodin, P.A. (1986) *Adult Cognition and Aging*, Oxford: Pergamon.

Saljo, R. (1987) 'The educational construction of learning' in J.T.E. Richardson *et al.* (eds) *Student Learning*, Milton Keynes: Open University Press.

Salmon, P. (ed.) (1980) *Coming to Know*, London: Routledge & Kegan Paul.

---- (1985) 'Educational psychology and stances towards schooling', in G. Claxton *et al.*, *Psychology and Schooling: What's the Matter?*, London: Institute of Education, University of London.

Smail, D. (1980) 'Learning in psychotherapy', in P. Salmon (ed.) *Coming to Know*, London: Routledge & Kegan Paul.

Stevens, R. (1983) *Freud and Psychoanalysis*, Milton Keynes: Open University Press.

Swann, W. (1985) 'Psychological science and the practice of special education', in G. Claxton *et al.*, *Psychology and Schooling: What's the Matter?*, London: Institute of Education, University of London.

Walkerdine, V. (1984) 'Developmental psychology and child-centred pedagogy', in J. Henriques *et al.*, *Changing the Subject*, London: Methuen.

---- (1985) 'Psychological knowledge and educational practice: producing the truth about schools', in G. Claxton *et al.*, *Psychology and Schooling: What's the Matter?*, London: Institute of Education, University of London.

Walsh, D. (1978) 'Sociology and the social world', in P. Worsley (ed.) *Modern Sociology*, (2nd edn), Harmondsworth: Penguin.

Warnke, G. (1987) *Gadamer: Hermeneutics, Tradition and Reason*, Oxford: Polity Press.

Chapter Four

RECONCEPTUALIZING THEORY AND PRACTICE

THEORETICAL AND PRACTICAL KNOWLEDGE

A dilemma exists in most forms of adult education, particularly continuing professional education, which has unfortunate consequences for research and professional formation. In the latter, for example, the stated rationale is invariably practical in terms of helping the practitioner by developing skills and capabilities and thus enhancing the quality of practice. Yet, in the main, content emphasizes theoretical knowledge with the result that the practical aim is not realized. That this should happen so consistently is surprising and in need of explanation. To locate the source of the dilemma we have to examine the effects of a particular conceptualization of practice and its implications for the relationship between theory and practice.

Schon (1983) has pointed out that a dilemma of rigour and relevance is also found within practice and he attributes this to the influence of the 'technical-rationality model'. In his view, this functions as both a dominant and an oppressive paradigm within practice. It assumes that professional knowledge is based on theory from which is derived general principles (or rules) which can be applied to the 'instrumental problems' of practice. Theory is therefore privileged as 'real' knowledge whilst practice, seen as consisting merely of skills, is taken to be the application of that knowledge to the solving of problems.

This leads to a differential value being attached to theory and practice and a differential status accorded the theorist as against the practitioner. We see the model's differentiating effect within professional education curricula in the division into theoretical studies based on 'foundation' disciplines, professional studies, and supervised practice; a division which is hierarchical rather than merely functional.

The model is a powerful one influencing the conceptions and assumptions of theorist and practitioner alike. The power lies in the assumption that the <u>application of theory</u> is the only certainty of 'rigour' in practice. At the same time, however, it is precisely this conceptualization which produces the dilemma of 'rigour or relevance' in practice, research, and professional formation. The achievement of rigour is purchased at the expense of relevance, since, according to Schon (1983), practice situations by their very nature are not amenable to a direct and linear application of theory - even practice of a routine kind cannot be so characterized. There are many practice situations which are not routine and manifest uncertainty, uniqueness, instability, and value conflict - where ends are not always known and given and the selection of means cannot simply be based on technical criteria of efficiency and effectiveness. Schon seeks to demonstrate that there is an 'epistemology of practice' which is quite different from theoretical knowledge. As a consequence, to be relevant, to address practice as it really is, practitioners may have to abandon the 'rigour' of technical-rationality.

Equally, the privileging of theoretical studies in professional education and training appears to guarantee rigour yet so often leaves students (practitioners) feeling that they have not learned anything of relevance to their everyday practice. This particular form of the dilemma is, of course, well known and is seen as a feature of the so-called 'gap' which is said to exist between theory and practice. The problem of the 'gap' is invariably seen in terms of how it can be bridged, either in terms of communicating theory more effectively to practitioners or in finding ways of implementing theory more effectively in practice situations (Carr, 1980).

It is clear, however, that the dilemma and its associated problems are not essentially ones of making theory simpler for practitioners to understand or of teaching theory which is directly and obviously relevant to the work of practitioners. Rather, the source of the difficulty lies in the predicated existence of the 'gap' itself and the consequent way in which it has been conceptualized and constructed.

One major problem is that theory and practice are both conceptualized in ways which seemingly are not congruent with the nature of education. As seen in Chapter 3, in certain kinds of practice like medicine and engineering this may be less of a problem, although even in these areas this is not always the case. However, since education, unlike medicine and engineering, is not obviously a practical field of knowledge, the nature and function of 'theory' in education have always been matters of controversy.

Clearly, the technical-rationality model is a version of the positivist paradigm of natural science, as discussed in Chapter 2. Here, the role of theory is to reveal the nature of the world; what is the case rather than what ought to be. Theory, ostensibly, is not concerned with values but with inquiry conducted in a scientific way. From this inquiry or research emerges a body of knowledge which, through explanation and prediction, enables the world to be controlled. In education, those working within this paradigm would claim that theoretical knowledge is the means by which practice is justified: practices can be assessed and thus warranted to the extent that they have theoretical backing. Practice therefore consists of solving technical problems through rational decision-making procedures. Theory tells us what is the case, and thus what would happen if certain things were done rather than others. Assuming given educational ends, then it is possible rationally to choose the means which will achieve those ends most efficiently and effectively.

This implies, first, that the theorist and the practitioner have to be different, since it is only the former who has access to the necessary scientific expertise. Second, therefore the practitioner is in a sense always a passive implementor, since ends are pre-given and means decided by the theorist; at best the practitioner is a skilled craftsman implementing the 'design' of others. Third, educational problems are essentially physical or resource problems capable of resolution through the use of 'objective' evidence, rational decision-making, and appropriate technical means.

The technical-rationality model has, of course, been subjected to sustained attack - to the extent that in education, at least, its position is beleaguered. Yet it still possesses some credibility and we will need to return later to why it does but, for the moment, we need to examine the nature of this attack.

THE CRITIQUE OF TECHNICAL-RATIONALITY

One important argument is that theoretical knowledge cannot be simply 'mapped' on to practice situations. These necessitate practical judgements about what is to be done which do not automatically follow from theoretical knowledge. The empirical data contained in the latter do not unequivocally point to certain kinds of action. As Hartnett and Naish (1976) point out, practical judgements are always made in conditions of 'bounded rationality' where theoretical knowledge is often incomplete and practice situations never fully understood. To put it another way, practice is always underdetermined by theory.

The relationship between the 'theoretical' and the 'practical', in relation to judgement, knowledge and problem-solving, is difficult and complex. However, we are not claiming that practical judgements have no connection with the empirical data contained in theoretical knowledge. In making practical judgements, appeals to the known nature of the world constitute an important element in both justifying and criticizing such judgements. The point we would make at this stage is that they are only one element and perhaps not the most important. Furthermore, whilst theoretical knowledge may be an element in a discourse of justification, it is the relationship of practical judgement and reasoning to action which most clearly demonstrates the function of theoretical knowledge.

Practical judgement and reasoning are exercised in a context where the emphasis is on action to bring about desired change. Problems requiring resolution are located in a context or situation where appropriate action is needed. The task of practical reasoning is to figure out what the appropriate action might be and put it into practice. In other words what might be termed 'action-reasoning' is involved. It is not a kind of contemplative, detached thinking where an ideal resolution is formulated which is theoretically acceptable but which is not expected to be practically implemented, or which could not be implemented without violating the 'ethics' of the situation. Practical judgement and reasoning must ultimately stand the test of practice not of theory. They are responsive and responsible to the situation, not to scientific rigour.

The emphasis therefore is on the taking of appropriate or right action which is crucially dependent on the context or situation. Every context is likely to have its own distinctive features which will both provide possibilities and impose constraints on what can be done. The practitioner therefore needs to have a situational or contextual knowledge which encompasses an understanding of these possibilities and constraints, and an awareness of their implications for action. Furthermore, contexts are also likely to be continually changing, and so the practitioner's situational knowledge must be correspondingly flexible and dynamic.

Theoretical knowledge is neither situational nor action-oriented. It is impersonal and universal (Bohme, 1983), concerned to explain the world not to act on it and in it, and is formulated in a discourse of generalizations. Although theoretical knowledge strives for empirical validity it is not simply a collection of 'facts' about particular situations or a set of prescriptions about what to do in those situations. Theoretical knowledge cannot, therefore, take account of contexts either in terms of their uniqueness or their propensity to change. Nor can it tell practitioners what is the right action that will resolve a specific problem in those contexts.

Theoretical knowledge does constitute an element in the justification of practical judgements. But there is a limit to this, since the justification itself requires a judgement as to which 'bits' of theoretical knowledge are relevant to the particular practice situation and, if these are in conflict, what criteria are appropriate for assessing relevance. The answers to these questions cannot be found in theoretical knowledge itself but require a process of deliberation and interpretation which is an essential aspect of judgement and action in practice situations. Clearly, therefore, the process involves hermeneutic understanding.

Another consideration is the distinction which can be made between theoretical and practical knowledge in terms of the well-known phenomena of knowing something 'in theory' and yet being unable to do it and its obverse, being able to do something but being unable to specify what one does in terms of 'theory'. In both cases this would seem to illustrate that doing something (practice) is not simply the application of sets of definable precepts (theory). Doing something in the sense of a skilled activity is often characterized by qualities of routineness and automaticity - in other words, there appears to be no prior theorizing

(Squires, 1982). Polanyi (1958) claims that 'doing something' is a matter of having tacit knowledge which cannot be specified in theoretical precepts. Furthermore, since there is considerable individual variation it would be impossible to specify the theoretical precepts in advance, since the latter would have to be infinite in number to accommodate the variations.

In many kinds of practice, action is not simply a matter of exercising routine skills. Whilst there is undoubtedly a tendency to make practice routinized for the sake of manageability, there is always a strong element in all practice situations of complexity and uncertainty which resists routinization. Teaching would be a good example in this respect. In considering the nature of teaching and the kinds of action required in specific practice situations it is clear that teachers do not apply a set of general theoretical precepts. If they were to do so they would literally be unable to teach. Non-routinizable skills are demonstrated through what teachers actually do, for example attending and being sensitive to developing situations, anticipating problems, making on-the-spot decisions, and experimenting. None of these actions depend on finding and applying theoretical knowledge. Furthermore, to reinforce the point, how teachers teach depends to a crucial degree on the kind of people they are.

Practical knowledge cannot therefore be derived purely from theoretical knowledge and practice is not something which can be merely 'read off' from theory. The learning of theory cannot tell anyone how to practice; in a very real sense practice is learnt in practice. Practice is located in practical knowledge which is situational and action-oriented.

So far, we have concentrated on two major issues in our critique of the technical-rationality model in education - the underdetermination of practice by theory and the related issue of the relationship of judgement, reasoning and knowledge in the theoretical and practical realms itself. At this point it is necessary to consider the nature of theoretical knowledge in education.

THEORETICAL KNOWLEDGE AND VALUES IN EDUCATION

In an earlier chapter we examined the problems resulting from attempts to reduce the social sciences to natural science and saw, among other things, how the nature of the objects of study resisted such a reduction. Furthermore, it was shown that the paradigm of natural science, with its positivistic features, itself embodies a conception of science which is oversimplified in relation to current, post-empiricist conceptions of the nature of science and scientific method.

We also noted that within social science there is fragmentation and conflict both between and within the constitutive disciplines. Their claim therefore to explain the nature of the social world is extremely shaky and to look to them to provide the theoretical knowledge upon which educational practice is founded would appear to be mistaken. As Carr (1982) points out, psychology, sociology, and philosophy mutually reject each others' theoretical framework and underlying assumptions. Moreover, within each of these disciplines there are conflicting paradigms; for example, in psychology between the behaviourist and the humanistic. Even pragmatically, therefore, it is difficult to see how, in education, questions of practice are supposed to be resolvable through appeal to theory. Even the most ardent supporter of the technical-rationality model would be hard pressed to find theory which would satisfy the three criteria of being scientifically 'respectable', ecologically valid, and commanding agreement beyond the immediate circle of its own proponents.

The educational practitioner is entitled to ask which of the conflicting 'bits' of theoretical knowledge is most securely established. The answer must be that there is precious little, in any sense, which is relevant to educational practice. However, this is not just because the positivistic search for such theoretical knowledge seems immune to success but that, given time, such knowledge will exist. Rather, because of the nature of education as a 'contested' concept (Hartnett and Naish, 1975), the search itself is essentially nugatory and, therefore, trying to find knowledge which would be the foundation for educational practice would seem to be wasted effort.

The notion of a 'contested concept' is useful in emphasizing the importance of means and ends in education.

In practical fields of knowledge, such as engineering and medicine, ends appear determinate and less subject to conflicts of value. In education, however, the opposite is the case. Ends are not given and are only temporarily determinate. Value conflicts about the nature of education, what goals it should be directed to, and what purposes it should serve, are endemic and intrinsic to the very nature of education. Therefore, there is no single theory that can determine its ends, goals, and purposes, and any principles derived from a theory which was supposedly the foundation of educational practice could only be appropriately 'educational' within a particular set of educational values. Since there is this 'contest' of values, choices always have to be made; it is not theory, therefore, which influences the making of choices but the choices which influence the relevance of theory.

This consideration suggests a very fundamental weakness in the technical-rationality model which, as we have seen, separates means from ends. In just the same way that ends must always be located within a framework of values, means must also be so located. The latter are not just about technical questions; indeed, in education, they hardly ever are. As Carr and Kemmis point out, means are not chosen on technical grounds in terms of their efficiency but in terms of 'what it is permissible to do to other people and what it is not' (Carr and Kemis, 1986:77). What may be most efficient may also be morally obnoxious and so, in education (which is essentially about changing people in desired directions through desirable ways), the framework of values must always be part of the enterprise.

This means that, in reality, ends and means cannot be separated. Ends are themselves the values which constitute means as essentially educational. The technical-rationality model sees means as instrumentalities which produce certain ends. More correctly, however, means are themselves imbued with values derived from ends, so the relationship between ends and means is intrinsic not instrumental. In which case, since there can be conflict over the choice of ends, there can also be conflict over the choice of means. The 'contest' in education encompasses both.

The argument so far has been that the technical-rationality model is inappropriate and misleading for education. Practice is equated with technique and thereby relegated to an instrumental and subordinate position in relation to theory. The theory-practice relationship is conceived as a dualistic opposition and a mechanistic application conveying a misleading picture of the nature of education. It has become both oppressive and limited in its usefulness (Eraut, 1985); although, as we have noted, its validity and usefulness have come under increasing challenge. Certainly, for many practitioners it no longer seems helpful as a working model of how to tackle the real world of practice.

However, the continuing power of the technical-rationality model has tended to prevent detailed examination of the nature of practical knowledge. Adherents of the model see the latter as essentially specific, intuitive, and unsystematic, and therefore not 'real' knowledge. The consequence of this position is one that concerns us, since it fails to address the problematics of practice (a matter which we would consider essential to an understanding of the theory-practice relationship).

RECONSIDERING THE NATURE OF PRACTICE

Pring (1970) maintains that the failure to problematize practice is inevitable, given the tendency to focus exclusively on 'theory' in considering the theory-practice relationship. If the nature of theory is clarified, so his argument goes, then the relationship is also clarified. Equally, the nature of practice requires clarification, otherwise the dualism we have noted is perpetuated.

Pring's analysis is worth considering, since it introduces an important argument about the nature of practice. Basically, he is saying that, since practice is concerned with action, the intentionality of the agent is a fundamental feature of the action. Actions can only be characterized by the concepts which the agent has - concepts which themselves are located within a social discourse of norms, rules, and meanings. In other words, all actions, since they presuppose intentions, are embedded within conceptual frameworks or paradigms which depend on social living. Given this, therefore, practice must presuppose an implicit or informal 'theory'. We have alluded to this in the previous chapter; essentially one cannot talk of 'practice' without also talking of the 'theory' in which it is paradigmatically located. Thus, as Pring points out, theory and practice are <u>conceptually</u>, not contingently, linked.

Carr (1980, 1986) also argues that practice consists of intentional activity located in conceptual frameworks through which practitioners make sense of their activity which he refers to as 'theory'. He points out that they enable practice to be characterized and assessed both in terms of the practitioner's own practice and that of others. De Castell and Freeman refer to practice as 'intrinsically instrumental action where theory is internally or conceptually related to the action itself' (de Castell and Freeman, 1978:19).

This way of analysing practice points to an alternative way of seeing the theory-practice relationship. By problematizing practice, the dualism of theory and practice is subverted and in its place we have a conception of the interleaving of theory and practice. This notion of theory as 'implicit' or 'grounded' in practice means that the latter is not 'some kind of thoughtless behaviour which exists separately from "theory" and to which theory can be applied' (Carr and Kemmis, 1986:113). Anything that is consciously and intentionally performed implies a conceptual framework or 'theory' which renders the activity meaningful. This implies that 'theory' is not something which is mechanically 'applied' to practice but is already present in any practice, such that without it practice would not be practice but merely random behaviour.

What then is the function of this 'informal' theory? To answer this we need to remind ourselves of the nature of education as a practical activity. Informal theory enables practitioners to work within the situations in which they find themselves, by relating their activities to both what is desirable and what is possible within those situations and to assess the outcomes of their activities in the light of these considerations. Since without such a 'theory' practice would be random and purposeless, we can say that it 'forms' practice. It enables practitioners to make sense of what they are doing and thus appears to have an enabling function.

This informal theory, however, has another function which is perhaps best explained through Schon's (1983) notion of 'reflection-in-action'. Schon problematizes practice by seeing it as a world of ill-defined problems where ends are often not known in advance. Practice situations are confused and tricky and the practitioner has to 'feel' his way through them. This is done through reflection-in-action which involves turning thinking back onto action. Through reflection, the practitioner brings to the surface the implicit and tacit knowledge in the action which is then integrated with the action and its outcome. The process therefore involves a relationship between understanding, action, and change. It is transactive in that an attempt to understand a situation through action leads to changes in the situation, changes which themselves generate new understandings and renewed action.

For Schon, practice involves 'action on the world' arising from practice situations where there is not only an inability to solve a problem but where the problem might be to actually define the 'problem' in the first place. Here we see a contrast with the technical-rationality model which sees practice as merely instrumental problem-solving. In practice situations, finding the problem requires 'problem-setting' action as a pre-requisite to any kind of problem-solving. Problem-setting requires 'understanding' the practice situation in new ways and acting appropriately through the new understanding. As the situation evolves, understanding both shapes and is shaped by the action taken and the resulting changes in the situation. The 'understanding', therefore, is not derived from abstract theory or general principles but is situational and action-oriented.

Through this reflection-in-action, new knowledge is constantly being generated. It builds up into a situational repertoire allowing the practitioner to cope with different kinds of problematic situations; the repertoire enables the new and unfamiliar to be related to similar but different situations successfully handled in the past. Every practice situation, therefore, potentially enables an extension and reconstruction of the repertoire and thus enriches reflection-in-action.

For Schon, therefore, 'theory' both 'generates' practice and is generated by it. The relationship is not causal but interactive. It enables practitioners to cope successfully, given that every practice situation, as we have seen earlier, has its distinctive features. The 'theory' is built on existing repertoires and enables certain kinds of actions and understandings appropriate to particular situations to be brought together. It is therefore not generalizable nor rigorous in a positivistic sense. Schon, however, is concerned to argue that the 'theory' is not merely a theory of the particular and that rigour is manifested in the quality of the understandings that arise and the action that is taken.

Clearly, he is arguing against the position that there is only one universal and invariant mode of rationality and type of rigour.

What Schon shows, therefore, is that informal 'theory' is located in the experiential world of practitioners and is a kind of knowledge which is not abstract and decontextualized yet is not merely intuitive and unsystematic in a 'scientific method' sense. It provides a means for informed action in coping with practice situations and therefore seems to have a regulatory function in addition to the enabling function noted earlier.

The notion of informal theory emphasizes the inseparability of theory and practice and therefore allows for the rejection of the traditional dualism and the confusing metaphor of 'gaps' which normally characterize the relationship. Theory is not projected as abstract and generalized knowledge applied to practice but as situational theory, both entering in and emerging from practice. Thus practice is not just instrumentality, a mere 'testing-ground' for theory but something which has a life and complexity of its own. It is socially-located, very often complex and problematic, and consciously and intentionally carried out.

Finally, as was noted in Chapter 3 in the discussion of practical knowledge, practice is not just action but proper or right action (Clark. 1976), because it is always responsive to situational values and concerns. The question for the practitioner is not 'what rules should I apply' but 'how I ought to act in this particular situation'? Practice therefore is not about instrumental control but about understanding and acting rightly within a framework of situational values and constraints. As de Castell and Freeman put it, the emphasis is on actions which 'constitute the merging of theory and practice and bridge the conceptual gap between theory and practice' (de Castell and Freeman, 1978:20).

The notion of 'informal' practitioner-based theory is clearly not compatible with the technical-rationality model. Instead, it has to be seen as located within an interpretive paradigm. This, as we have seen, emphasizes actions and their location in inter-subjective structures of meaning. Where technical-rationality emphasizes explanation and prediction, using the methods of natural science, the 'interpretive' stresses understanding and interpretation through the hermeneutic circle.

Implicit in the interpretive paradigm is a view of what 'theory' contributes to practice. If actions are embedded in frameworks, then their elucidation enables practitioners to be more self-aware of their actions. They may more readily understand their practice situations and their own role within them more explicitly. 'Practices are changed by changing the ways in which they are understood' and 'theory affects practice by exposing the theoretical context that defines practice to self-reflection' (Carr and Kemmis, 1986:91). Theorizing therefore functions to make the informal theory (which is already present in practice) open and explicit, enabling practitioners to surface and change their understandings and, hopefully, their practice.

As we have noted, practice is conceived as a species of 'deliberation', consisting of action which is not only informed by theory but also committed by values. This links up with the so-called 'practical' view of education, which locates the latter in a fluid and complex social world. Such a view would therefore reject any notion of educational practice as being about technical control but would see it instead as being about the exercise of judgement and the deployment of practitioner expertise. The practitioner is engaged in deliberation relating his/her understandings of the situation to experience and a framework of values. It is perhaps no surprise, therefore, that theory is seen to relate to practice through enlightening practitioners, deepening their insights and enabling them to probe the surface of practice (Carr, 1986).

THE LIMITATIONS OF INFORMAL THEORY

In the same way as we earlier considered some of the limitations of the interpretive paradigm, so, too, we now need to consider some of the limitations of the notion of informal theory. A crucial one is the status of this theory and the kind of knowledge which it presupposes. Informal theory, since it is implicit, is not always immediately present to the consciousness of the practitioner. The essence of practice as deliberation, however, is about the process of reflection and, in particular, reflection on the knowledge contained in informal theory.

A great deal of this knowledge is what might be called 'common-sense' knowledge, whose key characteristic is the 'unquestioned assumptions held by (groups) through which they tackle problems, (and) pick out features of experience as significant' (Pring, 1977:58). The kind of knowledge possessed by educational practitioners is very often of this common-sense variety. It is taken-for-granted knowledge, where assumptions are not subjected to reflection and critical scrutiny.

As Carr and Kemmis point out, educational practitioners, in common with all practitioners, possess a variety of different kinds of knowledge varying in its rootedness in common-sense, and therefore in its degree of taken-for-grantedness. As they aptly put it: 'Some of these kinds of knowledge have the roots of their rationality well hidden "underground" in the life of practice. Others have their heads in clouds of talk' (Carr and Kemmis, 1986:42). They conclude from this that both practice and 'informal' theory have to be problematized or, as Pring puts it: 'It is necessary to expose to critical scrutiny that which is believed uncritically' (Pring, 1977:77).

Squires (1982) in analysing the nature of informal theory isolates three possible weaknesses. First, given that it is practitioner theory it will by its nature be essentially private and, to a large extent, unique to the individual practitioner. Dialogue about efficacy, an essential part of reflection and critical scrutiny, may therefore be difficult. Second, the most common function of 'informal' theory is to eliminate practice problems rather than improve practice; the concern is with 'fire-fighting' rather than 'fire-prevention'. This is linked to the point made earlier that much practice consists of routinized, automatized skills. Furthermore, a great deal of practitioners' knowledge consists of 'survival' and coping skills - getting by rather than doing better. Finally, informal theory tends to 'tap only the most immediate and obvious causes, and explanations may be of a simple, linear kind rather than multicausal or interactive' (Squires, 1982:48). It follows that informal theory can be limited in the scope and depth of the reflection which it is able to incorporate.

It appears, therefore, that the problem with informal theory is that its strength is also its weakness. Inseparably rooted as it is in practice it may actually impede reflection and critical scrutiny. Although it is an essential element of informed and committed action in educational practice, informed commitment may only be potentially rather than actually present in certain contexts. As Carr and Kemmis put it: 'because these theoretical preconceptions are largely the product of habit, precedent and tradition they are rarely formulated in any explicit way or informed by any clearly articulated process of thought' (Carr and Kemmis, 1986:123). Their conclusion is that the knowledge contained in informal theory can only be the starting-point for reflection and critical scrutiny and 'cannot simply be taken-for-granted and systematized into theory nor can it be taken as definitive in prescribing for practice' (Carr and Kemmis, 1986:44). Furthermore, informal theory is not always reflexive; the knowledge it contains and the practice it guides is concerned, as we have seen, with what 'works'. In other words, the capacity to change interactively as the environment and circumstances change can be limited.

However, as we have seen in discussing Schon, informal theory can also function in a regulative mode where reflexivity is, in principle, possible. Problematic practice situations are resolved through an 'informed and committed action' which transactively relates the action to understandings and change in both. Schon talks of practice as 'a reflective conversation with a unique and uncertain situation' (Schon, 1983:130) which clearly implies that informal theory is no longer implicit. He describes the process in the following way:

> In this reflective conversation, the practitioner's efforts to solve the reframed problem yield new discoveries which call for new reflection in action. The process spirals through stages of appreciation, action and re-appreciation. The unique and uncertain situation comes to be understood through the attempt to change it and changed through the attempt to understand it.
> (Schon, 1983:132)

The process which Schon describes here is essentially hermeneutic and similar to Gadamer's (1975) description of the 'fusion of horizons'. Knowledge consists of a repertoire based on past instances of successful practice. This knowledge is not merely a set of taken-for-granted assumptions based on habit and prejudice. In using it to work with a problematic situation, understandings based on past situations are used only as an initial point of reference but without prejudging the question of identity. All new situations are not simply seen in routine and habitual terms as identical copies of past situations. In other words, they are seen as having 'truth', coherence and unity, an understanding of which can be revealed through dialogical encounter and the 'fusion of horizons'.

Theorizing, therefore, in going beyond the routine and habitual, becomes creative. This mode of theorizing is still situational but is capable of adding to the repertoire of knowledge which functions as a starting-point for the encounter with practice problems. Knowledge is not merely intuitive and unsystematic. Informal theory, in this sense, is not only a starting-point for reflection and critical scrutiny, but actually embodies it.

Even here, however, informal theory has its limitations. As Schon himself admits, even practitioners who might engage in reflection-in-action do not always do so. Part of the problem is that, since reflection-in-action is about experimenting in unique and uncertain situations, risk and unpredictability are inherently present. It is the very characteristics which give reflection-in-action its own particular rigour which may also lead to perceived 'threats' of unpredictability, uncertainty, and loss of control.

Any situation which involves change may prove threatening in this way. The essence of reflection-in-action is leaving oneself open, not merely trying to cope in routine and habitual ways, to 'go' with the situation as it develops. The element of risk is therefore considerable and practitioners may feel exposed and vulnerable. In reflection-in-action, experimentation may go wrong and, whilst one may not be 'blown up' literally, one could be figuratively. At the same time, reflection-in-action involves self-reflection as part of the process of changing situations - a process which can often lead to self-change. Schon refers to allowing your system 'to come apart' (Schon, 1983:270). However, individuals have a great deal invested in their intellectual and emotional systems, in their beliefs and values, and it is often easier and safer to be 'stuck' than to be productive.

There may also be other, more subtle, factors at work here. Informal theory has a particular relationship to experience and its use. It presupposes and requires that practitioners should be able to use it productively and creatively. Often being 'stuck' arises from a belief that experience cannot be coped with - a belief that arises not simply from the fear of risk but because using experience is itself seen as somehow not legitimate. As pointed out earlier, the theory-practice hierarchy assigns a lower status to practice and downgrades practice-generated learning and knowledge. However, there is also a further problem, in that, even if practitioners do not downgrade their knowledge, using experience productively may require certain prior conceptions which may not always be present in practice situations (Usher, 1985).

For these reasons, practitioners may not even initiate reflection-in-action and may remain enclosed in what Schon calls 'knowing-in-practice'. Even when practitioners do engage in reflection-in-action they may not be able to articulate what they are doing or unable to find an 'authority' for doing it. Working reflectively may often appear to have neither external justification nor generalizable value - it may 'feel' right for oneself but at the same time may appear to have no warrant outside of oneself. This may lead back to being stuck with its attendant feelings of anxiety and a consequent abandoning of working reflectively (Boxer, 1985).

The point is, therefore, that there are a number of individual constraints frequently found in practice which either prevent informal theory being used creatively or limit its scope and effectiveness. However, as well as these individual constraints, there are other kinds of constraint which are more commonly associated with institutionally located practice.

Institutions can, for example, impose constraints through the way in which practice roles are framed. Role frames influence the direction and forms of action and the kind of values which are brought to bear on problem situations. Within institutions, practice roles can be framed restrictively with certain modes of practice, the practitioner's role within these being defined in a taken-for-granted way. Institutions have what Schon terms their own 'learning systems'; like individuals, institutions have their own repertoires and exemplars which are geared towards coping and survival. Organizational learning systems may well be resistant to change and thus act as a constraint on reflection-in-action.

Argyris and Schon (1974) distinguished 'single-loop learning' (where, in practice situations, particular goals, values, and strategies are implemented rather than questioned) from 'double-loop learning' (where they were subjected to critical scrutiny). Single-loop learning seems to be present when goals, values, and strategies are simply taken for granted and the emphasis is on techniques and making techniques more efficient; it operates within a closed and self-confirming world of understandings. Double-loop learning, on the other hand, involves questioning the role of the framing and learning systems which underlie actual goals and strategies.

Single-loop learning is more commonly found because it seems to provide a degree of control and thus reduces risk both for the individual and the institution, although it is clear that risk is attenuated at the cost of creativeness. The only reflection that is possible is how to make strategies more effective, not whether the <u>strategies themselves</u> are the problem. Practice, therefore, becomes a closed world, routinized and ritualized, and ultimately ineffective in dealing with practice problems. Double-loop learning, however, can allow for reflection of a fundamental kind. As Argyris puts it: 'the basic assumptions behind ideas or policies are confronted ... hypotheses are publicly tested ... processes are disconfirmable not self-seeking' (Argyris, 1982:103-4). The world of practice is not closed, and thus problematic situations are not routinized, but at the same time uncertainty and the possible loss of control can be coped with.

Single-loop learning is perhaps another way of talking about those situations where informal theory is routinized and habitual, double-loop learning those where it is creative and reflexive. Clearly, however, there can be no guarantee that informal theory will always be the latter. This points to a distinction between reflective and unreflective practice. The latter contains informal theory but is not itself creative and generative, whereas the former can become so.

THE IMPLICATIONS FOR EDUCATIONAL THEORY

At this point, and in the light of what we have said about the nature of educational practice on the one hand and of informal theory on the other, we need to consider educational theory itself. In particular, we need to examine what the role of 'formal' theory is in relation to educational theory, taking into account our earlier critique of the role of the so-called foundation disciplines.

Clearly, we reject the traditional dualism of theory and practice on the grounds that it is impossible to conceive of practice without theory of the informal variety. The implication of this is that the term 'educational theory' can only refer to educational practitioners' informal theory and not to some 'theory' which originates outside that practice.

On reflection, we can see that the failure to recognize

this is the origin of the 'gap' between theory and practice. As Carr points out, the gap only exists because educational theory has been taken to refer 'to theories other than those guiding educational practice' (Carr, 1980:62). Theories with origins external to educational practice have been inappropriately seen as applying to the latter; for example, the 'theory' in the 'foundation' disciplines of psychology and sociology. Carr and Kemmis (1986) take the view that whatever 'gaps' exist between theory and practice arise from gaps between informal theory and educational practice. When practice no longer 'works', what actually happens does not 'mesh' with what was <u>supposed</u> to have happened, and it is informal theory which defines the latter. It is not just practice which has proved inadequate, but the informal theory also; indeed, it is the theory which directed the practice towards an end which was not in actuality realized. These gaps are therefore inevitable in any practice, including those practices which produce 'theory' in the foundation disciplines, since these in turn are also located in paradigms which contain informal theory.

This interpretation implies that educational problems do not denote a failure to apply a theory which originates outside a practice but rather a failure in informal theory. The resolution of problems lies in changing practice through changing informal theory, not the bringing to bear of new theory externally generated. The changes may be small, leading to marginal adjustments, or they may be of such a magnitude as to constitute a fundamental change in practice. In such a situation we would say that informal theory has undergone a Kuhnian paradigm shift.

Carr (1980) gives an interesting and pertinent example in this context. He points to changes that have taken place in educational practice from teacher- and knowledge-centred methods to more student-centred ones. These can be traced to changes in the conceptual frameworks and modes of understanding of informal theory. They have stressed the growth and development of the learner as the key factor, rather than the transmission of formal knowledge. As such they imply a radically different perspective of what education should be in terms of both its methods and goals.

Another example is one mentioned in the previous chapter. Maturational theories of age-related adult cognitive decline can be seen as psychological theories inappropriately 'applied' to adult education practice.

89

> Adult educators have thought of development as either the further elaboration or accumulation of knowledge or the growth of self-knowledge and understanding. Both of these functions focus upon types of content or knowledge and assume that the processes and thought structures which deal with the content are unchanging.
>
> (Allman, 1983:108)

Maturational theories, in setting limits to what adults could achieve cognitively, thus marginalized adults and affected both the quantity and nature of educational provision. Yet, practitioners were well aware that the theory was inadequate in relation to situations they encountered with 'real' adults who, in terms of cognitive decline, manifested a great deal of individual variation. Their informal theory in other words 'told' them differently. Hence, there was an educational problem which was only resolved when cognitive decline was no longer taken to be age-related but instead dependent on the quality of the adult's interaction with particular kinds of contexts. The shift in theory along the lines of seeing adults as cognitively competent at high levels in areas which they knew something about, or were skilled in, and being capable of 'post-formal' modes of thinking in those areas, led to radically different modes of practice both in terms of content and methods.

Our consideration of the nature of educational problems, and the ways in which they are resolved, leads us back to a reconsideration of educational theory. It is clear that the main function of educational theory is to help resolve problems arising in educational practice, problems which originate in the inadequacy of informal theory. This points unequivocally to the crucial role of practitioners' theorizing. The idea of education as a 'socio-practical field' (de Castell and Freeman, 1978) is relevant here. This is characterized by knowledge and understanding, which is instrumental in taking effective action to solve acknowledged practical problems. Essentially, the emphasis is on the immediately practical and the contextually acceptable.

Within the 'socio-practical', the 'gap' between theory and practice arises first, because of 'unarticulated practice' (in the sense that much of the understanding and knowledge underlying practice is tacit), a point which we have touched on earlier. Second, practice-constraining contingencies are inevitable in any social context. It is therefore suggested by de Castell and Freeman (1978) that closing the gap involves simultaneously improving the theoretical adequacy of practice and the practical utility of theory. They further suggest that the best way for this to happen is for theoreticians to become practitioners and practitioners theoreticians.

We noted earlier that educational problems arise as 'problems' for educational practitioners, and that these are not resolved by merely applying theory which originates outside educational practice. The site of origination of educational theory is educational practice, and the site of application and testing is the problems of this practice. Carr and Kemmis therefore claim that it is 'practice (that) determines the value of theory rather than theory that determines the value of educational practice' (Carr and Kemmis, 1986:52).

A possible consequence of this reasoning might be that no distinction should be made between theorizing and practising. Since practice is located in a theory and theorizing is an inevitable feature of practising (Vallance, 1982), the distinctions would appear to be artificial. Whilst one might not wish to accept entirely this argument, it does nevertheless point to an important consideration which should not be ignored. This is that practitioners must become aware of the place of theory and theorizing in their work, and that theorists need to take as their starting-point the actual situations and problems in which the work of practitioners is located.

This has two aspects. First, the kind of theory with which educational theorists are concerned starts with the concerns of practitioners. This, however, is only a starting-point. Part of the function of educational theory is to make explicit what is largely implicit in informal practitioner theory. As we have seen, although it is impossible to conceive of practice without informal theory, the latter may be limited in terms of its degree of articulation, coherence, and consistency. As such, its usefulness as a 'guide' to practice is limited, and it may actually hinder the development of new understandings in response to educational problems. The task of educational theory, therefore, is that of 'critically appraising the adequacy of the concepts, beliefs, assumptions and values incorporated in prevailing theories of educational practice' (Carr and Kemmis, 1986:115).

Second, a greater awareness of their informal theories, and the theorizing inherent in practice, could make practitioners more conscious of routine and habitual modes of working. The need here is for practitioners to convert practice into praxis - a form of practice which is both reflective and reflexive. The essence of being reflexive is that theory and practice are dialectically interrelated. Implicit theory is brought to consciousness and continually open to change in the light of practice, which itself changes as informal theory is modified. This process, therefore, clearly utilizes the hermeneutic circle of mutually-interactive backward and forward movement between understanding and action.

A problem still remains, however, concerning the role of 'formal' theory. If educational theory is concerned with the critical appraisal of 'informal' theory, with making the latter more coherent and rational and in enabling practitioners to use theory as a critical tool, then is there any role for theory originating outside education? The impression created so far might be that it has no role. However, this is not what we are trying to say.

A major difficulty that has to be considered is that the informal theory of practitioners does not exist purely as such. Moore (1981) makes the point that formal theory (she calls it 'academic' theory) is always already present, and that the common-sense knowledge contained in informal theory cannot easily be separated from formal theoretical knowledge. Educational practitioners could not help but have some formal theory incorporated into their informal theory. The fact that they have misunderstood or wrongly try to 'apply' it in their teaching is irrelevant, to the point that formal theory is already there. This implies, at the very least, that it should be made explicit, if only to correct misunderstandings, misapplications, etc.

However, there is a further, and perhaps more profound, point here. Moore puts it at its strongest by claiming that a 'genuinely' educational theory could not exist apart from formal theory. On the face of it, accepting this claim might bring us perilously close to accepting the 'foundation disciplines' approach to educational theory, which we criticized in Chapter 3. On the other hand, Moore's claim can be interpreted in a number of different ways, some of which would not be inconsistent with the line of argument we have been so far taking, whilst others would take the argument much further.

Reconceptualizing Theory and Practice

To illustrate the former, we return to a point made by de Castell and Freeman (1978), that educational theorists cannot ignore formal theory because this provides a critical perspective which allows a process of continual reassessment of informal theory in a socio-practical field, where theorizing is related to the immediately practical and takes account of contextual constraints. By a 'critical perspective' they mean that which is not concretely located in a specific context.

If the task of educational theory is to critically appraise the informal theory of practitioners and to enable practice to become praxis, then the 'tools' are needed to do the job. These tools are essentially to do with the facilitation of the process of critical appraisal, rather than with providing the content of educational theory. In that case, we could see formal theory as partly providing such tools. One way of formulating a possible relationship between formal and informal theory is by using the notion of 'review' (Usher and Bryant, 1987). This involves accepting that the purpose of formal theory is representation and explanation, and that of informal theory is judgement, interpretation, and understanding. The relationship between theory and practice is then not one where the former is 'applied' to the latter, but where representation and explanation can assist judgement, interpretation, and understanding.

A constant theme of our analysis so far has been that the informal theory of practitioners can easily become routine, habitual, and unreflective. In situations where 'problems' exist, the practitioner may become 'stuck'; normal practice is no longer helpful. Progress requires that practice be re-presented and it is here that formal theory can be a useful tool or resource by providing a means to view practice in a different way and hence to reformulate the problem. Here, therefore, theory is not applied to practice; rather, the process can be conceptualized as one where practice is reviewed (re-viewed) through theory.

This is not a smuggling in of formal theory 'through the back door' in order for it to re-assume its conventional place as a standard of veracity. Instead, the place of formal theory can be seen as a component in a process of dialogical engagement. The existence of practice problems indicates a failure of informal theory, and resolution requires an engagement of informal theory with something outside itself (the 'other' which we referred to in Chapter 3). The engagement between formal and informal theory has to be a two-way traffic - if one submerges the other, the resolution will be apparent only. The dialogical engagement is therefore constituted by the mutual interaction of formal and informal theory, the resolution being an emergent synthesis. A resolution where formal theory overwhelms informal theory would only be apparent, since it could not suggest situated action appropriate to practice. Equally, the overwhelming of formal theory would again only lead to an apparent resolution, since the latter would be but a reformulation of the original problem. It would be akin to the situation discussed where problems arising from the existence of single-loop learning can only be apparently resolved by endless reiteration of that learning mode.

What is missing from this analysis, however, is the point made in Chapter 3: that formal theories are bodies of knowledge which are themselves socially located and implicated in discursive and material practices. Without recapitulating the arguments put forward there, it is important merely to emphasize the point that disciplines can be seen as discourses, where theories and certain kinds of practice, including research, 'constitute' the objects studied.

The power of disciplines as discourses arises because the knowledge they generate normatively regulates social practices such as education. In the case of psychology and sociology we can see this clearly demonstrated in schooling and, less apparently, in adult education. Both disciplines have been intimately tied to certain kinds of educational policy and practice and have been committed to a positivistic conception of their own status and project. In this way, they have sought, through research based on the use of scientific method, to produce empirically valid knowledge which not only describes and explains the 'world' but also helps to regulate educational policy and practice. Through being empirically validated, knowledge appears to be about 'real' objects in the world; it provides 'truths' about the world and thus seems to have a warrant to regulate practice.

This is really only a variation on Foucault's (1979) theme of the relationship between power and knowledge which will be discussed more fully in Chapter 8. What is taken as 'justified true belief', knowledge, and 'rational' practice is intimately linked with forms of control within a society. It is hardly surprising, therefore, that formal theory is 'always already present'. It is knowledge constituted by a powerful discourse, which is not merely an abstract and disinterested pursuit of the 'truth', but which is present within practice itself. Educational practice, for example, involves pedagogies (in the case of adult education an 'andragogy') intimately connected with psychological theory. We have already noted that empirical 'truths' constitute the norms of these practices and the evaluation criteria for assessing the 'performance' of clients.

The power of formal theory is not always immediately apparent. It takes its most obvious form in the technical-rationality model, where theory is supposedly 'applied' to practice. We have seen that this is too problematic even within its own terms; at the same time we now have to recognize that formal theory is nevertheless there, and that the practitioner may often be unaware of its presence. Part of the problem which the practitioner faces, therefore, is to become aware of the place and power of models and formal theory. The development of this kind of critical consciousness, however, is (in a sense) the other side of the 'review' process mentioned earlier. There, formal theory's role was to bring a critical and positive dimension to bear on informal theory and practice. However, the problem is also one of becoming critically aware of the existence, power, and therefore potential oppressiveness, of formal theory within informal theory and practice.

REFERENCES

Allman, P. (1983) 'The nature and process of adult development', in M. Tight (ed.) Adult Learning and Education. London: Croom Helm.
Argyris, C. (1982) Reasoning, Learning and Action. San Francisco: Jossey Bass.
Agryis, C. and Schon, D.A. (1974) Theory in Practice, San Francisco, Jossey Bass.
Bohme, G. (1983) 'Knowledge and higher education', Studies in Higher Education 2, Stockholm: NBUC.
Boxer, P. (1985) 'Judging the quality of development', in D. Boud, R. Keogh and D. Walker (eds), Reflection: Turning Experience into Learning, London: Kogan Page.
Carr, W. (1980) 'The gap between theory and practice', Journal of Further and Higher Education, 4 (1), 60-9.
---- (1982) 'Treating the symptoms, neglecting the cause:

diagnosing the problem of theory and practice', Journal of Further and Higher Education, 6 (2), 19-29.
---- (1986) 'Theories of theory and practice', Journal of Philosophy of Education. 20 (2), 177-86.
Carr. W. and Kemmis, S. (1986) Becoming Critical, Lewes, Sussex: Falmer Press.
Clark, C. (1976) 'Education is not an academic discipline', Educational Studies, 2 (1), 11-19.
de Castell, S. and Freeman, H. (1978) 'Education as a socio-practical field: the theory-practice question reformulated', Journal of Philosophy of Education, 12, 12-28.
Eraut, M. (1985) 'Knowledge creation and knowledge use in professional contexts', Studies in Higher Education, 10 (1). 117-37.
Foucault, M. (1979) Discipline and Punish: The Birth of the Prison, trans. by A. Sheridan, New York: Vintage/Random House.
Gadamer, H.G. (1975) 'Truth and Method', London: Sheed & Ward.
Hartnett, M. and Naish, A. (1975) 'What theory cannot do for teachers', Education for Teaching, 96 (1). 12-19.
---- (1976) Theory and the Practice of Education, London: Heinemann.
Moore, P. (1981) 'Relations between theory and practice: a critique of Wilfred Carr's views', Journal of Further and Higher Education, 5 (2), 44-56.
Polanyi, M. (1958) Personal Knowledge: Towards a Post-critical Philosophy, London: Routledge & Kegan Paul.
Pring. R. (1970) 'Philosophy of education and educational practice', Proceedings of the Philosophy of Education Society, 4, 61-75.
---- (1977) 'Common-sense and education', Proceedings of the Philosophy of Education Society. 11, 57-77.
Schon, D.A. (1983) The Reflective Practitioner: How Professionals Think in Action, London: Temple Smith.
Squires. G. (1982) The Analysis of Teaching. University of Hull, Department of Adult Education.
Usher. R.S. (1985) 'Beyond the anecdotal: adult learning and the use of experience', Studies in the Education of Adults, 17 (1). 59-74.
Usher, R.S. and Bryant, I. (1987) 'Re-examining the theory-practice relationship in continuing professional education', Studies in Higher Education, 12 (2), 201-12.
Vallance. E. (1982) 'Practical uses of curriculum theory', Theory into Practice, 2 (1), 4-10.

Chapter Five

THE PRACTICE OF ADULT EDUCATION RESEARCH IN CONTEXT

INTRODUCTION

We are now in a position to examine the nature of research itself as a type of practice embodying elements of theorizing and empirical discovery, and to do so in a way that will allow the adult educator to begin to interpret the process of research and its products in a more critical and 'meaningful' way, in terms of accessing material for his/her own practice. Our intention in this and subsequent chapters is not to show how the results of particular investigations can be 'applied' to educational activities, since the burden of our argument so far has been that this would imply a simplistic conception of the theory-practice or research-practice relationship.

In the 'applications model', the importance of research to the practitioner or policy-maker is taken to lie in the use-value of its products - indeed, research is commissioned and evaluated in terms of the anticipated and assessed benefits of the 'results' or 'outcomes' which inform decision-making and implementation. One of the reasons why attempts to apply or incorporate the findings of research directly into practice are frequently disappointed lies in too literal a reading of research. It is not just that any reported disclaimers or qualifications may be ignored, but that an operating paradigm derived from the foundation disciplines of research as the practice of investigative precision directed towards discovering the 'true facts' of situations forces such a rendering - a non-reflective acceptance of research terms and of statements that such-and-such were the conditions of the research which necessarily dictated the general character, if not the specific empirical details, of the outcomes.

The immediate concern is to look at research as a methodical attempt to gain knowledge of reality, in this case the practice of capturing and making intelligible selected aspects of educational activity. Since any kind of research is not just random observation, but involves purposeful looking (i.e. is directed by some notion of the general characteristics of what is being sought), questions of 'method' must be addressed. We are not concerned, however, with the correctness of particular investigative techniques in and of themselves. To achieve an educationally appropriate understanding of research, it is necessary to go beyond questions of methodology - which, although of theoretical and procedural significance, are addressable only within the contexts of inquiry itself - and to take these contexts as given. Here the task is a more complex one of actually examining the 'given-ness', or situatedness, of research in relation to theories and practices in adult education.

To understand what is involved in pursuing research into education as a practice, which has been described as 'the attempts to bring about desirable change through desirable means', one has to consider the paradigmatic nature of educational research, as typically conducted, in terms of the available theories and methodological requirements of the foundation disciplines. For this task, research has to be re-read as both a product and a process of giving accounts (describing and explaining) instances of educational activity.

CONVENTIONAL REPRESENTATIONS OF RESEARCH

Research has been conventionally understood as one of the ways of relating theory and practice. 'Systematic research methods are the means of linking theory to the empirical world' (Ackroyd and Hughes, 1981:15). Taking the 'empirical world' for present purposes to include practices of all sorts (familial, occupational, political, etc.), research can thus be viewed as a connective activity - one which links theory and practice in a triangular relationship such as the following:

Adult Education Research in Context

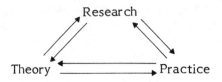

In this simple model, research is given the task of clarifying, through a systematic investigation, those theory/practice or theoretical/empirical relationships which are imperfectly understood. Its role is to develop new theories to account for known facts or to discover new facts requiring an explanation. Whether treated as a set of dependent, independent, or intervening activities, research is regarded as connecting theory and practice in a number of different ways. There are four analytically distinct sub-models, each of which locates research with respect to the theoretical and the substantive in a particular way:

1. Theory ⟶ Research ⟶ Practice

Here, research is 'theory driven'. Theory-derived hypotheses suggest particular problems for research to pursue and the task of the investigator is to measure only those theoretically relevant aspects of the practical/empirical that are required to test propositions. The controlled laboratory experiment is the archetype of this kind of research.

2. Theory ⟵ Research ⟵ Practice

In this sub-model, the relationships are reversed; researchable problems are 'grounded' in empirical/practical circumstances, which are then investigated in order to generate evidence for which explanations (theories) are sought. Research is dictated by the occurrence of events and not by theory. In the social sciences, participant observation is often considered to exemplify this kind of inductive research.

3. Theory ⟶ Research ⟵ Practice

The investigative agendas in this sub-model are independently suggested by theory on the one hand, and practice on the other. It is unlikely that they will coincide on all points; at given times the research will be required to decide between the dictates of theory and the 'real' world. For example, many of the compromises demanded in interview and survey research can be located in this type of relationship.

4.   Theory ←——— Research ———→ Practice

Although this sub-model is not a substantive possibility, it is logically possible in suggesting that research occupies an independent position outside both theory and practice which is somehow available to inform them both. However, it cannot do so independently of both at the same time. Research cannot be anything other than theoretical and/or empirical, since without them it would have no agenda.

Now, although the relationships suggested by this simple typology are apparently exhaustive, it can be readily seen that it grossly oversimplifies the nature of research and the activity of discovery. We have presented it merely in order to show the logical context in which research is often presented with respect to theory and the world of the empirical/practical, and as necessary ground-clearing for a better understanding. All that the general model actually does is to delineate different types of research and identify particular examples of inquiry (e.g. the experimental-deductive or participant-inductive) in terms of a given sub-model. But only the dependent relationships of research with respect to theory and practice are supplied. No sense is given in this mode of understanding that research itself is conjointly the situated practice of theorizing and the theorizing of practice. It is this way of looking at research that we wish to develop.

THE FOUNDATIONAL AND INSTITUTIONAL LANGUAGE OF RESEARCH

Certain characteristics of any investigative field, what it is that one is looking at or for, will be pre-given in the inquiry languages of psychology and sociology in those disciplines' characteristic foundational terms and concepts which denote instances of human activity. In arguing for a reflexive understanding of research it is therefore necessary to look at the language of its practice, whether that practice be the discovery, explanation, provision, or judgement of educational events. Language is taken to be a constituent force of practice; re-thinking practice (in this case the practice of doing educational research) therefore requires an examination of the language of practice. For this task, it is not necessary to accept the strong sense of language constituting practice (i.e. that it is the practice itself and that is all that the practice is). Whether or not such is the case is not the issue here. What can be said, however, is that the way in which either psychological or sociological language is used to constitute its own research objects, does provide evidence of the kind of practice that educational research is taken to be. The paradigmatic force of the 'normal' research methods of psychology and sociology, and of the accepted foundational nature of their relationship to education, has been such that both psychological and sociological research into educational subjects are regarded as being educational research. Educational research does not therefore have its own methodological integrity. It is a dependent practice.

In fact, educational research displays a double dependency. On the one hand, the conceptual and operational language of the foundation disciplines provides the accepted scientific vantage point from which to theorize about and research into educational matters, and which are then approached as instances of basic or underlying sociological or psychological phenomena; for example, 'organization', 'participation', 'attitudes', 'learning', etc. On the other hand, the topics or objects of research are themselves pre-interpreted through the institutional language of the controllers of educational events; for example, in the demarcations that they utilize to distinguish different forms of provision, by categorizing 'courses', 'students', 'qualifications', 'modes of study', etc. Such demarcations constitute the adult as a (potential) object of educational intervention. It is not possible for educational research to break free of this dependency by employing its own private language of investigative practice, and it cannot provide the reflexive means whereby practitioners themselves might critically assess the processes and products of inquiry without subjecting the derived language of its own practice to careful scrutiny.

Part of the value of research as a product for the user lies in the form that it takes as a report, and this form exhibits a high degree of standardization regardless of the subject matter or methods of investigation. Research reports are concerned with the production of findings, and with the processes or methods by which these are achieved. Methodology texts are largely concerned with the techniques of extracting information on site and/or drawing inferences from sample surveys about the characteristics of larger populations. Reports are accounts of situated discoveries, in which the boundaries of the 'situation' are drawn by or for the investigators themselves. These may be the naturally-occurring or stimulated events in the field (as, for example, in participant observation or action research studies), or the controlled occurrences of the formal survey or laboratory experiment. For whatever kind of study, an accounting of 'what happened' in the form of discovery procedures, description, and analysis of findings takes the research 'situation' almost exclusively to mean that in which the subject is to be found. In addition to finding things out and providing these things with an explanation, the practice of doing research is also concerned with the construction of an acceptable narrative of discovery. Generally, this means one that is impersonal and disengaged. The construction of such a narrative is a discursive performance in which the language of research practice that is learned and employed within the social science community constitutes the 'correct' way of reporting.

The paradigmatic force of reporting practices as the 'normal' ways to convey research findings does more, however, than carry messages in an acceptable medium to the would-be users of research. The language of a paradigm actually constitutes the meanings of discovery objects themselves - i.e. in those conceptual categories employed to represent them and in the methods by which any instances of these categories are recorded.

In an examination of the language of sociological practice, Phillipson (1981) rejects the dominant idea that sociological (and by extension psychological) speech provides the researcher with an observation language in which concepts stand in a relationship of literal correspondence to 'real' referents. This notion has been accepted both within and outside the foundation disciplines of education:

> Because the common culture within which sociology lives is itself primarily empiricist in character its version of authentic sociology coincides with that of the sociologist as empirical observer. The relevance, weight and influence of sociology as one discourse among others is judged in terms of its ability to assure

those who might listen to it of its empiricist commitment, that is first of all observation and reproduction of untransformed 'facts'.

(Phillipson, 1981:138)

As Phillipson sees it, the failure hitherto of social scientists to attend to the constitutive nature of language is that they have not critically examined their own practices as forms of alternative discourse to those having currency in the worlds that are the objects of their investigations. Indeed, he states that:

> Empiricism is constitutionally incapable of reflexivity because of the very ways in which it relates the observer to the observed and the world in which the observer's speech negotiates its place.
>
> (Phillipson, 1981:139)

We have already noted in Chapter 3 that there is a recognition by social scientists of the 'second order' nature of the constructs that they employ. The possibility is acknowledged that at any time research subjects may answer back from the point of view of their own first-order understandings. It is Phillipson's charge, however, that such a recognition has not yet come to terms with a further implication - namely that in addressing a pre-interpreted world, and the practices that routinely sustain meaning therein, the researcher as empiricist is accepting and thereby unwittingly reinforcing other theoretical practices as his/her own. The result of this acceptance is that the product of empiricist research is not knowledge but information which is accumulated and accommodated within -or what is more likely, ignored by - existing practices and frameworks of understanding (both of the researchers themselves and of those for whom the research is ostensibly conducted). For the educational researcher or practitioner there is a paradox here. The educator looks to the researcher to supply information that would be useful for practice, but that information as supplied is an empiricist product having no transformative potential. It has little of significance to say in itself to those who take education as a practice to be concerned with understanding and change.

Phillipson concludes with the following observation on sociology that is also applicable to the educator who, as either a producer or consumer of educational research, accepts uncritically the epistemology of empiricist social science.

> If sociology works within and accommodates to the conventional definition by others of sociology as empirical observation that produces information for use ... then <u>it fails to take a radically analytic stance towards either itself or those cultural practices that produce the culture itself as empiricist</u>. It maintains sociological practice as superior 'technically' to other discourses and this technical superiority carries a latent morality that underpins the practice and represents its deep commitment (for example, that 'more information of the kind we produce is good in itself').
> (Phillipson, 1981:146)

(It should be noted that the underlining in the above extract has been added for emphasis by the present authors.)

The point that is being made here by Phillipson is that the 'radically analytic stance' that is required by reflective practice is precluded by the mutually conventional empirical expectations and products of foundational research.

SOME RECENT RESEARCH INTO ADULT EDUCATION PARTICIPATION

In the light of our discussion so far, we are now in a position to examine an actual piece of adult education research as the practice of giving meaning to a set of activities, and to suggest how that practice might be read critically. The idea is to try and show how the distinctions that have come to be accepted between research and practice (or theory and its supposed applications) might be dissolved, and the relationships reconstituted by proposing alternative discursive forms to those of empiricism that would help to promote reflexivity in the reader of research. Whereas it could be argued that it is possible to develop an educational philosophy in a disengaged manner, the argument that we are trying to develop here implies that the obtaining of actual educational knowledge is only to be had by locating oneself as theorist or practitioner within a context of empirical problem-solving. Any debate about the value of research needs to be grounded in the actual tasks of discovery and giving meaning, the practice of actually 'doing' research rather than just thinking about methods or meta-theorizing.

Large-scale surveys of adult education are rare. Woodley et al. (1987) Choosing to Learn: Adults in Education (hereafter CTL) report and interpret the findings of one such study of participation in adult education which was commissioned by the Department of Education and Science (DES) in 1979/80 in order to provide information on the access to, and progress through, further and higher education of mature students in England and Wales. The intention was to determine 'how well the existing pattern of courses met their needs'. A consortium of three institutions carried out the research which was conducted primarily by means of a questionnaire survey of a 1980/81 sample of 12,500 adults attending both qualifying and non-qualifying courses 'of a substantial nature'. The research objectives as outlined by the DES were as follows: to identify and compare the characteristics of mature students, non-continuing students and non-participants; to establish how far particular factors acted as incentives and barriers to participation; to analyse perceptions of the relevance of courses to the participants.

The authors of CTL describe one of their purposes as going beyond the immediate task of describing the characteristics of mature students 'to develop, if not a theory, at least a conceptual model of adult participation in education' (Woodley et al., 1987:1). At the research proposal stage, barriers and incentives were characterized as being 'intrinsic' (pertaining to the adults themselves) and 'extrinsic' (associated with the substance and structure of course provision) (see Woodley et al., 1987:xv). Subsequently, a number of theoretical approaches to mature students are reviewed in terms of their suggestiveness for specific areas of inquiry. First, there are those derived from psychological theories of individual motivation, which claim to explain participation in structured learning activities as stemming from a desire to satisfy certain needs or achieve some goal. It is acknowledged that individuals may have multiple needs/goals and also that the strength and direction of motives to participate may change over time. Second, there are those theories derived from sociology which locate adult study (or its absence) in the social class membership and life-cycle concerns (e.g. occupational/family role requirements) of particular individuals and groups, and which are intended to account for differences in the amounts and forms of participation. Third, there are the 'supply side' models, or institutional theories, which focus on the content and organizational factors of provision which encourage or discourage participation. It is acknowledged that these models are relatively underdeveloped when compared to the first two kinds, but that they are necessary to a more complete understanding of the opportunity structures in which participation does or does not occur.

The researchers' review of existing theories underscores the complexity of the phenomenon of adult education participation and the difficulty for any particular theory, or even a combination of different types of explanatory approach, in accounting for the many qualitative and quantitative distinctions that need to be drawn. Of necessity, and as a true reflection of the state of research into participation, we are presented with a set of partial and overlapping existing explanations in which the different approaches each offer plausible suggestions for lines of inquiry - in effect, they are investigative pointers - rather than testable propositions. The different theories are reported as plausible, and to some extent overlapping partial perspectives, but they are not compared in terms of any contradictory propositions that might thereby be derived and which might in principle be tested by an appeal to some discoverable 'facts'. This research does not therefore take the form of hypothetico-deductive theory-testing, nor indeed does it claim to do so. Rather, it is directed towards discovering those 'facts' about participation through the suggestions offered by different theories about where to look and what to measure. However, what is only acknowledged at a procedural level - and what, we want to suggest, may be a source of the 'relevance problem' in the research/practice relationship - is that the complexity is made researchable only by constituting the phenomenon of participation in particular ways.

One of the purposes of any macro-survey is to identify differences within the survey population (in terms of respondents' possession of particular characteristics) and so distinguish them from other respondents, and to group these distinctions in comparable ways. CTL represents a case of what might be called 'category analytic' understanding which is typical of social survey research, one in which the categories that are employed are necessitated by the scale of the investigation and the requirement to produce comparable data. Therefore, although it is not possible for this kind of research to dispense with categories, since the data collected has to be ordered and typified in some way so that one can make sense of it, the key question is the constitutive nature of the categories themselves and the meanings that they convey.

In this particular study of participation, as with any similar kind of research, the categories are suggested in a number of ways - by the original terms of reference of the research, by the types of available theory of adult education participation (i.e. motivational, situational, institutional), by pre-survey pilot interviewing 'to confirm and develop our questionnaire design and our analysis of the statistical data' (Woodley et al., 1987:10), by practical considerations in conducting the survey (e.g. sampling restrictions), by the response options offered to the subjects in the main survey instrument, and by analytical and presentational decisions to use a tabular format for the aggregation and reporting of findings.

Since the mode that is chosen by the researchers to represent participation is a statistical one, discrete units of response are required of their subjects. Specificity and formality characterize the questionnaire, so that in reporting their own circumstances and experiences the adult students must first translate these into the option categories supplied by the investigators (even including the places where they themselves can specify 'other'). Now, for the kinds of questions that have a discrete answer, this reporting requirement may be easy enough to satisfy. This is not always the case, however, and a consideration of one important exception will allow us to highlight the 'relevance' issue for the practitioner who hopes to be informed by enquiries of this type.

The exception concerns a set of questions on aspects of mature students' experiences of participation, in which respondents are asked to record a judgement about the extent to which each item in a list of possible study/learning difficulties, aspects of teaching/learning facilities, and study benefits are regarded as problematic, satisfactory, or beneficial respectively (Woodley et al., 1987: 187-9). The multiple categories within each question are quite extensive but they permit the respondents to reply only in a manner that will allow individual responses to be grouped, and it is these grouped responses that are subsequently taken to represent aspects of 'experience'. 'Experience' is therefore construed as aggregated dispositions to respond in pre-given ways and only in discrete ways, and consequently in a formal manner that is dictated by the empirical and procedural requirements of the survey. We do not know from this investigation how any individual respondents would qualify their answers to questions about their 'experience' if they were given an opportunity to do so, or how they might describe them differently in terms other than those supplied. In fact, the survey necessarily sets aside the complexity, contingency, and self-constituted nature of experience itself.

If we consider for a moment some of the findings from the CTL survey on mature students' experiences, we learn, for example, that 'although the checklist allowed people to indicate negative experiences of learning, few were mentioned by either qualifying or non-qualifying students. The great majority of respondents had gained many positive benefits' (Woodley et al., 1987:95); and 'there were high levels of satisfaction with almost all of the items listed under teaching/learning facilities' Woodley et al., 1987:99). All items on the checklist of possible problems with 'study and learning difficulties' are located within the individual, so that 'coming to terms with the academic's way of looking at things' was recorded as somewhat of a problem by three out of ten students (Woodley et al., 1987:120, 172). Yet no policy implications are drawn for a re-assessment of teaching practice in those cases which are clearly statistically significant in the concluding chapter of the study, which is content to report that 'the experiences of our respondents indicates generally a high level of satisfaction with the services provided by their institutions' (Woodley et al., 1987:178).

Torbert (1981) has criticized conventional educational research, of which CTL is a prime example, on the grounds that the institutional practices that sustain it are characterized by what he calls 'the effort at unilateral control' in which the researchers have a knowledge of what is significant from the outset so that they can 'implement the pre-defined design as efficiently as possible' (Torbert, 1981:142). Since this kind of research is self-regulatory, it is also to a large degree self-confirming. There are no suggestions that teaching practices need to be reconsidered and these could not be deduced from the contrived nature of the responses. Indeed, the 'academic's way of looking at things' is regarded by the researchers as potentially problematic only if owned by the students in their difficulty in 'coming to terms with' it, rather than as a matter for self-examination by the academics. Given the generalizing purpose of the research, there is little in the survey findings, as presented, that resonates with the particular conditions that individual students or practitioners face. According to Torbert, 'such descriptive, disembodied knowledge' does not provide an educational means for practitioners to improve their practice, and he considers that this is so whatever the level of educational practice one looks at (teaching, administration, policy-making), since 'descriptive theory cannot help acting systems learn how to act better next time - no matter how defensible it may be in analytical and statistical terms' (Torbert, 1981:143-4).

CTL does not allow adults to make their own sense of their experiences of education. In contrast, Weil's (1986) ongoing research into non-traditional learners in higher education asks the question: 'how in fact do adults make sense of their experiences of (higher) education?'. She starts with the suggestion that all adults are 'of necessity experienced learners' (Weil, 1986:220), and that it is the meaning that they give to their earlier experiences of 'being a learner' that influences the sense that they make of subsequently becoming a learner within the formal context of higher education.

Using a qualitative design and grounded theory procedures suggested by Glaser and Strauss (1967), the research is conducted by way of unstructured depth interviews with twenty-five mature undergraduates ('non-traditional' learners in four departments of a British polytechnic). Weil's inquiry avoids the prior categorization of educational activities and attitudes by giving currency to any and all aspects of prior learning considered significant by her interviewees. In short, the conditions of the research are such that participants are given the opportunity to theorize about their own practices as learners. Equally importantly, however, what is an opportunity for her subjects is treated as an obligation upon the investigator, i.e. that this 'methodological approach demands a reflexive stance on the part of the researcher' (Weil, 1986:222).

In considering the mature students' identification of barriers to learning as they are experienced within higher education, Weil (1986) develops two related constructs to account for their perceptions. The first is that of a 'learning context' which incorporates all the structures, values and relationships which operate in a given learning environment

- both those which are evident and those which are less apparent but are experienced as 'real' by the actors involved. It is in such a context that any contradictions between the espoused purposes and intentions of education and the actual experiences of learning are felt. The second construct is that of a 'learner identity', introduced in order to represent an emergent and conditional set of dispositions towards the activity of learning, together with the following: a developing understanding of the conditions in which learning takes place; its consequences for the self as they are revealed during the course of the interviews.

Learner identity and learning context are related, in that their characteristics at any given time shape the expectations and the experience (i.e. the 'making sense') of any subsequent education. Weil discovered that the individual's sense of personal efficacy, and those positive expectations derived from earlier supportive learning contexts (provided, for example, by self-help groups and community education activities), were in many cases threatened and thwarted as a result of the personal experience of higher education:

> these forms of non-traditional education seemed to have heightened their awareness of 'hidden agendas' operating in formal education. Many expressed 'shock' at the gross contradictions between espoused values (e.g. fairness, objectivity, the development of critical thinking, etc.) and actual practices. Many experiences of higher education were retrospectively perceived by non-traditional learners as an assault on the identity which had begun to emerge through learning in other contexts.
>
> (Weil, 1986:226)

Although this is not Weil's immediate purpose, the accounts that she reports are exercises in learner self-examination which contain important implications for researching the practice of teaching adults. They establish the legitimacy of her methods of surfacing and rendering intelligible the informal understandings of learners and what are referred to as the 'disjunctions' between these and the 'competing perspectives of teachers who have been socialised largely within the formal education system' (Weil, 1986:232). Her point is that we could not actually know of these conflicts and associated problems of the perceived 'relevance' of learning through a purely formal understanding of meanings. By extension, her methods and the general constructs of 'learning context' and 'learner identity' are equally applicable to practitioners, since they are also learners who operate in formal and informal contexts. It is to these dimensions of the 'relevance' question in relating research to practice that we now turn.

THE FORMAL AND THE INFORMAL IN RESEARCH AND PRACTICE

'Learner identity' incorporates beliefs concerning what is to count as 'knowledge'. The discounting or downgrading of informal knowledge lies at the heart of the relevance question. Academic educational research is generally viewed in a formal manner, through the institutions which sustain it and the foundation disciplines which theorize its practices in various methodological dicta. At the same time, there is a recognition (not least by students, as we have seen) that it is somehow 'not real', in that it does not speak to experience.
One particular dimension of the relevance problem is addressed by Baldamus in his concern to establish a closer integration between theory and research in sociology (Baldamus, 1977). He focuses on the formal and informal dimensions of theory and research as generators of knowledge and he borrows some ideas from organization theory in order to examine the 'actual production processes of theorizing and researching itself' (Baldamus, 1977:287). When we look at 'processes of administrative organization' and the structural conditions in which practitioners operate, what we find is that two sets of activities are occurring within two frameworks of understanding - the formal and the informal. Analysts such as Schon (1983) insist that we cannot answer the question 'what is going on?' in any organization simply by accepting the formal accounts of its activities. Science presents itself to the world as being formally organized in the way that it orders and reports its own activities (e.g. as 'academic work' meeting certain criteria). Yet we know from experience and the informal admissions of scientists (as revealed by studies in the sociology of science) that much of the work that they do as theorists and empirical researchers relies heavily on the informal (guesses, common sense, serendipity, etc.). Furthermore, we also know, from studies in the history of

science, that the motivations and actions of scientists are not always of the purest. The myth of a disinterested pursuit of knowledge for its own sake and the automatic power of critical reasoning in conquering all obstacles conceals intense rivalries, intrigues, and false trials.

Baldamus offers a tentative model for examining the production of theoretical and empirical work in its informal and formal aspects. We have simplified this while retaining the sense of his representation as follows:

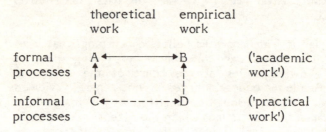

This model presents a way of locating research with respect to practice. Research is normally thought of as the activity of generating formal knowledge by doing theoretical and empirical work and the association of categories A and B is a comparatively strong one, at least in the natural sciences. It is also accepted that formal theorizing and factual discoveries rely to some extent on informal processes. What is less clear is the actual and potential influence of formal processes upon categories C and D, which jointly represent a larger category which Baldamus (1977) calls 'pragmatic knowledge'. This is the domain of the 'practical', with which formal knowledge as the domain of the 'academic' may be contrasted. But academic work is also a species of practice and as such incorporates much that is pragmatic (though this may not be admitted in the formal reporting practices of science).

Now let us consider the informal processes of obtaining knowledge through practical work and try to situate research therein. These are activities which encompass the development of 'know-how' and tacit understandings, the 'making sense' of the world in ways that have already been referred to in a learning context and in the development of a learner identity. All practitioners do 'empirical work' in that their activities involve what might loosely be called 'finding things out'; some of these things are the result of their being socialized into practice, the learning of rules (and the conditions under which they can be bent), routine exchanges between colleagues, and the discovery of facts of all kinds about the situations in which they find themselves. There is a problem about calling this 'informal research', since research suggests direction and intention, both of which are thought to be absent in this case. This is apparently so, however, only because, as academics, we operate with a formal sense of what research is/ought to be about (i.e. we think of research as being only the doing of A and B).

Category D can perhaps be more fruitfully thought of as 'personal research', grounded in the experience of practice but having some direction and intention as suggested by C (know-how, informal understanding, etc.). We have shown in an earlier chapter how formal understandings can speak to the informal attribution of meanings (through what we have called a process of 'review'). This is not possible, however, if research as an enterprise is concerned solely with the discovery of 'category facts' of a formal kind that is located outside the practice of teachers and learners. The rendition of the 'facts' of participation in adult education, in terms of comparative statistics of social class membership, levels and types of learning, and experiences thereof (all formally defined), and the consequent explanation of access and experience in these terms, does not resonate either with the understandings of practitioners who routinely have to cope with the inherent uncertainties of practice, nor with adult students who experience participation and account for it in highly contingent ways - unless of course the practitioners are operating (as will usually be the case with policy-makers) with congruent formal categories of understanding in their work.

At best, formal empirical studies may provide interesting facts, but they are not facts which in themselves can be expected to make a difference to the practice of learning or teaching because they do not speak directly to experience. Furthermore, it is not enough to relate or to attempt to make 'relevant' the results of formal research to practice simply through the drawing up of recommendations while those results are not given in the currency of 'real' experience. As Popkewitz (1984) has noted:

> The language of research does not 'sit' as a logical artifact, outside social discourse and devoid of human

interpretation and manipulation. Theory enters a world in which there are pre-defined institutional arrangements, linguistic conventions and established priorities ... the theory of participation, for example, may 'treat' the world as highly integrated and people as rational. These assumptions guide people in 'seeing' participation as a rational involvement in publicly sanctioned groups ... The assumptions about participation also contain beliefs about how institutional structures should be challenged. Lack of participation ... may be viewed as lack of individual motivation rather than as an institutional defect.

(Popkewitz, 1984:11)

Categories pre-determine the form of research outcomes, and, while they may be logically coherent, they may not be instantially relevant. If, however, they are grounded in informal or common-sense understandings (which are no less concerned than formal theory to draw distinctions) then they are better able to speak to these understandings in a practically relevant way. We have seen in Weil's study how her subjects can be encouraged (in effect through a process of engaging in personal research on themselves as learners) to reach understandings that have important implications for practice, since they surface the contradictions that require attention.

Having situated research and shown how its practices can be read, we can now turn to a consideration of so-called 'action research' as the variously intended ways in which the distinctions between the formal and the informal, the categorical and the grounded, can be bridged. Having introduced the notion of 'personal research', we also anticipate an examination of the location of the 'self' as practitioner/researcher in different operational contexts.

REFERENCES

Ackroyd, S. and Hughes, J.A. (1981) <u>Data Collection in Context</u>, London: Longman.

Baldamus, W. (1977) 'The category of pragmatic knowledge in sociological analysis' in M. Bulmer (ed.) <u>Sociological Research Methods</u>, 283-300, London: Macmillan.

Glaser, B.G. and Strauss, A.L. (1967) <u>The Discovery of Grounded Theory</u>, New York: Aldine.

Phillipson, M. (1981) 'Sociological practice and language' in P. Abrams et al., Practice and Progress: British Sociology 1950-1980, London: Allen & Unwin.
Popkewitz, T.S. (1984) Paradigm and Ideology in Educational Research, London: Falmer Press.
Schon, D.A. (1983) The Reflective Practitioner: How Professionals Think in Action, London: Temple Smith.
Torbert, W.R. (1981) 'Why educational research has been so uneducational', in P. Reason and J. Rowan (eds), Human Inquiry: A Sourcebook of New Paradigm Research, 141-51 London: Wiley.
Weil, S.W. (1986) 'Non-traditional learners within traditional higher education institutions: discovery and disappointment', Studies in Higher Education, 11 (3), 219-35.
Woodley, A. et al. (1987) Choosing to Learn: Adults in Education, Oxford: OUP/SRHE.

Chapter Six

THE LOGIC AND PROBLEMS OF ACTION RESEARCH

INTRODUCTION

The term 'action research' refers in general to a style of inquiry which incorporates a set of procedural ideas in adult education and other practices that have become prominent of late. These ideas are advanced in order to overcome some of the difficulties associated with the applicability thesis of the theory-practice relationship on the one hand and the foundational character of educational knowledge on the other. We have examined such difficulties as they relate to discipline-based theory and research in adult education in earlier chapters. Action research also contains a theory of its own practice; it has been legitimated as a practice, for example, in terms of certain theories of educational appropriateness.

In this chapter we consider the question of whether either the theory of action research or action research as it has been practised is actually capable of providing an educational resolution of the theory-practice problematic. In order to do this, it will be necessary to address two general issues - one concerning the justification for action research in terms of its relevance claims, and the other concerning the epistemological claims of action research as a logic of reflective practice. Proponents of action research have justified it as an educational science having its own procedural integrity by making its case in either scientific (theoretical) or practical (action) terms. By doing so, they have unwittingly preserved a distinction that we regard as false - one which leads ultimately either to foundationalism (the grounding of action research in the 'scientific'), or to

Action Research

practicalism (action research as a type of superstructural social engineering).

A more fruitful approach is to consider action research as a form of hermeneutical inquiry concerned with widening understanding beyond, rather than developing knowledge within, the confines of academic disciplines on the one hand and 'practical concerns' on the other. Before proceeding, a certain amount of ground-clearing is necessary. There are a number of overlays and relationships between action and research that are suggested by the combined term 'action research' that would not actually qualify as examples of its educative potential. As a vogue term, it is also a seductive and deceptively vague term. The seduction lies in its promissory character - that it is the only kind of research that will 'get results' or 'make a real difference'. The deception arises by taking a part to be the whole; 'action research' is not simply about testing research in action to see if it works according to the prescriptions of formal theory. This would be a simple pragmatic justification of theory. Neither is it concerned merely with informed procedure or the appropriation of techniques of inquiry in support of social action. In such cases one can say that the strategy, but not the tactics, of action have already been decided. For example, the strategy of action could include: gathering information to support the activities of pressure groups; market research in pursuit of commercial objectives; determining the likely impact of a given social policy. Nor is it research which is simply intended to generate further action, as though the findings that are conveyed through research will automatically stimulate an action imperative which was previously absent.

Such views of 'action research' - which in relation to practice might conveniently be labelled justificatory, supportive, and generative, respectively - are all particular aspects of a more holistic and complex set of ideas that we are trying to understand. Each aspect may well have its appropriate place in a developing course of action and research, and may indeed be specifically suggested at a particular moment of reflective practice, but none adequately conveys the educational sense of the phenomenon as a whole. In examining some of the proposals towards a general educational theory of action research, it will be necessary to look at the kinds of problems that are raised by attempts to realize the promise of 'action research' in actual practice. It should be noted that the following critique has a recursive theme, drawing on a previous analysis of the relationship between theory and practice to deconstruct 'action research', and using this exercise as a means of furthering the understanding of that relationship. The overall purpose is to reveal the educational sense of action research - i.e. in terms of education being an integral part of the intention to change through a development of one's understanding of the situatedness of <u>any and all</u> actions, including the doing of research itself.

THE IMPETUS TO ACTION RESEARCH AND ITS PROMISE

How are we to account for the trend towards action research as a preferred style of research in adult education? Part of the explanation lies in the fact that, for the funder or sponsor, action research offers the opportunity to be identified with 'initiatives' of an apparently dynamic kind. The possibility of greater 'value for money' is implied through the stress on both diagnosis and innovative provision. Correspondingly, given the scarcity of funds for basic educational research and the current emphasis on the accumulation of research contracts as a mark of 'excellence' and as a licence for continued institutional survival, those who seek research funds often feel the need to build an action component into their proposals. To be convincing, a defence of the value of research has to be located within a discourse of relevance. Increasingly, there is an implicit recognition that, in the competition for funds, research must be 'relevant', 'practical', and relate to the 'real world'. Action research is supposed to demonstrate a commitment to these desirables.

The promissory character of action research which is attractive to the adult educator is that it offers a mode of inquiry and understanding in which the conventional distinctions between teacher and taught, researcher and researched, are dissolved. Understanding is to be achieved through an emphasis on participative and collaborative procedures. At the same time, action research as a form of investigation has a strong theoretical warrant within educational contexts, in the interpretive requirement, to study the situated aspects of human action by getting involved, not simply as a participant observer but as an active change agent. In addition, action research is congruent with andragogical models of practice, in which educational provision is viewed as a dynamic process of adjustment to emergent needs and an impositional mode is rejected in favour of change through negotiation.

The relationship between research and practice, particularly as it is mediated through the teaching of adult education studies, is also important in the above context. Action research more readily facilitates links between research and practice than conventional styles of investigation, with their emphases on linear models of research utilization. It is claimed that action research findings can be readily 'translated' into practice and that its methods and procedures can stimulate and support practitioner-based inquiry. Essentially, therefore, the developing emphasis on action research in adult education is no mere passing fashion. It arises partly from the pragmatics of funding and emergent priorities of research policy, but also and perhaps more importantly from current models of practice in adult education in which there is a perceived need for clearer and closer links between theory and practice. In addition, there is the overriding policy concern and institutional discourse of 'relevant' educational provision which constitutes the adult as an object of intervention or regulation.

ACTION RESEARCH AS CONVENTIONALLY UNDERSTOOD

Action research as it has developed since the 1940s has tended to take the form of theories of change-agency in formal organizations. It derives from Kurt Lewin's (1947) post-war work and has a pedigree in wartime operational research. The academic theorizing of action research to justify its methods and analyse its claims did not gather momentum until the early 1970s. Lewin's model of action research was based on a cycle or spiral of conceptual discovery, planning, executive, and evaluative activities. In this scheme of formal operational requirements, the primary change agent was to be the researcher and not the researched (who was a secondary change agent, consigned to implementing the research evaluations). Until recently, theories of action research have been cast within a positivist applications paradigm, notwithstanding their claims to be sensitive to the contingencies of action. An examination of some representative theorists will allow us to highlight the problems associated with such views of action research.

Sanford judged that, by the end of the 1970s, practitioner dissatisfaction with the institutional separation of research from practice and the increasing intra-disciplinary fragmentation of research had put action research back on the agenda (Sanford, 1981). He describes Scriven's work in formative evaluation as going 'a long way toward filling in Lewin's cycle with precise operations. Although (such) authors assume a division of labour between the evaluators and those responsible for execution, their work shows beyond question that much can be learned from studying the effects of actions' (Sanford, 1981:175).

Evaluation research, however, does not qualify as action research but is just one type of applied research. As Sanford puts it: 'nearly all of applied social science emphasizes the application to problems of what is already known, rather than the study of action as a means for advancing science' (Sanford, 1981:175). It is significant that Sanford is not thinking here about action research as a means of advancing action, but only science. He sketches a model of 'research action' in which the questions to be asked would be multi-disciplinary, practical, problem-focused, and open-ended. 'Action' would consist of reporting to the client with the aim of promoting individual development in the client. There is also the suggestion (which is unfortunately not developed) that collaborative research should involve reciprocal studies, in which practitioners research each other's culture of practice.

Gouldner's attempt to provide a theory for applied social science (Gouldner, 1957) requires that any applied social science must consider those lay values which guide practices that are not themselves 'scientific', and that, although the researcher is exhorted to be 'professionally oriented' to these values, he/she is not required to incorporate these into the methods of social science. Since the interest in application is change, the applied social scientist has to identify those variables in his or her research which are amenable to change, i.e. those which can be controlled, and not necessarily the variables that formal theory suggests as having the greatest predictive power. The 'corrective' to lay hypotheses is the identification of those actions which result in negative 'unanticipated consequences', and it is these actions which require change. The assumptions underlying this kind of approach to 'action research' is that experiential knowledge is full of 'mistakes' that the academic researcher can be called upon to correct through the application of a more formal understanding.

Clark (1972) also considers that the judgement of what is to count as 'valid knowledge' in action research is the extent to which it relates to 'lay hypotheses', in the sense that the researcher must find a way of relating his understandings to those of his sponsors. Consequently, action research imposes rather different demands upon the researcher than academic research does. Here, action research is seen as a means of connecting formal propositional knowledge to experiential knowledge. This is to be accomplished by developing a mutually acceptable framework of inquiry as a kind of 'linking device'. A way has to be found of giving freedom to the academic, within the terms of reference of the research, for testing some formal hypotheses while at the same time addressing the 'problems' as defined by laymen. To do this, the action researcher must undertake activities which are 'seemingly scientifically senseless but actually sociologically necessary' (Clark, 1972:72).

Clark recognizes that the extension of rational strategies of academic research outside the scientific community may not be successful in the world of practice because of the differences in orientations to knowledge in the two domains. The kind of theories used by practitioners is part of the 'problematic' of action research. This will not be a single theory-in-use but an amalgam of pragmatic and situated understandings of what is necessary to get things done, or 'informal theory' as we have previously described it. What matters to the practitioner is not the logical consistency of the theories but that the understandings he/she has will actually allow things to get done. Practitioners cannot keep asking themselves 'am I being logical?'. The practitioner wants <u>performative</u> 'action'-knowledge, not merely empirically validated and logically consistent knowledge. However, we are not told by Clark how and what kind of research action would provide this (i.e. we are not presented with a theory of action to connect propositional to experiential knowledge). The principal interest of the academic researcher remains with the former and the principal concern of the practitioner with the latter, and Clark is ultimately content with this division.

A different concern is that of Rapoport (1970) who considers existing understandings of action research to be focused too exclusively on the existence of a client with a problem to be solved. Consequently, the identification of the 'problematic' of action research has been one of securing the investigative means to solve a client-based problem. As such, theories of action research have not been concerned with the social scientists' legitimate interests in the research but only with the clients'. The balance is tilted too far in the direction of research 'applications'.

To redress this balance, Rapoport regards action research as having joint legitimate aims, as follows:

> Action research aims to contribute <u>both</u> to the practical concerns of people, in an immediate problematic situation and to the goals of social science by joint collaboration within a mutually acceptable ethical framework.
>
> (Rapoport, 1970:498)

The inherent tension in action research is that serving its aims in one way leads one away from action, and in the other way 'towards the sort of action that is not theoretically informed and does not have a cumulative scientific character' (Rapoport, 1970:503). If we read further, we find that Rapoport wants action researchers to create the conditions that would optimize both practical and intellectual interests (Rapoport, 1970:510). So here we have a recognition of a problem of action, within action research itself, of the need to serve competing interests. Scientific and practical interests are considered to have equally legitimate claims, but within their own and not in each other's domains as it were. There is a taken-for-grantedness about the separate requirements of academic research ('the goals of social science') <u>as science</u>, unaffected by the nature of practice in its own domain. It is difficult to see how 'a mutually acceptable ethical framework' to reconcile the claims of science and practice could be established, since the positivist foundational nature of social science remains unquestioned in Rapoport's model.

Denzin (1970) explores the action problematics of doing research in a rather different way. He examines, in considerable depth, the nature of the relationships between the activities of the researcher and those of the researched. His argument is that the conceptualization of researchable objects and the determination of investigative methods are themselves ways of 'acting' on an environment in order to render it meaningful. Working within an interpretive paradigm, specifically symbolic interactionism, Denzin requires that the researcher 'takes the role of the acting other' (Denzin, 1970:8) in order to understand actors' everyday conceptions of reality which govern their practices. But he then insists that the 'situated aspects' of human conduct be translated back into the formal language of sociological discourse in order to reach a proper understanding of action (Denzin, 1970:10-11).

Although the process of engaging in social research is itself one of symbolic interaction, the researcher 'must maintain the distinction between everyday and scientific conceptions of reality' (Denzin, 1970:19). However close to the action (practically or conceptually speaking) the researcher is, the real loyalty is to the consensual formalism of an academic discipline.

The conceptual representations of human action are ultimately derived from everyday actions, but 'commonsense terms only validate and reinforce what is known' (Denzin, 1970:40). Although the characteristic of grounded sociological concepts is their openness to new perspectives, 'they must have a meaning that is strictly and totally sociological' (Denzin, 1970:39). Thus Denzin's purpose is to argue for the appropriateness of research actions for sociology, and not for action as such.

More recently, Susman (1983) has argued that the focus of action research in any organizational context is with concrete problems rather than the problems suggested by formal theory. Practitioners' concerns are 'problem-driven' whereas researchers' concerns are 'theory driven'. Accordingly, action research proceeds by making a conceptual representation of problems and the context in which they are set. In organization-theory terms this will be a systems context of interrelated variables. One then theoretically 'solves' the problem by a process of observation and reasoning. The theoretical 'solution' is then tested through action, which is the attempt to put the solution into practice. For Susman this is the appropriate and sufficient means of relating theory to action: 'Since the "solution" is tested by acting on it to see whether it produces the consequences it implies, action research unites thinking and doing or theory and practice' (Susman, 1983:96).

This approach to understanding action research simplifies, to the point of eroding, an early logical justification for action research actually developed by

Dewey, to whom Susman refers with approval. Dewey's justification is a pragmatic one but it is not simply about testing the consequences of a theory by acting on it to see if it works (Scheffler, 1986:227ff.) The activist conception of knowledge is more than an applicative conception of useful or valid knowledge as seen from the point of view of the client or practitioner. Knowledge has an artefactual character in that the impetus to know is an 'action problematic' - what to do in a situation of uncertainty - where we can say that the intent to know lies in the reduction of doubt. Knowledge in this sense is the satisfaction of intent, the result or consequence of figuring out what to do in situations of uncertainty, i.e. it has a procedural component.

Susman's theorizing of action research takes the procedural problematic only to be that of designing procedures for obtaining knowledge within organizations and subsequently creating the optimum conditions for its use therein. It does not problematize the context by explaining how the system itself contributes to the determination of the knowledge structure and content - i.e. it takes knowledge within the system as problematic, but not the knowledge-constitutive character of the system itself.

TOWARDS AN EDUCATIONAL UNDERSTANDING OF ACTION RESEARCH

All of the above interpretations of action research are limited by virtue of the fact that they do not consider the possibilities of practitioners doing their own research. The net result of their particular orientations is to 'save' action research for positivism and foundationalism through maintaining a separate domain of academic research expertise and preserving those theory-practice distinctions that we have previously criticized.

In contrast, Ebbutt (1985) defines action research as being about:

> the systematic study of attempts to change and improve educational practice by groups of participants by means of their own practical actions and by means of their own reflection upon the effects of those actions.
>
> (Ebbutt, 1985:156)

This definition is useful in a number of respects. First, it emphasizes that action research is carried out by practitioners or, at least, that researchers are actually participating in the practices being researched, and working collaboratively with practitioners. The point here is that action research is concerned both to understand and change particular situations, and that researchers (who are not in and of the situation) are not in a position to do either. They cannot share the informal theory of practitioners and cannot possess the situated knowledge essential for change. By being detached from the situation, the researcher does not have to 'see the research through' in all its possible consequences. This is not only a matter of ethics, it also means that the researcher cannot act 'rightly' or in a committed way in the situation, thus endangering the success and validity of the research.

Second, the use of the terms 'change' and 'improve' in the definition points to the importance of improving practice in action research through 'transformation' of the practice situation. In action research there is a particular kind of relationship between transformation and understanding. Schon (1983) puts it this way: 'The practitioner has an interest in transforming the situation from what it is to something he likes better. He also has an interest in understanding the situation, but it is in the service of his interest in change' (Schon, 1983:14).

There is thus an interplay between understanding and change, such that understanding is oriented by the interest in change and the change itself increases understanding. Schon characterizes this process as 'reflection-in-action' and we examined this in some detail in Chapter 4. The vital ingredient in this process is, of course, action; we can, therefore, see action research as akin to reflection-in-action. This implies that action research does not have to be something carried out by a special group of people called researchers but is in fact what practitioners can do in their everyday practice, given certain conditions (which we also explored in Chapter 4).

Third, and related to the above, there is the emphasis in the definition of reflecting upon the effects of actions. Reflection is a key aspect of action research as research. The action research process has been compared to a spiral where action is followed by reflection, and greater understanding followed by more action and reflection. When we reflect we do not do so aimlessly, but because the situation towards which reflection is directed demands action. Reflection has intentionality, which is grounded in the situation and thus involves 'thinking', not in a purely abstract sense but thinking about something - in other words it has both form and content.

As Kemmis (1985) points out, the fact that reflection goes on 'inside our head' should not lead us to see it as something purely mental and subjective. To do so would be to privilege the thinking component over the action component. If reflection always involves action then it inevitably has a social dimension. At the same time, reflection is not simply a mental problem-solving activity or thought experiment. This is not to deny that reflection cannot be part of the process of problem-solving, although to see it purely as this is to have a technical-rationality view of reflection; to see it only as a technique for solving problems more efficiently. Schon puts it in the following way: 'reflection tends to focus interactively on the outcomes of action, the action itself and the intuitive knowings implicit in the action' (Schon, 1983:56). In action research, given the concern with change, there is always an interest in the outcomes of action but, at the same time, given the concern with understanding, there is an equal interest in the 'knowing' or informal theory which is implicit in the 'doing' or action. Here, therefore, thought and action are united both in the practice which is being researched and in the practice of the research itself.

Action research is concerned with understanding action and its outcomes and with acting through understanding. In this process, reflection plays a key part but, as we have seen earlier, it is not the reflection of abstract contemplation nor yet the reflection of instrumental problem-solving but a reflection which is practical. The concern is with acting appropriately in a particular situation, given the circumstances and constraints of that situation. In other modes of reflection this is either ignored or manipulated to achieve a pre-given end. Action research seeks to understand the practical reflection of practitioners and to incorporate it within its own situated understandings and action.

Finally, the definition uses the term 'systematic study' which poses the question of the extent to which action research is research. Practical reflection, since it is situated, is inevitably value-laden. Actions and understandings are always concerned not only with what is possible but also with what is desirable, and thus the ends towards which action is directed and the means used to achieve those ends are co-implicated within value-frameworks. Understandings are not simply technical, of how to achieve a given end most efficiently and effectively, but of how to act rightly and appropriately in a particular situation. Since the <u>consequences</u> of action are a key consideration this provides a further rationale for the involvement of practitioners in action research.

This, in turn, has a number of consequences for the perceived status of action research. First, the implication of action research within value-frameworks must of necessity pose a problem if we see research solely in terms of a natural science paradigm. Whilst it is possible, as we saw in Chapter 2, to distance ourselves from such a paradigm and indeed to recognize the existence of more appropriate alternatives, we also have to recognize the power of the natural science paradigm in defining what is to count as <u>legitimate</u> research - a legitimacy which practitioners themselves may often accept.

Second, the status of action research is criticized on the grounds of bias and lack of objectivity. As we have seen, the action researcher is part of the action and not detached from it. Furthermore, the researcher is not only attempting through reflection to understand his/her own understandings but also the understandings of the practitioners with whom he/she is working. The researcher is not simply trying 'impartially' to discover the facts but to transform and improve a situation, and thus in a very real sense is 'creating' the facts. In doing this the researcher is, by definition, changing, or at least challenging, the status quo. Through collaborative working, practitioners are also engaged in the same process. All this can lead to a problem, succinctly summed by Finch, that action research is 'much more likely to offer up findings and insights which will disturb the status quo, while at the same time the methods employed make it impossible to claim credibility on the grounds of objectivity' (Finch, 1986:197).

Third, action research is thought to face a problem of generalizability. Since action research is situated and since every situation is different, then the product of action research must necessarily tell us only about that situation and no other. Related to this is the fact that action research does not use a hypothetico-deductive but a grounded model where 'hypotheses' emerge during the course of the research and are subject to change as the research proceeds. Since action research is not located within a natural science paradigm and is not concerned to provide 'scientific' explanations of the world or make a contribution to formal theory in foundation disciplines, the lack of generalizability is neither a serious problem nor an apposite criticism. One could equally well argue that: 'an enhanced understanding of the particularity of a teacher's situation is more important than generalisability, and that replicability and transferability are less important than authenticity and accountability' (Kelly, 1985:131). Although Kelly is here talking specifically of the teacher-as-researcher, the point being made is generally relevant.

None the less, if action research is 'systematic study', then we have to have some means of distinguishing it from, for example, good teaching or simply good practice in general. Ebbutt comments:

> If action research is to be considered legitimately as research, then participants in it must, it seems to me, be prepared to produce written reports of their activities. Moreover these reports ought to be available for some form of public critique.
> (Ebbutt, 1985:157)

The call for written reports and the possibility of public critique is, in essence, a call for accountability in the sense that all parties to a piece of action research must be in a position to account for what happened to a wider audience.

Action research can be as systematic as more conventional forms of research, but such a case can only be made if certain things are accepted beforehand. First, that there are forms of rationality other than that found in the nature science paradigm; second, that the attempt to be 'objective' is itself a prejudice; third, that because all human action is meaningful, the researcher cannot adopt a detached and neutral position since he/she is located within a social context; fourth, that knowledge is conventional, and pragmatically rather than foundationally related to 'truth'. We have already discussed these issues, so we will not reiterate them. Suffice it to say that a case can be made for action research having its own rigour and 'logic'.

In view of Susman's more recent interpretation of action research, it is somewhat surprising that in an earlier article (Susman and Evered, 1978) he comes close to the above understanding. He correctly identifies the 'crisis' of the increasing irrelevancy of much of academic research for practitioners as being one not of applicability as such, but of epistemology or the way in which knowledge-claims are grounded in conventional scientific research. Susman and Evered argue that action research could not meet the critical tests of positive science, but that it should not have to. They list a number of characteristics of action research as correctives to a narrow understanding of what research ought properly to be about and which would provide action research with its own integrity as a mode of understanding:

1. Future-oriented: it is not restricted to discovering and explaining existing or past states of affairs, but to informing practitioners' own planning processes.
2. Collaborative: stressing interdependence and the requirement for a mutual clarification of values between researchers and practitioners.
3. Developmental: in building competencies to improve communication and problem-solving.
4. Generates action-grounded theory: neither practitioner theory nor formal theory but the joint consequence of acting on theories and theorizing actions.
5. Agnostic: methods are generated during the process of research itself and cannot be specified in advance. They are tools with which to examine particular moments of action, other moments will require their own contextually appropriate tools.
6. Situational: recognizes the situatedness of all knowledge and its own situatedness. Actions not only change situations but change the knowledge of situations.
7. Continuity of action: actions cannot be understood simply as discrete occurences. They have both a history and an intentionality.

While we would concur with many of these features of action research, which make it a different kind of animal to research as normally undertaken, or action research as it has often been conceived, a number of problems remain. These include the 'practical' ones of instituting programmes of action research in a culture where more conventional scientific values and a deference to positivist expertise exist. In this context, the philosophical viewpoints that legitimate action research - by drawing on concepts and traditions such as 'praxis', hermeneutics, aspects of existentialism, phenomenology and pragmatism - are not without their own difficulties. They have to be argued for within an academy still influenced by a culture of positivist scientific practice, and in the outside world of practice which itself still largely operates with a discourse saturated by positivism.

ACTION RESEARCH AS REFLECTIVE PRACTICE

One possible representation of 'action research' in relation to theory and practice is as follows:

Figure 6.1 Action research

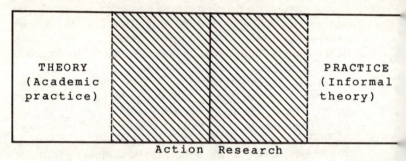

Formal theories are the result of certain kinds of academic practice, notably foundational or discipline-based research. Any kind of practice, including academic practice, contains its own informal theory. The promise of action research is that it will effect a unification of theory and practice since it proceeds from the assumption that their separation is educationally unwarranted. If action research is concerned at the same time with the theorizing of practice and the practice of theorizing, then a proposition that we can put forward in its support is that, by examining in action our own informal theories or 'theories in action', we will come to know better the structures, rules, and assumptions which govern our performances, both as researchers and practitioners. The action researcher would thus become a reflective practitioner.

Any model of action research must also contain a theory of communicative action in which different understandings are conveyed by different forms of discourse

- including those of the theoretician and the practitioner. Here, it is instructive to turn to Habermas (1972, 1974), whose proposals for a critical social science have important implications for action research as reflective practice. According to Habermas, forms of discourse and associated knowledge-claims are socio-culturally situated in and reflect different <u>interests</u>. His arguments present two sorts of problems for the educator as action researcher. These are the problems: first, of being reflective and second, of having interests.

Reflection is taken to be a higher form of thinking or a capacity to be critical in the service of autonomy and responsibility. These are both ideals that many, if not all, adult educators would certainly subscribe to. In the relationship between researcher and practitioner in action research, a key question is 'do we want practitioners to be able to operate at the same level of discourse or within the same argumentative sphere as the theorist-researcher?'. One of the tasks of action research is to establish discursive symmetry - to make sure that participants are at least 'talking the same language' even if their interests in the research are not identical. At first, the various parties to the research are likely to face a situation of <u>discursive asymmetry</u> and a differential willingness or capacity to reflect critically upon their practices.

Let us suppose for a moment that the adult educator as a researcher exemplifies the characteristics of the 'reflective practitioner' and wants to put into practice some ideas about critical self-reflection, using participative or collaborative research as the vehicle for this. The acid test of whether the researcher is really being 'critical' in a reflexive way is that he/she is open to the criticism of those who are not at this stage of thinking. An important question is whether the researcher is willing to authenticate the experiences of others as a means of assuring the authenticity of critical self-reflection itself. There would be no purpose in education if there was an <u>unconditional</u> willingness to do so, since <u>all</u> renditions of experience (i.e. of both the academic researchers and the lay participants) would be regarded as equally valid. The educational requirement of action research is that the academic researcher must reveal, in discourse and action, the way in which his/her own informal understandings of what is going on is situated, and under what discursive and action conditions these are open to change. In effect, the educational action researcher would be acting as an exemplar of reconstructive possibilities to those whose understandings he/she wishes to influence.

Habermas establishes an identity between knowledge and interests in which the rootedness of knowledge in human interests is the requirement for having any kind of knowledge at all. The knowledge-interests identity creates both a 'theory problem' and a 'practice problem'. If theoretical knowledge and practical knowledge are both tied to interests in the way that Habermas insists, then how is it possible to step outside one's interests to examine either one's theories or one's practices, let alone the relationship between them? Habermas promotes the idea of a 'critical social science' as a reflective practice of freeing oneself from one's interests and as the discursive reconstruction of undistorted knowledge.

Critics of Habermas have argued that this is a complex and unsatisfactory idea. Critical social science is promissory, but unrealistic. It cannot justify the potential risks of abandoning one's interests in advance. Also there still remains, according to Ottman, a 'reflection problem', in that the power of interests is such that Habermas overestimates the power of reflection, so that it is extremely doubtful if reflection can reveal interests in an interest-free way (Ottman, 1982). There are several aspects to the 'reflection/interests problem':

1. It is not in the interests of stabilized behaviour to be continually asking questions about the status of validity claims - one has to exercise trust even while recognizing that what one is trusting may very well be a distortion.
2. It is not practically possible to establish the conditions for continuous reflection, and action research cannot do this.
3. It presupposes the artificial conditions for an unburdened self-conscious behaviour yet, as Ottman points out, 'even when these conditions are fulfilled, one still has to take into account the pressure of time, the necessity of having to decide, the limited capacity to take up or alter topics of communication, and the fatigue of those participating in the dialogue' (Ottman, 1982: 95-6).

The above issues raised by Habermas' theory of a

critical social science are manifestations of a general problem of 'the gap between the empirical conditions of discourse and its idealization' (Ottman, 1982:96). However, Ottman considers that all is not lost, and he suggests that:

> the possibility arises of re-integrating the ideal of an unconstrained communication into the framework of traditions. <u>Within the practical interest</u>, 'critique' could play the role of a 'regulative idea' which is not itself a form of life but a necessary and unrenounceable idea with the help of which we examine distortions in our communication.
>
> (Ottman, 1982:96)

(The underlining has been added to the above excerpt by the present authors for emphasis.) Such a regulative idea, for example, is the Rawlsian notion of justice as fairness which, by positing equality and the absence of constraint (Rawls' so-called 'veil of ignorance' upon which a system of justice is constructed), lays down ideal criteria by which to identify the extent to which any actual system of justice is 'fair'. The 'regulative idea' is a tool for examining the discourse of one's practice. This is an important concept in both educational practice and action research but, to emphasize its importance properly, we need to examine further Habermas' analysis of discursive assymetry or distorted communication.

His central concern is with the problem of how communication can be distorted through the influence of power and ideology. He fears that, because of this influence, our horizons of understanding remain permanently limited and hence dialogue will be constrained. His answer to this problem is to bring together causal explanation and self-understanding in a process of 'guided' self-reflection. Reflection is guided through the recognition and acceptance of causal explanations. The process would be one where I thought I was doing X because of reason Y, but I am offered an explanation Z which imputes my action to ideological factors of which I was entirely unaware. If I now accept Z, I recognize that my previous understanding Y is no longer adequate in itself. The causal explanation (Z) is now taken into account alongside my self-understanding (Y) and both can now contribute to the process of self-reflection.

It is only by accepting such explanations that the conditions are created for reflection. The latter is thus guided by explanations allowing us to understand the 'objective' conditions of power and ideology. We can also begin to see how our self-understandings or 'subjective' meanings, because they are located in these conditions, are thereby systematically distorted.

Habermas bases his analysis of distorted communication on a psychoanalytic model which functions both as an analogy providing us with insights into the process of distorted communication and an approach to overcoming it. Put at its simplest, the problem of distorted communication is that people do not always speak 'truly'. Psychoanalysis purports to provide causal explanations in terms of the unrecognized influence of the unconscious, repression, and so forth. Using this model in a more general sense we could say that practitioners do not speak 'truly' because of the equally unrecognized influence of power and ideology.

In psychoanalysis the patient engages in self-cure through reconstructing his/her life history in the light of the causal explanations offered by the analyst. Generalizing this again, we could say that what seems to be involved here is the reconstruction of situated understandings (Anderson et al., 1986). Habermas would claim that, in all cases, causal explanations are a necessary feature of the reconstruction, whose outcomes are undistorted communication and an opening of horizons.

If people can speak 'truly' then unconstrained dialogue is possible. We would also emphasize that by 'dialogue' we do not simply mean people talking to one another but also the wider sense of the process of 'encounter and engagement' between the interpreter and what he/she seeks to interpret. This is a dialogical process which brings together the situatedness of the interpreter and the object of interpretation in what we have earlier called the 'fusion of horizons'. The fusion can only occur, however, through participation in the dialogue, in the process of 'encounter and engagement'; being a disinterested 'objective' observer will not do.

This implies that understanding and interpretation are not contemplative but performative. Given our situatedness, if we were to be simply objective observers and contemplative theoreticians, then our horizons would indeed be very limited. But if we are participants, then our horizons can be open and creative and our situatedness, far from being a 'problem' is the basis for the 'fusion of horizons'. In effect, the problem lies precisely in seeing this

Action Research

as a problem.

This consideration allows us to see more clearly the weakness in Habermas' analysis. In grappling with the legitimate problem of constrained communication he fails to recognize the implications of the performative nature of dialogical understanding. Ultimately, he is forced into the position that it is possible to step outside one's situatedness and engage in 'guided' (critical) self-reflection, whereas our position has been that it is impossible to do so. Habermas clearly believes that relying on hermeneutic understanding is never enough to penetrate the ideological veil, whereas we would take the view that it can, since it always contains a critical potential.

The thrust of our argument is that action research is a form of inquiry into situatedness which is itself situated. As such, the constraints on inquiry are dialogical. As Habermas rightly points out, a problem arises because the dialogue may be implicated in power-ideology relationships. We have seen in an earlier chapter how disciplines, for example, are not just neutral collections of knowledge but an essential feature of regulative practices. Communication can therefore become distorted, dialogue constrained; the question is how these distortions and constraints can be removed so that dialogue becomes edifying rather than oppressive.

If action research is a form of situated inquiry, then we can see its purpose as one of widening understanding rather than 'discovering knowledge'. The first task in this inquiry must be to understand situatedness and thus the initial limits of horizons. To paraphrase Gadamer, inquiry must start with an understanding, by the inquirer, of his/her 'historicity'. This involves recognizing that one's knowledge has a specific cultural and historical location, and is the result of social practices both past and present - or what we have earlier called 'tradition'.

This allows the openness to other horizons which we have already described, and which is the condition for unconstrained dialogue. Through a participative openness, both the action researcher and those with whom he/she is researching attain a position where they are no longer divided into the subject and object of research, researcher and researched. The recognition of 'historicity' on the part of both is therefore the first stage in the 'fusion of horizons' and the possibility of unconstrained dialogue.

We would claim, therefore, that action research as

inquiry is hermeneutic and as such is well able to take account of the influence of ideology and power, despite Habermas' claims to the contrary. Hermeneutic understanding does not merely operate at the level of the explicit but, through its recognition of situatedness, can penetrate beneath this level to the more underlying factors to be found there. It is not merely a matter of subjectivity but of examining the context in which this subjectivity is located. Habermas' 'causal explanations' are thus unnecessary, since hermeneutic understanding can undertake the task of reconstruction which Habermas (as we have seen) considers essential.

Furthermore, the recognition of 'objective' constraints is not something which necessarily requires 'causal explanations', because these constraints are <u>already</u> part of the 'tradition' towards which hermeneutic understanding is interpretively directed. For instance, in an earlier chapter, we saw how the knowledge contained in disciplines is always already present in practitioners' understandings. Similarly, 'objective constraints' have already 'entered our world'; the tradition incorporates them 'as part of its self-understanding, whether expressed or unexpressed' (Warnke, 1987:114). Warnke further makes the point that if they were not so incorporated they would have no meaning. Yet it is manifestly the case that it <u>is</u> possible to talk meaningfully about 'objective' constraints; indeed, by describing them in this way, they have already been interpreted or hermeneutically understood.

Hermeneutic understanding, therefore, can be critical. In being critical, however, it does not do so from a position which is outside situatedness. In our view, this is where Habermas' analysis is flawed - in attempting to locate the possibility of undistorted communication and unconstrained dialogue in a 'rational consensus of universal discourse' which is free of distortion and constraint. Such a 'consensus' will itself inevitably be situated. Gadamer's position, as summarized by Bernstein (1985), is that because we cannot escape our 'historicity' there is no 'absolute knowledge, finality in understanding or complete self-understanding of the knower. We always find ourselves in an open dialogical or conversational situation with the very tradition and history that is effectively shaping us' (Bernstein, 1985:63). In the end, we can be aware of the distortions and constraints of ideology and power but our recognition of their influence must always be <u>practical</u>.

Essentially, what Habermas is trying to point to is that in order to be critical we must be in a position to appeal to some standards or criteria which are outside our situatedness. He tries to find these through the idea of a rational community, in which consensual agreement can emerge about appropriate standards and criteria. Such a consensus is based on the possibility of non-distorted communication which, although an ideal, Habermas believes is conceivable, if only because a concept of 'distorted' communication must presuppose such a possibility. The problem here is that it is difficult to understand how such a rational community could itself not be situated and how, therefore, it too would be free of the distortions of ideology and knowledge. We are thus forced back to the position that there can be no universal and neutral standards or criteria to which a final and authoritative appeal can always be made.

What we are left with, therefore, is an appeal to the practical and the pragmatic. As Rorty (1982) points out, we do not need a theory allowing us to ground communication and providing a warrant for 'undistorted' communication. Communication is a social practice 'hammered out in the course of history', and we cannot expect to have standards outside those practices which will tell us absolutely and finally what is true communication and what is not. We can only evaluate our communication within the context of the practical, the standards and criteria that are available to us at a particular point in time and within a particular cultural location.

The important thing is openness to dialogue and keeping the dialogue going. Bernstein describes dialogue as 'mutuality, the respect required, the genuine seeking to understand what the other is saying, the openness to test and evaluate our own opinions through (dialogical) encounter' (Bernstein, 1985:113). By opening ourselves up we can surface our prejudices, interests, and distortions, and interrogate them critically. We can never entirely escape these but we can transcend particular prejudices, etc. (Wain, 1987).

Essentially, therefore, we do the best we can; we seek the truth and we try and make the best case we possibly can within the dialogical encounter. Naturally there are problems and obstacles, and any dialogical inquiry recognizes these. But the hermeneutic process is ultimately dependent on the possibility of understanding and communication. If we conceive of dialogue in the way described, it can provide us with a 'powerful regulative ideal' which gives direction to practice. In other words, whilst we may not always be able to organize practice in a dialogical way, and whilst dialogue may often, in actuality, be constrained, there is always an ideal of the way things could, and should, be. As Bernstein puts it:

> whatever the limitations of the practical realisation of this ideal, it nevertheless can and should give practical orientation to our lives. We must ask, what is it that blocks and distorts such dialogue, and what is to be done, what is feasible, what is possible, what is correct, here and now to make such genuine dialogue a living reality?
> (Bernstein, 1985:114)

People can therefore 'talk the same language' and talk it 'truly', but what this depends on is not so much Habermas' 'regulative idea' but an ideal which directs their discourse and practice. Now, this 'ideal' is clearly normative. We are not, however, merely arguing prescriptively. Our claim is a stronger one, to the effect that such an ideal always exists (even if only potentially) in any dialogue. The hermeneutic understanding associated with it recognizes the multiplicity and submerged meanings of discourse and is thus capable of revealing the ideological constraints of situatedness.

Habermas' project is that of formulating a critical social science which synthesizes the natural science paradigm's emphasis on 'objective explanation' with the interpretive paradigm's emphasis on 'subjective understanding'. Such a critical social science would thus resolve the theory-practice problem. We have seen how in the technical-rationality model of the theory-practice relationship the justification for a course of action is ultimately foundational. Can the action be warranted by a theory which corresponds to or mirrors reality? Guided by the formal corroboration of causal relationships between independent and dependent variables, proper action is suggested by the rational choice of means towards the attainment of given ends. Even some theories of so-called 'action research' are actually set in this vein.

We have also seen that the interpretive corrective to positivism does not necessarily prescribe for a course of action at all. This is potentially a weakness in all approaches based on interpretive paradigms. For example, although Weil's approach to understanding the meaning of adult education participation (see Ch. 5) is a valuable corrective to the categorical understanding of participation as supplied by formal survey research, there is nothing in that approach which suggests in itself how the problems that are revealed by non-traditional mature students are to be solved. It remains research without any action imperative. Weil's grounded theories do not entail action but merely point to the consequences of past actions.

Carr and Kemmis have pointed to the possible limitations of interpretive theories as follows:

> Many critical theories will be interpretations of social life created by individuals or groups concerned to reveal these contradictions. In this sense, critical theories may be the outcomes of interpretive social science, subject to criticism on the same ground as other interpretive theories. Most particularly, they may be subject to the criticism that they transform consciousness (ways of viewing the world) without necessarily changing practice in the world.
> (Carr and Kemmis, 1986:144)

For the adult educator, Habermas' scheme for the realization of a critical social science that would transcend both positivism and interpretivism is beset with difficulties. In the final analysis, as we have seen, it is probably untenable. However, it does highlight the task of the educator in action research as one of creating with others conditions for the reconstruction of action through discourse. Carr and Kemmis explore the practicality of Habermas' scheme for the construction of an education science through action research, and introduce a number of refinements into his ideas.

The knowledge that is generated through action research is the consequence of a process of continuous construction and reconstruction of theory and practice. It entails a theory of symmetrical communication and contains the idea of 'being strategic' in action - that is, of informed, committed doing, which recognizes the limits of its own situatedness and has an understanding of what is prudent in given circumstances. This 'being prudent' in action research therefore requires the acceptance of 'real' limits which cannot simply be thought away or reflexively dissolved. The idea is that one theorizes and takes action to identify and reach a limit situation; once one arrives at the limits, the situation is effectively changed, and the change opens up new possibilities for action that could not be conceived before the earlier action was taken.

An important issue remains. Can the authenticity and communicability that is required within action research be preserved 'outside' the domain of the research? Action research requires participants to be co-researchers. Unlike the knowledge generated by the observations of 'objective' science or the empathetic verstehen of interpretive science, the knowledge generated by action research is 'insider knowledge'. As such, it is difficult to validate its truth claims to outsiders, or to those not party to the action research itself. Outsiders may have commissioned action research in the mistaken belief that it will generate understandings that can be applied to approvable actions. This raises questions of whether the truth claims of action research can properly be assessed by outsiders, and, indeed, the wider issue of whether action research can and should be required to meet public tests beyond those suggested by Ebbutt, in particular those of the academic community of professional educators. Public tests will be given by 'other situated' criteria. The action researcher's reply would be that these criteria need themselves to be deconstructed and to be brought into action, so to speak - the only 'proper' judges of action research being those who themselves are prepared to be engaged.

It is in the face of such problems that Carr and Kemmis review Habermas' arguments for a critical social science in terms of the practical difficulties of creating the conditions for realizing what would otherwise remain as ideals of curriculum practice. They note that 'for educational theory, the problem is to articulate a conception of educational research which could bring about the emancipatory aims and purposes that are characteristic of critical social science' (Carr and Kemmis, 1986:151). The problem is thus posed by Carr and Kemmis as being one of the enactment of educational research.

The action that is taken in action research is the conscious working towards the limits of situated horizons. In the process, one's understanding of these limits will change and hence the judgement of possibilities for further action. Much of what is called 'action research' would not therefore qualify, being characterized by what Carr and

Kemmis refer to as 'a single loop of planning, acting, observing and reflecting'. They continue: 'if the process stops there it should not be regarded as action research at all. Perhaps it could be termed "arrested action research"' (Carr and Kemmis, 1986:185). Candidates for arrested action research include research that is confined to problem-solving and aims-achievement models of evaluation which do not result in 'the establishment of more educationally defensible situations and institutions' (Carr and Kemmis, 1986:185).

At the same time, it is important to retain the sense of action research as 'research', by insisting on its systematic nature. It is not content with random or sporadic reflection on practice, even if its own practice is included. Both reflection and action have to satisfy the requirements of research as a consistent and persistent practice. Action research therefore requires a 'theory' of research to authenticate it, in the sense of a defensible understanding of its own situated actions or practices, and an understanding which is not foundational.

Summarizing the necessary conditions for educational action research, Carr and Kemmis require:

> freedom of discourse, a common commitment to assuring scope for unconstrained dialogue, proper precaution against self-interested domination and control of the process, and the freedom of decision-making for those involved.
> (Carr and Kemmis, 1986:223)

In essence, we return to the conditions for unconstrained dialogue, to the 'dialogical encounter' which we described earlier.

SOME ACTION RESEARCH IN PRACTICE

The above requirements are formidable. The community development projects (CDPs) of the 1970s provided adult educators in the UK with an opportunity to test some early pre-critical thinking about action research.

In their work with public housing residents in Liverpool, jointly examining the implications for tenants of the Housing Finance Bill, 1972 which proposed a reduction and redistribution of rent subsidies, Ashcroft and Jackson (1974) suggested that the idea of action research 'requires letting theory determine practice to a much greater degree than would be allowed by accepting institutional norms as they apply to regular provision' (Ashcroft and Jackson, 1974:45).

For these educators, action research is about creating conditions for putting their theories into play. They do, however, correctly identify a shortcoming in existing community action practices which confine understandings of the problems of community development to localized and particularized concerns. Any educational inputs into deprived communities, in terms of an instrumental curriculum of 'coping' with local problems, are properly rejected.

Ashcroft and Jackson organized community meetings to consider their own diagnoses of discrepancies between the political justifications for the Bill and its likely effects. These meetings resulted in the formation of a rent action committee. The researchers were able to theorize about the appropriate conditions for the dissemination of knowledge, some local community members were able to engage in informed actions, and there were 'educational outcomes', e.g. the formation of 'an organised class in social theory and social problems' (Ashcroft and Jackson, 1974:61). However, the educators' own reflection-in-action was confined to a consideration of the strategic and tactical issues in engendering community participation, and not extended to an examination of their own situated understanding of housing legislation. In effect, education was separated from actions to protect tenants' rights, Ashcroft and Jackson had an understanding of public housing legislation in terms of a macro-theory of the position of social classes in relation to the housing market, but they claim that this was 'held in reserve' when the Housing Bill was represented to residents as a community issue. The overall exercise could be characterized as an attempt to stimulate action on the basis of the researcher's own prior understandings, to 'act on a theory' rather than to theorize a set of actions including their own.

Few situations can be more highly charged than those that exist in Northern Ireland. The conflicts of sectarianism perhaps exemplify as well as any 'issues' the embeddedness of knowledge in interests as claimed by Habermas. And few other locations could provide as stiff a test for the practicalities of implementing action research.

A Community Action Research and Education (CARE)

project was established at the Institute of Continuing Education, Magee University College, Londonderry, in 1977. Reflecting on the work of CARE in 1983, Lovett and his team described their involvement with community activists from both sides of the sectarian divide who represented a variety of trade union, religious, political, and community interests. Lovett et al. (1983) report that, in general terms, they could be seen as possessing three broad philosophies of change through education: the welfare/ameliorative; the personal/developmental; and the structural/transformative. These were deeply rooted positions that proved to be difficult to work with in joint sessions with representatives of different groups. Among the problems experienced by the team were the following:

1. The divisiveness of political views from entrenched positions and the fact that these were real conflicts which got in the way of open discussion.
2. The acceptance of a 'theoretical' requirement to compromise between the pressing claims of reflection and action was not sufficient to overcome a differential sense of urgency about what should be done.
3. 'The reluctance of those involved to let the project provide a structure which would have assisted the learning process' (Lovett et al., 1983:82).

This raised the question in participants' minds about the legitimacy of a purely educational agenda; and for the project team there was a problem of maintaining a harmonious working relationship between their own educational agenda and the hidden agendas of some of the participants.

One aspect of the work of CARE was to encourage those involved in the project to participate in community research. A modest research and information centre was established and an evening class in social research was started, but the commitment was not sustained. Reflecting on this aspect of the project, Lovett et al. state that:

> We introduced ourselves to some important sources and items of information, but did not manage to consolidate this into a rational flow of knowledge let alone an active audience eager to pursue the implications of what we had discovered. The project remained incoherent and academic in a bad sense.
> (Lovett et al., 1983:101)

Examining their relative 'failure' in this area of work, Lovett et al. reviewed the benefits and dangers of participatory research in general, and sounded an important cautionary note. If the opportunity for action research is offered in response to criticisms of the actual methodologies and conduct of much academic research, then one must resist the notion that it is not necessary to be concerned about method at all. This is not the case, and Lovett rightly argues that disciplined and purposive inquiry is a necessary part of the actual terms of participation, whatever research methods are chosen in practice. In its absence, any 'research' that is conducted, however well-intended, may just serve to confirm existing interests, be mere descriptivism, and lead to the avoidance of 'inconvenient facts'. Lovett et al. also caution against the naive assumption that joint participation in research can bring about change by itself. Only action will do that, and the issue becomes one of the extent to which action can be informed by sensible, critical, and sustainable research.

THE REQUIREMENTS FOR ADULT EDUCATION ACTION RESEARCH

Avowing that people have a right to knowledge is an empty recognition without providing them with the ability to create and legitimate that knowledge for themselves. Action research has no automatic claim to be a 'better' kind of research than any other as a generator of knowledge, and must argue its case alongside other claims. The strength of that case lies in a recognition of the situatedness of any and all inquiry.

In setting down some of the theoretical requirements for educational action research, there is no intention here to supply hard and fast principles. If one asks the question 'what ought action research to do?' then at the end of the day the answer can only be 'it all depends on the situation'. A more productive approach to theorizing the possibilities and problems of action research is perhaps to ask 'what would a genuine theory of action research look like?' and to this question the following is suggested:

1. It would not prescribe specific investigative action in advance.
2. It would entail an interactive search for the limiting

conditions of its own action.
3. It would require a theory of action possibilities.
4. It would require reciprocal research between participants having different views.
5. It would not be promissory in the sense of guaranteeing certain outcomes, but in terms of the educational value of its own processes.
6. It would embody a contingency rather than a deterministic theory of human action and would be cautiously eclectic.
7. It would have an activist conception of knowledge-construction.
8. Its theory of action would be a theory of its own action in relation to the actions of others not involved as participants.
9. It would have a theory of the relationship between 'insider' knowledge and 'outsider' knowledge.
10. It would identify the situatedness of its own knowledge in relation to other-situated knowledge.
11. It would have the means of reflecting on its own truth claims in terms of their situatedness and experiential validity.
12. It would require making a commitment to reflective practice which in principle would be open-ended.
13. It would identify opportunities for participants to adopt appropriate roles as situations and their readings changed.
14. It would identify for itself the circumstances in which any formal theories of behaviour might provide relevant explanations of conduct or guides to action.
15. It would be neither optimistic nor pessimistic, but prudent.
16. It would be self-consciously critical, but not to the point of prejudicing its own action.

We recognize these as desiderata that are nowhere near being matched in current adult education research and practice. In a recent examination of the uneasy relationship between the theorizing and practising of adult education, Welton argues that the required theoretical basis for giving greater credibility to the discipline within the academy is not to be found within current adult education discourse. He says: 'adult education as now constituted is a "normative discipline" teaching students organisational/institutional principles in the name of theory' (Welton, 1987:50).

Adult education theories are characterized by accounts of the supposed characteristics of mature learners rather than by theories of the socio-cultural situatedness of knowledge. Current thinking is typified by a Knowlesian decontextualised concept of the 'self' in relation to 'knowledge'. Adult educators have situated knowledge in terms of a professional construct of 'needs', and have justified the supply of that knowledge through a 'needs-meeting' ideology. By so doing, they deny to adulthood both the role of the self in authenticating its own 'knowledge' and the role of knowledge in contributing to a responsible sense of 'selfhood'. This can only be achieved by creating the conditions for reflection-in-action in which the self has a controlling and not merely a responding role.

It is to the location of the self in the research process that we now turn, and which is the subject of Chapter 7.

REFERENCES

Anderson, R.S., Hughes, J.A., and Sharrock, W.W. (1986) Philosophy and the Human Sciences, London: Croom Helm.

Ashcroft, R. and Jackson, K. (1974) 'Adult education and social action', in D. Jones and M. Mayo (eds) Community Work One, 44-65, London: Routledge & Kegan Paul.

Bernstein, R.J. (1985) Beyond Objectivism and Relativism, Oxford: Blackwell.

Carr, W. and Kemmis, S. (1986) Becoming Critical: Education, Knowledge and Action Research, London: Falmer.

Clark, P.A. (1972) Action Research and Organisational Change, London: Harper & Row.

Denzin, N.K. (1970) The Research Act in Sociology, London: Butterworths.

Ebbutt, D. (1985) 'Educational action research: some general concerns and specific quibbles', in R.G. Burgess (ed.), Issues in Educational Research: Qualitative Methods, Lewes: Falmer Press.

Finch, J. (1986) Research and Policy, Lewes: Falmer Press.

Gouldner, A.W. (1957) 'Theoretical requirements of the applied social sciences', American Sociological Review, 92-102.

Habermas, J. (1972) Knowledge and Human Interests,

London: Heinemann.
---- (1974) Theory and Practice (tr. by J. Viertel), London: Heinemann.
Kelly, A. (1985) 'Action research: what is it and what can it do?', in R.G. Burgess (ed.), Issues in Educational Research: Qualitative Methods, Lewes: Falmer Press.
Kemmis, S. (1985) 'Action research and the politics of reflection', in D. Boud, R. Keogh, and D. Walker (eds), Reflection: Turning Experience into Learning, London: Kogan Page.
Lewin, K. (1947) 'Frontiers in group dynamics: channels of group life: social planning and action research', Human Relations, 1 (2), 143-53.
Lovett, T. et al. (1983) Adult Education and Community Action, London: Croom Helm.
Ottman, H. (1982) 'Cognitive interests and self-reflection', in J.B. Thompson and D. Held (eds), Habermas: Critical Debates, 79-97, London: Macmillan.
Rapoport, R.N. (1970) 'Three dilemmas of action research', Human Relations, 23, 499-513.
Rorty, R. (1982) The Consequences of Pragmatism, Brighton: Harvester.
Sanford, N. (1981) 'A model for action research', in P. Reason and J. Rowan, Human Inquiry: A Sourcebook of New Paradigm Research, 173-81, London: Wiley.
Scheffler, I. (1986) Four Pragmatists: A Critical Introduction to Pierce, James, Mead and Dewey, London: Routledge & Kegan Paul.
Schon, D.A. (1983) The Reflective Practitioner: How Professionals Think in Action, London: Temple Smith.
Susman, G.I. (1983) 'Action research: a socio-technical systems perspective', in G. Morgan (ed.), Beyond Method: Strategies for Social Research, London: Sage.
Susman, G.I. and Evered, R. (1978) 'An assessment of the scientific merits of action research', Administrative Science Quarterly, 23. 582-603.
Wain, K. (1987) Philosophy of Lifelong Education, London: Croom Helm.
Warnke, G. (1987) Gadamer: Hermeneutics, Tradition and Reason, Oxford: Polity Press.
Welton, M.R. (1987) 'Vivisecting the nightingale: reflections on adult education as an object of study', Studies in the Education of Adults, 19, 46-68.

Chapter Seven

THE SELF IN RESEARCH AND REFLECTIVE PRACTICE

INTRODUCTION

In previous chapters we have exposed some of the assumptions underlying the pursuit of foundational research in the social sciences, and have done so by concentrating on the epistemological grounding of knowledge-claims and various problems associated with their intended applicability to practice.

The traditional methods of social science research have also been found wanting in terms of one of the central purposes that we take to be characteristic of adult education research as a practical endeavour - namely the intention of the discovery process itself to achieve change in all parties (teachers and researchers as well as learners and research subjects), through the joint development and refinement of critical understanding. Although they are not without their own difficulties (as we have seen in Chapter 6) 'action research' practices are now being adopted by adult education researchers, where the principal feature is that of <u>engagement</u>.

This entails more than simply 'being involved'; rather, it necessitates, on the part of researchers themselves, a commitment to their own reflective practice of inquiry by acting as exemplars of a process that they wish to encourage in others. In this process, researchers act together both as teachers and investigators. The relationship is that of co-explorers of a variety of practices - including the practice of doing research itself. This will not be possible if participants assume the roles of teacher and/or researcher as conventionally understood. The researcher-researched and teacher-taught dualities, along with the positivist and transmission models of knowledge production and communication, need replacing. For this to be a realizable prospect, however, rather more work has to be done on understanding the nature of engagement in the research process than has been evident to date, even among those advocates of educational action research as a preferred mode of understanding.

Our purpose is therefore to 'personalize' the action inquiry process by considering the <u>agency</u> of research as it has been, and might better be, understood. To the extent that adult education research is committed to reflective practice, it must <u>embody</u> research itself as a practice of critical self-reflection. In contrast, formal considerations of different research methodologies have contributed to the disembodiment of research, as if it were a purely technical process that somehow happens outside of human agency. This approach has had the unfortunate consequence of allowing the protagonists of different methodological schools to separate matters of investigative technique from broader research questions, including 'problems' of an ethical or political nature and, by so doing, to split the self as technician from the self as a responsible participant. Action research that is to be educational for all parties requires that these matters be treated jointly.

Advocates of the 'normal' methods of social science research have a particular view of the 'self' in the research process. It is one in which the agents of inquiry are required to maintain a necessary and appropriate distance from their subjects in order to satisfy the transpersonal canons of objectivity and consistency. This is the case both for hypothetico-deductive and grounded-theory research. Discoveries are to be made, and explanations given in the absence of personal valuations which are held to contaminate and thereby invalidate any findings. There is a paradox here; while insisting that the best efforts are required by researchers to avoid making value judgements, yet at the same time acknowledging that any attempts to avoid the intrusion of values can only be partially successful, such an insistence artificially writes off the researcher as a situated, construing and self-critical reflective practitioner. If action research is itself to be thought of as entailing a commitment to reflective practice, then the self as an evaluating and problem-solving agent has, in Homans' sense, to be 'brought back in' to the process

(Homans, 1964).

If research is to be of value to practitioners, then in whatever way it is made available to them - through participation, collaboration or joint action - researching into the practices of others must also involve a consideration of research itself as a practice. Furthermore, as Kemmis notes 'a research programme for the improvement of reflection must be conducted through self-reflection' (Kemmis, 1985:140). First, it is necessary to expose the shortcomings of conventional and disembodied notions of research which require the researcher to be an outsider, as a writer and/or director of the investigative script rather than being on stage as a performer and thereby accepting a share of immediate responsibility for the performance. Second, the implications for the self as a researcher/practitioner in moving 'beyond method' (Morgan, 1983) and engaging in what has become known as 'new paradigm' research (Reason and Rowan, 1981) need to be examined.

THE SELF IN THE RESEARCH ARENA

Mead's classical concept of the self is one of a developing entity which 'arises in the process of social experience and activity' (Mead, 1962:135) and has four principal and interrelated characteristics. First, the self is both subject and object: it is reflexive, that is to say it has the quality of being an object unto itself. Second, it is relational: it is implicated in the construals of others 'in relation to whom he acts in any given social situation' (Mead, 1962:138). Third, the self is communicative: it is engaged in symbolic exchanges in which the content of communication is addressed not merely to others but also to the self. Fourth, the self is rule-governed and has a structural quality, which Mead illustrates through the notions of role-taking and game-playing and in relation to his concept of the 'generalized other' as a performative reference.

The model (Fig. 7.1), which can be taken to represent a summation of the doing of social science research as theorized by Blumer (1969), Denzin (1970), Mills (1959), Sjoberg and Nett (1968), and others, has a Meadian pedigree. It projects the self as a purposeful, normatively-guided role player and skilled practitioner within a number of concurrent relationships. The presence of a self within the

The Self in Research

Figure 7.1 The self in the research arena

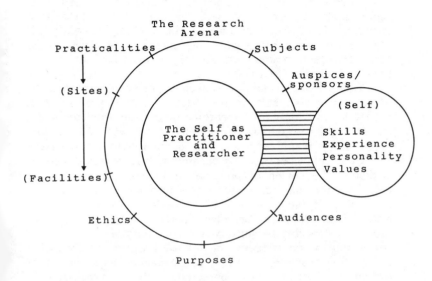

research arena that has to deal with the multiplicity of issues that characterize research as a practice is problematized in terms of the conditions for successful role performance. 'Good' researchers are those who are adept at solving a whole range of problems that confront them by the application of foreknowledge, and the drawing on skills and personal experiences as refracted through the self's own personality and set of values.

Of course, the self as a researcher is a problem-solving practitioner, not only in relation to the analytical aspects of a chosen substantive topic of inquiry, but also in relation to those cultural, economic, and political problems that are entailed by that choice. Indeed, topics may be chosen as much for their 'safety' (thus solving some of these latter problems by avoidance) as for their theoretical significance. So this notion of researchers as problem-solving selves in interaction is a useful one. Among other things, it alerts us to the following considerations: that there is more to doing 'good' research than having a good technique; that 'significant' research may put the self at risk (and as a corollary 'safe' research may not be very significant); and that certain kinds of research are likely to be more or less suited to certain kinds of selves as personalities and/or holders of particular values.

The politics of doing research involves the presentation of an acceptable self as practitioner within the research arena. In drawing on a repertoire of accumulated technical skills in their own practices, researchers will also display particular personal 'styles' - the accumulated result of the self's own experiences, temperament, and personal values. Although the notion of personal style has received a good deal of attention from researchers into the study practices of adults, it has received little reflexive attention from either methodologists or advocates of particular research practices (possibly because of the fuzziness of the notion of 'style' as a constituent or characteristic of research conduct). It cannot, however, be discounted as a formative ingredient within the personal, albeit 'professional', relationships of doing educational research. This is especially so if we take adult education to be concerned with engaging persons in the totality of their personhood as affective and situated, as well as cognitive, beings. To be consistent, we have to recognize these dimensions of adulthood in the researchers' own learning as well as in that of their subjects.

The research situation itself, or 'arena' as we have called it, has been extensively analysed from interactionist premises. Although it is not our intention to rework this analysis here, a brief interrogative list of some of the 'issues' for the self as a researcher (as identified in Fig. 7.1) is in order, particularly as they are likely to concern the adult education action researcher.

Subjects

What is implied in terms of procedural possibilities and

obligations by the defining of subjects as 'partners', 'clients', 'respondents', or in some other way?

Auspices/sponsors

What support and 'formal' legitimacy can researchers claim for their inquiries, and how is this related to the various senses of legitimacy that other parties to the research may apply?

Audiences

Who are the audiences for one's performance as a researcher and how is one to cope with differential expectations of, and satisfaction with, the research both in terms of its processes and outcomes?

Practicalities

What limits are to be set by the research exercise, and within the available facilities how is the disposition of time, money and specific research tasks to be managed? What are the implications for access and negotiation of choosing particular research sites, and what are the continuing implications for directing and sustaining the research effort?

Ethics

Is there an over-arching set of adult education research responsibilities, and if so, to what/whom? If identifiable, how do these claims relate to any 'situational' or 'personal' ethics of inquiry?

Purposes

What distinctions can properly be made, and by whom, between any manifest and latent research purposes in a given domain? In any contradictions of purpose who is to bear the cost of any 'failure' of the presumed intent of research?

The above issues are sufficient to indicate the kinds of problems that the researcher as a practitioner will be taking on, consciously or unconsciously, as an engaged self in the research process. They have all been identified by previous analysts as exemplifying the problems of socially-situated performances. They are of special concern to adult educators as action researchers, both because of the ways in which these practitioners orient themselves towards their 'subjects' as active and responsible learners and because of their concern with personal and/or social change.

There is one major problem with this interactionist approach to locating the self in the research process, however. It does not demonstrate how the complexity of those relationships and issues that confront the researcher as a self - the actual <u>experience</u> of doing research - <u>is a factor in the constitution of knowledge itself</u>. If we accept that all parties to the research will be making knowledge - claims that are grounded in their own situatedness, then we will need to take account not only of the self as an interacting party to the research but also as a sense-maker and knowledge-claimant within an arena of multiple senses and contested claims. The educational action researcher's purpose is to try and sort out at least some of these, in the hope that by so doing there will be a refinement of all parties' knowledge including the researcher's own.

THE SELF IN DISCOURSE

A major objection to the research orthodoxy of the foundation disciplines of education lines in its model of the person both as a subject of inquiry and as the agency of research. We have suggested that the idea of an interacting self in the research process can be of some value in helping us to understand the critical areas of diplomacy and management that must be addressed, in order to maximize the satisfaction of the research experience for all participants. Nevertheless, the primary purpose of research is not to achieve satisfaction, however laudible that aim; it is to generate warrantable knowledge (which may be disturbing). It is therefore necessary to consider the knowledge-constitutive aspects of the personal experiences of selves in making claims and making sense for themselves, and in relation to others who are similarly occupied. Here, a discourse-analytic approach to understanding the 'self' may help us.

Potter and Wetherell's approach is one which:

> takes discourse as a research topic in its own right rather than treating it as a transparent medium through which the 'real facts' of attitudes, events or behaviours can be recovered ... it takes a social perspective which focusses on the role of discourse in interaction and sense making rather than being concerned with, for example, abstract questions of semantics.
> (Potter and Wetherell, 1987:184)

They argue that the notion of the 'self' is dependent on the linguistic practices used in everyday life to make sense of our own and others' actions (Potter and Wetherell, 1987:95). Traditionally, the self has been characterized in three general ways:

1. As a set of personality traits. With respect to practice, this approach has been adopted by judges of the prospective suitability of individuals for task performance, e.g. in relation to job recruitment, counselling and career development, where the self is projected as being an appropriate character for role-occupancy.
2. As a role-player. This is the 'public' self of actual performance rather than the 'private' self of propensity. It is a mediating concept between individuals and their situations. The role-player self is also impersonal; it separates the identities of individuals from their situations, so that it is possible to talk for example of 'the researcher' without having any particular person in mind. As we have already seen, this leads us to a conception of research as a set of conflicting role requirements that any incumbent has to manage. The self-reflection of the role-player would be a mirroring, in Mead's sense, of the expectations that others have of one's role performance.
3. As an 'authentic' or 'true' self. This is the focus of Rogerian personal growth therapy and some forms of humanistic psychology which aim to reveal and/or to realize the 'whole' or 'potential' self.

Potter and Wetherell invite us to consider what is being assumed in the above kinds of modelling of the self. They conclude that each makes a claim to understand selfhood as a definable entity but one having different attributes for different purposes - such as diagnosing, knowing how to act towards, or intervening on behalf of, the self. This multiplicity of selves is a consequence of different linguistic practices. According to Harre, 'to be a self is not to be a certain kind of being but to be in possession of a certain kind of theory' (Potter and Wetherell, 1987:262). A theory of the self is a theory of the subjective and objective characteristics of personhood employed for practical purposes. A discourse-analytic approach to understanding the constitution of the self would therefore examine the functions served by the different interpretations in situations where talk about the self is revealed.

Now this has important implications for understanding the conditions under which it might be possible to improve practice through participative educational research. In so far as we have identified the improvement of practice as resting on acts of critical self-reflection, we can now go further to suggest that it also depends upon acts of critical self-description. Empirical research on the discursive construction of the self is in its infancy (Potter and Wetherell, 1987:110). However, it is possible to identify ways in which the self is constituted through the everyday language transactions of affirming, crediting, blaming, and so on - i.e. in discourse which is not merely descriptive but is 'an automous part of particular social practices' (Potter and Wetherell, 1987:179).

The key, then, to a better understanding and improvement of practice lies in recognizing that the so-called 'problems' of practice do not refer to some kind of extra-linguistic impedimenta. 'Problems' exist only in discourse and by virtue of the ways in which practitioners so describe aspects of their own practice and their restricted capabilities as problem-solving selves. Challenging the notion that there is 'a world out there' as a non-discursive reification, Potter and Wetherell argue for the inherently reconstitutive possibilities of discourse. Matters which appear to be insoluble can always be described and thereby acted upon by the self as a practitioner in different ways and with potentially different consquences.

CRITICAL THINKING AND RESEARCH AS ENGAGEMENT

Educational researchers share with other practitioners the fact that they are expected to be 'problem solvers' within their own domain of expertise. Research expertise is conventionally thought to lie in the application of standardized techniques to a substantive field in order to reveal and explain aspects of behaviour therein. Research involves both finding out and theorizing about what is found. An additional dimension of 'critical thinking' in the shape of some formal analysis is therefore necessary for an explanation of their discoveries to be accepted. Normally, critique is taken to apply only to alternative conceptualizations of what is uncovered through research. If criticism is only directed 'outwards' as it were, i.e. toward interpretations of objects of discovery and not at the same time directed 'inwards' towards the self as an interpreter, then this will prevent the researcher becoming a reflective practitioner. The expectation that guides the conduct of research is one in which researchers are normally expected to be theorists with respect to their objects rather than towards themselves as subjects.

If we consider those dimensions of constructive self-criticism that are essential to reflective practice, then it should be clear that we do not regard such a thinking exercise simply as a detached cognitive activity that has its own self as an object. As Brookfield (1987) argues, critical thinking about the self is not something that one can suddenly decide to engage in by taking a new and radically different set of principles down from the shelf, hoping that henceforth they will displace one's conventional modes of practice. On the contrary, it is a developmental process of becoming, or a 'practical accomplishment' in itself. In that process, it is necessary to establish what Brookfield calls 'lines of communication' and the structural supports to maintain these between the self and other parties to the research process. Given this support, it is then possible for the critical thinker to venture into uncharted territory, to be an opportunistic and exploratory self with respect to action possibilities. In addition, critical thinking is 'contextually aware' - it recognizes the situatedness of all practices and thoughts about practices ('informal theories' as we have called them), including its own. The open and possibilistic aspects of critical thinking in reflective practice are conjectural. This quality relates situations to aspects of other, seemingly dissimilar situations - for example, in using metaphor for thinking 'as if ...' and in speculating 'what if ...?'.

For Brookfield, the critical self-awareness of reflective practice is both required by and is a product of, action research. For this to happen, however, the conditions of the research must be such that there is at least a temporary consensuality among participants, even though there may be differences about the relevance of particular exploratory domains at any given moment. The process of critical thinking 'involves alternating phases of analysis and action' and the capacities which characterize critical thinking are 'developed and refined in active inquiry' (Brookfield, 1987:23). The medium of critical thinking is an argumentative rather than an affirmative discourse. For action research to be directed towards reflective practice, it must therefore avoid the exchange of premature ultimates.

By inviting researchers to move 'beyond method' in considering their practices, Morgan wants us to understand research as a set of activities and understandings concerned with the construction of knowledge, rather than being concerned with the discovery of knowledge 'out there'. As a practice, its characteristic is neither the innocent gathering of facts nor the revelation of their supposed causes. Research is the more or less systematic and critical accomplishment of meaning - the active conferral of sense upon the world. In a weak connotation, all actors are 'researchers'. In a stronger one, different research methods and styles can be distinguished by their degrees of systemization and the extent to which they are consciously self-critical of their procedural assumptions.

This view is one of research as the continual and active reconstitution of knowledge rather than an activity of 'innocent exploration' to attain knowledge of the previously unknown. Morgan brings the notion of 'engagement' to the forefront of the research process, and invites a consideration of research as the realization of possible knowledges:

> Scientists engage a subject of study by interacting with it through means of a particular frame of reference, and what is observed and discovered in the object (i.e. its objectivity) is as much a product of this interaction and the protocol and technique through which it is

operationalised as it is of the object itself ... The view of research as engagement emphasizes that researcher and researched must be seen as part of a whole and, therefore, questions the idea that it is possible to stand outside the research process and evaluate it in any absolute way.

(Morgan, 1983:14)

Any activity can be seen as involving the making of knowledge claims. That which is called 'research' simply claims to be more systematic about it. The important thing to note here is that the situated character of any and all activity means that there can be no independent point of reference from which to judge the validity of knowledge claims. This seems to land us back in the 'relativism problem', but this is not so according to Morgan, as we shall see.

First, it must be noted that one important implication of Morgan's view of research is that it completely avoids another difficulty - the 'applicability problem'. This is only a problem if we think of research as being about the production of knowledge for use; here, 'applicability' refers to the use-value of a definitive product. Alternatively, if research is thought of as a process of engagement concerning the sensibility and contextuality of claims and counter-claims to knowledge, and engagement as the considered realization of 'new' knowledge, then its value is not as product but as edification in the generative and ultimately educative process of doing research itself.

Morgan draws together a number of social scientists and invites them to reveal the base assumptions behind their different modes of engagement. The various assumptive logics of inquiry that are presented are then decoded in terms of how and for what purposes researchers constitute their objects. Any particular mode of engagement will only result in the realization of one possible form of knowledge among many possible forms. No particular form is epistemologically privileged and cannot therefore stand as a test of validity or veracity for the rest.

Positivists and correspondence theorists attempt to minimize the influence of subjective processes in research. Neither researchers nor researched as sense-making selves have a legitimate place in their programmes. Interpretivists and phenomenologists require subjectivity as the agency of sense-making among the researched, though they have been less comfortable about admitting it as a primary vehicle of their own understandings as researchers. In taking a view of a wide spectrum of research practices as multiple forms of engagement, Morgan sounds an important note of caution about pronouncing foundationally on where the 'truth' between the rival claims of subjectivity/objectivity might lie:

> the idea that scientific research is a process of 'engagement' ... does not of itself establish the supremacy of knowledge that systematically explores the relation between subject and object. In order to be able to make such foundational claims regarding the priority of subject, object or some relation between the two, one has to be able to see and evaluate their claims from a perspective that transcends the presuppositions that shape the subject/object problematic.
> (Morgan, 1983:372)

The necessary relativism of any research stance can best be seen as an <u>opportunity</u> for regarding knowledge in a different way, rather than as a constraint on the production of truth. Relativism, as we have seen, is only a problem if knowledge is regarded as foundational, since there can be no 'true knowledge' in the sense of corroborated theories which are not themselves derived from situated research practices. If, as Morgan suggests, relativism is 'an inevitable feature of the process through which knowledge is generated' (Morgan, 1983:373), we can look at different varieties of research as forms of practice that are particular and partial means of expression concerning the relationship of the self with the world. This has affinities with Gadamer's understanding of research as a process of making and re-making oneself, as well as Rorty's approach to research as a process of (self-)edification.

THE PROMISE OF 'NEW PARADIGM' RESEARCH

While sympathizing with the general tenor of the arguments marshalled by Reason and Rowan (1981) towards a 'new paradigm research manifesto', we need to examine some specific details of the case that is being made for the location of the self as a practitioner in the research process.

The authors describe 'new paradigm' research as the

working through of a set of ideas towards 'a synthesis of naive inquiry and orthodox research' and refer to this synthesis as something that would be 'objectively subjective' (Reason and Rowan, 1981:13). They acknowledge that the influence on their own approach is the stance towards human beings taken by humanistic psychologists such as Kelly (1969). Their position has important implications both for the relationships that are held to be proper within the conduct of research and for the status of knowledge that is generated therein. If we are to understand research as something that is neither purely objective nor subjective but rather as a synthesis that is a product as much of artistry as of science, then we must disabuse ourselves of certain notions concerning objectivity and subjectivity and find space for research as their creative interplay.

Orthodox assumptions about the stability and determinateness of 'fact', which are subsumed in the idea of a detached collecting of data, involve the researcher in what Harre (1985) calls 'a strategic retreat to certainty' (cited in Reason and Rowan, 1981:9). The room for manoeuvre that is required by negotiating actors in the kind of research that Reason and Rowan prefer, implies the continual re-(creation) of 'facts' through discourse. Harre argues that by offering, through talk, our actions to others as open sets of possibilities, we come to a different understanding of what knowledge is and also to a different view of the self as a researcher who accepts responsibility for the creation of knowledge by engaging with others.

The problems that attend the 'application' of the results of conventional research are not solved but relocated and deepened by the determination to follow a course of 'action research'. A descriptive shift whereby 'subjects' become 'clients' will not of itself alter their relationship with researchers. If action research as co-operative inquiry is to treat subjects or clients as 'co-researchers', then the relationship will indeed have changed. But this is still insufficient. Given that genuine collaboration requires subjects or clients to be co-researchers, there will be an additional requirement for researchers to become co-subjects, with all that implies for an examination of the self as a sense-making agent. As Heron says: 'to give a full and sufficient explanation of research behaviour, some reference must be made to the notion of intelligent agency or self-direction' (cited in Reason and Rowan, 1981:21). The characteristic of intelligent agency is the 'construing-and-intending' of creative actors (Reason and Rowan, 1981:22). Interpretivists accept the need to examine this in subjects, but do not necessarily require it of themselves as researchers.

There is a further obligation, and also a payoff. If the researcher is to be regarded as a co-subject, then this imposes a duty of exposure to the reflections of others in order to become self-reflective as a practitioner of inquiry. Heron notes that in so far as subjects' construing-and-intending may contain rationalization and/or delusion, then there is no reason to suppose that this might not also be the case for researchers as subjects, regardless of their technical proficiency. Hence there will always be the need for what Heron calls 'corrective feedback' (cited in Reason and Rowan, 1981:24) to be applied to all parties.

If new paradigm research is to fulfil the kind of promises set out by Reason and Rowan, then a condition of such research must be the granting to co-inquirers as selves in interaction the freedom to make their own sense of what is revealed through collective investigation. Rowan regards 'making sense' as a key phase of the research cycle (Reason and Rowan, 1981:ch. 10). If one were to follow the canons of a strict Aristotelian logic of inquiry, however, there would appear to be little opportunity to do so. Were the laws of contradiction (requiring that propositions not be both true and false) and the excluded middle (requiring that propositions be either true or false) to apply, then there would be no room for the kind of manoeuvres that sense-making demands as a practical activity of negotiating meaning.

At the very least, some of the operations of any kind of practice, including research, are conducted on the basis of naive beliefs and subjective knowledge - and necessarily so. The point is that, although from a strictly logical point of view these suppositions may be 'weak' or 'mistaken', we also know that objective truths do not exist which would satisfy the above canons. They are inapplicable for several reasons: i) the impossibility of knowing everything, even about a finite domain; ii) the multiple and mutual causality of interacting systems, and especially in this context the complexity of self-other relationships, iii) the universal human experience of contradictions; iv) the need to find some meaning in actions even at the cost of logic.

Reason and Rowan want the experience of doing research to be one where the engaged self together with other engaged selves moves to a state of 'realized knowledge' through a continuous working on the data of experience, and it is this practice of 'making sense' or reflecting on experience that they commend. There is no end to this process. Certainly, realized knowledge is neither the 'truth' nor a logically consistent set of beliefs. Rather, it is the <u>necessarily incomplete</u> resolution of contradiction. In principle, the commitment of the self to others in any joint venture of making sense must be open-ended. However, what is perhaps more important in the context of our present discussion (although not specifically alluded to) is that <u>the process will be educational in the sense that we understand it</u> - i.e. by effecting change through the effort to understand.

This theme of the need to find meaning and the making of sense as the task of any self (including the 'professional researcher' self) is the performative condition of selfhood. Selves are situated and scripted. Rowan consequently invites us to consider the potential contribution of hermeneutics as a way of recognizing the ontological fact of situatedness and of accessing meanings that are both 'given' or scripted, yet are at the same time open to alteration through interpretation (Reason and Rowan, 1981:132-5). The goal of interpretation in the research process thus becomes one of achieving a 'maximal reasonableness' through an 'oscillation of interpretations' between part and whole, the outcome of which is a coming-to-understand and to act in new ways. So-called 'naive' beliefs and subjective knowledge will never finally be eradicated, since this is neither the purpose nor the promise of hermeneutic practice.

The practice of doing research encompasses a multiplicity of experiences in which the self embraces shifting and contingent theories of what is going on (working hunches, etc.) in order that the research itself can proceed. But these experiences need to be rendered down in any formal or public discovery accounts, and in this process not even everything of significance is sure to be related (there may be a <u>post hoc</u> significance not recognized at the time). For the researcher to submit to the dictates of a predetermined method or logic of inquiry would be for the self to deny at least a portion of its own experience that may later turn out to be relevant to the realization of knowledge. Although the self cannot conceivably attend simultaneously to all of its experiences, it must admit, encourage, and be prepared to speak of different aspects of experience within the research process. Conventional research epitomizes the practice of premature closure. While there is obviously a sense in which specific research projects must end, research as such (even within an apparently limited domain) cannot ever be said to do so, being but a species of perpetual human inquiry.

How is one to think about the capturing of experiences and their incorporation into research that makes it something other than a random process? Kelly speaks of 'creativity cycles' in research which he depicts as a three-fold recursive process of circumspection, pre-emption, and control (cited in Bannister, 1981; Reason and Rowan, 1981:ch. 16). In the first phase of circumspection any and all suppositions are permitted, including those which do not have any apparent basis in one's own or even others' experiences. Speculation is allowed which may literally be fantastic; the techniques of 'brian-storming' and lateral thinking are examples of this phase. In the second phase of pre-emption, concrete experiences supply material out of which seemingly relevant issues are drawn. Another way of putting it is to say that 'issues' are pre-emptions that are experientially referential. But they are not as yet focused. It is the third phase of control, necessary if research is to be considered as a relatively formalized version of ordinary human inquiry (or the rational attempt to make sense of the making-sense of others), that is directed towards specific elements of experience and sense-making in their situatedness. The cycle as a whole is depicted by Kelly (1969) as an alternating sequence of 'loose' and 'tight' construals, first by a relaxed and then by a disciplined self in examination of his/her personal constructs. In the context of educational action research, the relevance of Kelly's creativity cycle is in suggesting a complementarity of loose construals which allow for change and invention and tight construals which give more specific directions for action.

A remaining issue is the extent to which so-called 'new paradigm' research is realizable in practice, given the actual circumstances under which much adult education research is conducted. One point to be made here is that if we are to take Kelly and like-minded theorists of alternative research practices seriously, then, for reflexivity in research to occur as they would wish, the conditions for researchers must be such that issues are experienced as part of the self's own personal constructs. There must be a feeling that the research actually 'belongs' to them, not in a private or possessive way but as an inalienable condition for making sense. Short-term contract research acts against this. There is a danger (which is unfortunately all too apparent on occasion) of what one might call a 'false attachment' to research, i.e. it can be regarded as being a necessary job by the researcher and a tolerable incursion by the researched rather than as being a reciprocal engagement. Such research can easily become a type of alienated labour for all parties to the process.

THE VALIDITY ISSUE

The confrontation and public presentation of the researcher as a self is one in which the kinds of assumptions that are necessary for all practitioners to make in order to make sense of the 'messes' with which they have to deal are exposed and explored through conversation or dialogue (Morgan, 1983:381-2). Morgan recognizes, however, that in any exchanges, especially those involving the sponsors of research, there will be conflicts with the affirmational demands of institutionally-sponsored research which favour a 'production-oriented mentality that emphasizes the importance of achieving significant, useful results' (Morgan, 1983:384) and the tentative and self-doubting revelations of the reflective research practitioner. Such conflicts often raise questions about the validity and generalizability of research.

If the processes and results of research are self-referential, then conventionalist requirements of validity, which are regarded as objective and trans-personal, will not be satisfied. One implication of locating selves in the research process in the way that we have tried to do here, and which now needs to be made more explicit, is that these agents of sense-making are 'on trial' with respect to the validity of any knowledge claims that are made, or which may emerge dialectically. But they are on trial in a rather different way and under different rules than those applying to conventional scientific research. For a start, they are engaged with counter-claimants during the research itself. Some claims will be rhetorical. If all parties agreed about everything then there would be no need for reflective practice, and there would be no politics of research. It is because there is such a need, and because there is an internal politics of claim-making that action researchers do not have the luxury of working in conditions where judgement is suspended until conclusions are reached and the results offered for peer assessment. The self is less protected within the research, if not afterwards.

Traditional validity principles cannot appropriately be applied in new paradigm research or to the kinds of research for reflective practice that we are advocating. A logic that insists on true measurement, the attribution of true cause, and warranted generalization - all conventional dimensions of validity - is misplaced. A different kind of multivalent logic is required which recognizes the dialectical quality of sense-making. Its validity principles are properly based on an experiential coherence which is neither insistently 'objective' nor ineffably 'subjective'. Validity thus becomes a matter of the <u>authenticity</u> of shared knowledge among a community of sense-making, reflective practitioners. Although knowledge-claims cannot be substantiated in any formal manner, they must resonate with experience so that it is meaningful and insightful for practitioners to 'know' in a particular way rather than in some other way.

The strength of the conventional view of research as foundational has been that even its critics have felt uncomfortable about replacing conventionalist criteria for research <u>evaluation</u>. There can be no absolute and 'objective' criteria of validity, though this does not mean that any kind of research is as good as any other. Indeed, Morgan insists that the absence of such criteria places an even greater responsibility upon the researcher as a construing self, since he/she cannot hide behind a convenient screen of impersonal and supposedly 'objective' facts speaking for themselves. The responsibility that is placed upon the engaged researcher is the requirement for reflective exploration to be made public, in what Morgan calls 'reflective conversation'. This is seen as both an opportunity and a duty for researchers to engage in exchanges where they will confront their professional 'selves' (Morgan, 1983:374).

Traditionally, the privileged position of academic researchers as knowledgeable authorities has been achieved by following the prescriptions of 'normal' scientific practices. In so far as these are 'distanced' from research subjects and adopt formal validity criteria, a measure of protection from counter-claims to knowledge is assured. However, here and in the previous chapter we have suggested that the self as a reflective practitioner of action research requires protection from 'unreasonable' claims upon his/her practice, since these are likely to follow from the process of engagement itself. In wanting to 'loosen' the constraints of validity as conventionally understood, we are not advocating a lessening of responsibility upon the self to produce 'good' research, but wish to emphasize that both 'good' research and the conditions necessary for its realization depend upon the continuous negotiation and reflection-in-action of all parties in the process - before, during, and after any investigation.

REFERENCES

Bannister, D. (1981) 'Personal construct theory and research method', in Reason and Rowan, Human Inquiry: A Sourcebook of New Paradigm Research, London: Wiley.
Blumer, H. (1969) Symbolic Interactionism, New Jersey: Prentice-Hall.
Brookfield, S.D. (1987) Developing Critical Thinkers, Milton Keynes: Open University Press.
Denzin, N.K. (1970) The Research Act in Sociology, London: Butterworths.
Harre, R. (1985) 'The language game of self-ascription: a note' in K.J. Gergen and K.E. Davis (eds) The Social Construction of the Person, New York: Springer-Verlag.
Homans, G.C. (1964) 'Bringing men back in', American Sociological Review, 5, 808-818.
Kelly, G.A. (1969) Clinical Psychology and Personality: the Selected Papers of George Kelly, New York: Wiley.
Kemmis, S. (1985) 'Action research and the politics of reflection' in D. Boud et al. (eds), Reflection: Turning Experience into Learning, 139-63, London: Kogan Page.
Mead, G.H. (1962) Mind, Self and Society, Chicago: University of Chicago Press.
Mills, C.W. (1959) The Sociological Imagination, New York: Oxford University Press.
Morgan, G. (ed.) (1983) Beyond Method: Strategies for Social Research, London: Sage Books.
Potter, J. and Wetherell, M. (1987) Discourse and Social Psychology, London: Sage Books.
Reason, P. and Rowan, J. (eds) (1981) Human Inquiry: A Sourcebook of New Paradigm Research, London: Wiley.
Rowan, J. and Reason, P. (1981) 'On making sense' in Reason and Rowan, op. cit.

Sjoberg, G and Nett, R. (1968) A Methodology for Social Research, New York: Harper & Row.

Chapter Eight

LEARNING ABOUT RESEARCH: CURRICULUM IMPLICATIONS

INTRODUCTION

In this chapter our intention is to examine the implications of the themes discussed so far for a curriculum concerned both with learning <u>about</u> research and learning to <u>do</u> research. Such a curriculum needs to be based on an understanding of adult education both as a field of study and a field of practice. In previous chapters, we outlined the problematic elements in both areas. The task now is to extend this analysis and we begin by focusing on the way in which the study of adult education can be seen as a practical field of knowledge. This will allow us to proceed to an alternative conceptualization of adult education 'theory' and thus its role in a curriculum for research.

Adult education as a practical field of knowledge is supposedly an inter-disciplinary composite with elements drawn from various social science disciplines. A practical field can be distinguished from a theoretical field in terms of an orientation - the latter has an orientation concerned with finding out about the world, discovering 'truths', the way things are, whereas the former is concerned with acting in the world and changing it in certain ways.

As we have already seen, this analysis has been used by Bright (1985) to demonstrate that adult education as a field of study cannot be a theoretical field even though it has claimed to be one. The more important question, however, is whether it can be characterized as a practical field of knowledge, comparable for example to engineering. Bright's answer on this point is not entirely clear. He argues that if adult education abandons the disciplines model it could be characterized as a practical field of knowledge, but he also wants to support the de Castell and Freeman (1978) notion of a 'socio-practical' field of inquiry and assimilate adult education to that.

The latter is an argument we would want to support, since it highlights a particular characteristic of adult education as an activity directly concerned with human welfare where value judgements and the context generally must be taken into account. This is reinforced by other factors to do with clientele, location outside of schooling, and humanistic orientation.

Unfortunately, adult education as a socio-practical field is not the same as adult education as a practical field of knowledge. The latter is still based on disciplines, albeit not independent but an inter-disciplinary composite with an integrating theory and concepts. However they are still disciplines, whereas the socio-practical is not based on disciplines in any sense. There is a place for disciplines but that place is pragmatic not foundational. The knowledge in the socio-practical does not derive from disciplines but is the knowledge to be found in practice.

Clearly, the pragmatic nature of the socio-practical is congruent with the critique presented in an earlier chapter of disciplines as foundations and foundationalism in general. It is, therefore, a potentially fruitful conceptualization for our present purpose so some of its main features can usefully be highlighted at this point. It is characterized as a field of enquiry where considerations of welfare and contextual constraints are paramount and where theory (knowledge and understanding) is 'instrumental to taking effective action to solve acknowledged practical problems' (de Castell and Freeman, 1978:17).

The 'theoretico-practical' as a field of enquiry, in distinction, assumes context and value questions to be irrelevant to its concerns. The problems towards which inquiry is directed are instrinsic to itself and are identified by the theory within the field, a theory which we have earlier called 'formal' theory. The socio-practical, on the other hand, assumes variable social contexts, and the problems towards which inquiry is directed are intrinsic to these contexts and are identified by the need for continually effective action 'as a matter of urgent concern' (de Castell and Freeman, 1978:15).

Socio-practical fields can be characterized in terms of their particular content, method, and goals. There is no restriction on substantive content - the only consideration is the 'necessary concern' with purposeful action, the urgent solution of problems and the practical use of knowledge. Method is defined in terms of function so there is no methodological restriction on theory, since any theory which facilitates effective action is acceptable. Thus, it is eclectic and its justification pragmatic. In terms of goals, the reason for action is always the need to solve urgent problems involving human welfare. The generation and use of knowledge is therefore always instrumental and never an end in itself.

Given this orientation, it is clear that the role of practitioners is crucial. It is they who are in the best position to define and resolve problems since they have the knowledge and understanding of the specificities of contexts, the immediacy of problems, and the limitations and possibilities of action. Within the socio-practical, the practitioner is not seen merely as a technician. This has implications for the relationship between theory and practice, since the practitioner is involved in 'internally instrumental action' which is 'similar to the concept of praxis' (de Castell and Freeman, 1978:19).

Praxis is the dialectical bringing together of theory and practice, where generalized theory or prescriptions cannot be adopted per se but must be filtered through the contextual constraints within which action is located. Practice, therefore, is not the application of theory nor is the action involved in practice 'mindless' or atheoretical. Theory provides the reasons or motives for purposeful action and thus 'guides' practice, but within situations where contextual variables have to be taken into account.

Adult education has not systematically conceptualized itself as a socio-practical field of inquiry. As Bright (1985) rightly argues, adult education as a field of study has used a body of knowledge drawn, in an untransformed way, from social science disciplines, and a methodology (or more accurately methodologies) drawn from the same sources in an undifferentiated way. He concludes, therefore, that adult education as a field of study has neither its own theory nor its own methodology. What adult education 'theory' there is, would appear barely to merit the epithet, and methodology seems to be chosen entirely on the basis of the particular social science discipline possessed by the theorist or researcher. This has unfortunate consequences for curriculum design, teaching, and research, and we shall explore these later in this chapter. Our purpose is to locate adult education within a modified version of the 'socio-practical' and to see what curricular implications this has.

'THEORY' IN ADULT EDUCATION AS A FIELD OF STUDY

First, we need to discuss the current content and position of 'theory' in adult education as a field of study, bearing in mind the criticisms we have already presented. The theory of andragogy as elaborated by Knowles (1978) is perhaps the best known and still very influential. It is hard to characterize Knowles' views as a 'theory', since he puts forward a number of 'principles' appropriate to adult education. These are the self-directedness of the adult, the constitutive nature of experience, and the need for adults to learn things that are relevant to them. From these are then derived two further 'principles' which are specifically curriculum related - adults immediately want to apply what they have learnt and they learn best through a problem-centred rather than a subject-centred approach.

Theories of adult development are more readily recognizable as 'theories'. We have commented on these in an earlier chapter, so only a brief recapitulation will be provided here. Essentially, they seek to challenge a static conception of the adult and replace it with one which emphasizes change and growth. Riegel (1979) put forward the notion of 'dialectical' modes of thinking which is both a higher mode than Piaget's 'formal' mode and uniquely characterizes the thinking of adults. This post-formal thinking involves an acceptance of contradiction, ambiguity, and change, and, unlike formal thinking, emphasizes 'problem-finding' rather than problem-solving.

There is no doubt that this conceptualization has become increasingly influential in adult education. In recent work (Chickering et al., 1981; Cross, 1982; Allman, 1983; Nottingham Andragogy Group, 1983) a 'contextualist' paradigm of adult development has been elaborated. This puts forward the notion that adult thinking and learning is not invariant but something which very much depends on the nature of the context. It challenges the conventional view of adult maturity as a kind of plateau followed by inevitable decline. Contexts themselves can vary according to life stages and the kind of developmental 'tasks' associated with them.

In Chapters 3 and 4 we noted the status of these theorizations as part of an emergent discourse which constituted the adult in particular ways. The question of their 'truth' is a problematic which it is not our purpose to examine. What we are concerned with is a critical examination of the nature of the discourse within which andragogical and developmental theories are formulated.

The main element in any critique would be the individualistic assumptions upon which both these theories are based. This individualism appears to be derived from psychology, particularly that variety based on humanistic paradigms. Welton talks of the 'colonisation of the territory of adult education by psychology and the intrusion of individualism into the conceptual framework of adult educators' (Welton, 1987:52). There is an uncritical acceptance of the notion of the autonomous, rational self, hence the assumption of 'self-directedness' in Knowles and of 'post-formal' thinking in Riegel.

It is also an abstracted individualism, however, in the sense that it fails to situate the individual within any kind of context. Self-directedness, for example, fails to situate adults in their society or culture - the assumption is that it is already present, simply waiting to come to fruition through andragogical teaching. As Squires points out 'Teachers and students do not exist in isolation; they are always acting in a context of institutions, roles, regulations and norms' (Squires, 1987:183). He also points out that to talk of problem-centred approaches to teaching in an abstract way neglects the essential contingency of teaching - its dependence on the kind of students a teacher has, the nature of the content to be taught, and the kind of setting in which the teaching takes place.

There are similar problems in the theory of adult development. On the face of it this seems curious, given that the theory is based on a contextualist paradigm. The problem here, however, is that the paradigm is one of abstracted contextualism. This is exemplified by the uncertain status of dialectical thinking. Is it a necessary developmental stage, as Piaget's stages are meant to be, or is it something that is learnt? If it is the former, then there is little that the educational practitioner can do, and if it is the latter, then a general theory of adult development needs to be replaced by a number of local theories. But the matter goes further than this - Squires (1987), for example, makes the point that the concepts used, such as 'abstract thought' and 'concrete reality', are taken as givens and treated unproblematically. Is the latter, for example, something that is just unproblematically 'there' or is it itself constructed?

Clearly, therefore, theories of adult learning and development are all, in the final analysis, psychological theories. Welton (1987) talks of the 'colonisation' of adult education by psychology and Griffin (1983) reminds us that the theory of andragogy is derived solely from psychological learning theory.

At one level there may be no problem here. After all, one could argue that if adult education is a field of knowledge in the Hirstian sense, then why should it not be based upon the discipline of psychology in the same way and for the same reasons that education has been? However, a number of counter-arguments could be made. First, a field of knowledge is meant to be an inter-disciplinary composite and therefore not dependent solely on one discipline. In the case of adult education as a field of study this would no doubt be endorsed by those who have criticized the failure to bring in the discipline of sociology and, through this, understandings of societal contexts. Second, as we have already seen, a field of knowledge is not only meant to be based on more than one discipline but is also meant to have a theory of its own which functions to integrate the various disciplines and, in the case of a practical field of knowledge, to provide the link with practice.

In our view this is a much more serious criticism, for it points to a fundamental problem in the relationship between the theories we have been considering and adult education as a field of study. As Bright (1985) points out, certain psychological concepts related to adult learning, thinking, and development are deployed but have not been elaborated from within adult education itself. Riegel's (1979) concept of 'dialectical thinking', despite its apparent relevance to adult education, is actually not part of a theory which has been generated, or at the least refined, within adult education as a field of study and certainly has no link with adult education as a field of practice. This leads to an important point which we shall explore in detail later but is worth making in general terms now. It has always been implicitly assumed that the study of adult education does not commence with the field of practice to which the study is related but with knowledge contained in formal theory, in the main in the discipline of psychology.

This could well throw some light on a rather curious aspect, so far not touched on, which is that the theories we have been considering are not in any sense self-referential. We can illustrate this, first, in general terms with the following quote from Allman:

> The 'contextualist' paradigm assumes that what people think and how they think emerges from people's transactions and interactions with their social and historical contexts. Since these contexts are dynamic, it is impossible to predict the most adaptive competencies which humans can develop or to predict an end stage in the developmental process.
> (Allman, 1983:110)

This appears to be a perfectly acceptable statement completely in line with 'contextualism'. However, if we consider the matter more closely, we can see that this is not quite the case. First, if what and how people think emerges from socio-historical contexts, then we need to ask about the context from which theories of adult development have emerged, since they too are examples of what and how people, in this case psychologists, have thought. In other words, theories which theorize contexts must themselves be contextualized.

Second, we are told that we can neither predict 'the most adaptive competencies' nor an end to the developmental process. Yet it is very clear from the writings of theorists of adult development that they do not really mean this at all. Riegel (1979), for example, clearly intends dialectical thinking to be seen as a post-formal mode which is both a later and higher form of thinking and is thus both the 'most adaptive' stage and the culmination of the developmental process. The same sort of assumption is to be found in Cross (1982) and Perry (1970). Squires points out in relation to their work that 'they attempt to identify a path of development which is not based on any coherent or consensual view of human existence' (Squires, 1987:191). We would simply add that the reason for this is the failure to contextualize one's own theorizations.

Theories of adult learning and development, despite their supposed location in a contextualist paradigm, fail to be self-referential. The interesting question is, why do they fail to be so and what is the consequence of this failure? One possible explanation is that, despite being theories contexts, they are still 'formal' theories generated from within the discipline of psychology. Formal theory is cast in a discourse which is meant to be universal even when it is about contexts - it describes the world in general and cannot therefore be itself contextualized. If it were to do so, it would no longer have the explanatory power which formal theory is supposed to have.

More specifically, we note that whatever theory there is in adult education as a field of study has been founded on the notion of the adult learner having unique characteristics. The adult as learner is supposed to be different from the child as learner; this is found in Knowles (1978), for example, in terms of self-directedness, experience, etc., and in the developmentalists in terms of post-formal modes of thinking. However, if we refocus our gaze from the question of differences to the common element of the 'learner' in theories about both the adult and the child, then an important but largely unacknowledged issue comes to the surface. The 'learner' in both cases is the abstracted individual of psychology whom we first encountered in Chapter 3. Without restating the critique made there, all we would say here is that this abstracted individual is not the contextualized, situated subject, and cannot be as long as theory itself is not contextualized.

There is another aspect of this, however, which needs emphasizing and, again, was touched upon in Chapter 3. It will be recalled that we talked about theoretical discourses which both constituted their own objects and were implicated in material practices of a regulatory kind. This line of analysis is useful for the specific point we are trying to make here. We commented there that adults are increasingly becoming a site for intervention, the objects of various regulatory practices; for example, re-training. These practices are always bound up with, indeed require, appropriate knowledge and hence appropriate theorizations. The theorizations we have been considering fit this bill admirably.

Here, we must remind ourselves of a point made earlier concerning their location within a humanistic paradigm and its assumption of the autonomous, rational self, capable of 'self-realization'. This theorization is admirably appropriate because it enables a discourse which is essentially voluntaristic and optimistic. Welton makes the point succinctly: 'Knowles' assumption that adulthood is an uncrinkled psychological movement towards self-direction dampens our fears that we are not masters of our own destiny' (Welton, 1987:52). This voluntaristic and optimistic discourse is suitable not simply for educational intervention but for intervention of a particular kind. It is a benign intervention which emphasizes 'facilitation' and making people more 'self-aware', and where training is no longer seen as merely a matter of imparting skills but of inculcating the 'right' attitudes.

In effect, the discourse is normative and, indeed, if we look closely at theories of adult learning, thinking, and development, we can see that they, too, are essentially normative, although this is partially concealed by the fact that they are couched in a 'scientific' language of objectivity and truth. This ambivalence is, however, no coincidence. They have a certain power because they are normative, since as such they appear to be saying something important about what the adult needs and what the adult can become if those needs are met. Equally, they have power because of their seemingly scientific nature, since this appears to be giving secure access to truths about adults; the knowledge they contain appears to have foundations which are secure because they are more than what is 'merely' desirable.

A body of seemingly secure knowledge is necessary for any profession and the more secure it is the greater the recognition afforded the profession. Whilst there is still considerable debate as to whether adult education is 'truly' a profession, a debate which we do not intend to enter, there is undoubtedly a growing number of adult educators both in the 'field' and in the academy. The latter have attempted to provide theorizations which the former can 'apply' - a procedure which is inherently problematic and which we have criticized in Chapter 4. It is clear from what has been said that the theorizations we have considered have been influential in providing a body of knowledge which has helped the growth of an adult education profession. What is not clear, however, is whether this body of knowledge actually relates to practice in adult education. In so far as there are problems in the relationship between adult education as a field of study and a field of practice which are displayed most acutely in the design and implementation of curricula, there is reason to be doubtful.

The picture that emerges, therefore, is that adult education as a field of study does not have its own theory but borrows from the disciplines, principally from psychology, and in so doing adopts their problematic features. Whilst we can recognize that the dependence on psychology has been a necessary part of professionalization and a growing implication with regulatory practices, we would claim that it has had a distorting and unhelpful effect on the development of both adult education theory and practice.

At one level the distorting effect is clear. As Welton puts it: 'Contextual frame factors blur into the background, and adult education as a complex socio-political process conflates to learning as a psychological process' (Welton, 1987:52). At the same time, 'needs' are treated psychologically as 'learning' needs and objective givens which can be measured. Thus, the emphasis is placed on positivistic research and knowledge designed to 'discover' needs and on appropriate organizational strategies to 'meet' them (Griffin, 1983). Adult education becomes a matter of management and adult education research the marshalling of 'facts' in support of managerial recommendations.

At a deeper level, the distortion arises through theory becoming ideology. Foucault (1979) reminds us that power and knowledge are inseparable. The emphasis on the objectivity and measurability of needs opens the door for the adoption of the technical-rationality model of practice, which we criticized in earlier chapters as an example of an oppressive ideology where adult education practice becomes merely a matter of structures and techniques. Furthermore, the derivation of theory from humanistic psychology, with its assumptions about the nature of the self and self-realization, conceals the situatedness of the adult and of adult education practice in the unequal distribution of power and the oppressions of class, gender, and race.

The failure to be helpful arises because theorizations seek knowledge which is foundational. Whilst such a status may be needed for professional and academic 'respectability', what the practitioner needs is not foundational but <u>pragmatic</u> knowledge. Since the practice is always situated, knowledge is to do with coping and understanding, with acting rightly and appropriately in particular situations, with the process of 'creating' oneself through practice rather than with certainty and objective 'truth'. It is, in other words, concerned with practical knowledge, a form of knowledge which is already present in practice.

Adult education as a field of study has systematically

failed to recognize practical knowledge and the mode of understanding associated with it. Since it is the latter which characterizes adult education as a field of practice, this means that the study of adult education does not actually relate to the practice of adult education. The former only appears to do so when it takes the form of a normative discourse, which is in reality an ideology that systematically distorts practice. Where the normative elements are missing (for example, in attempts to construct a 'scientifically valid' theory of adult education), such attempts fail to have any resonance with practice. Practitioners, who it is designed to help, fail to see its relevance.

What adult education has failed to do, therefore, is to interlink its study with its practice. By vainly seeking for knowledge in disciplines it has failed to see that there is knowledge in its practice, and that generating its own theory must start from that knowledge. Adult education as a field of study must therefore be located in the 'practical' and we now turn to what is involved in doing this.

THE NATURE OF PRACTICAL KNOWLEDGE

In earlier chapters we presented a critique of the technical-rationality model to which we have just returned. In setting the scene for an analysis of practical knowledge we need to bear this critique in mind, and also to remind ourselves of the notion of the 'socio-practical' which was discussed earlier in this chapter.

Any analysis of the nature of practical knowledge takes as its starting-point the Aristotelian conception of different kinds of knowledge, with associated modes of reasoning distinguished in terms of their purpose. With theoretical knowledge, the mode of reasoning is scientific and contemplative and the purpose is to discover the nature of the world, to describe what necessarily exists in the world, and to provide explanations in the form of universal laws. With technical knowledge or 'know-how', the purpose is to achieve some pre-defined end-product or end-state, and the mode of reasoning is instrumentally concerned with deciding the most appropriate means to achieve the defined end in an effective manner.

With practical knowledge, the purpose is to act rightly and appropriately in the world, and is associated with praxis as a mode of reasoning. It differs from the other variants as it is not knowledge just of the world but of how to act in the world in an informed and committed way. As a form of 'know-how' it has a similarity with technical knowledge but also differs very significantly from it in three important respects (Bernstein, 1986).

First, because people are always situated, they cannot help but act in the situations in which they find themselves, and thus cannot help but use practical knowledge to cope with the circumstances of these situations. Using technical knowledge, on the other hand, is not situationally dependent; so, for example, we can know how to make something when required to do so but if not we can 'forget'. But since we are always in situations we cannot 'forget' how to act within them, although the outcomes of our actions may be more or less successful. Practical knowledge is action-oriented knowledge that is always 'with' us.

Second, practical knowledge is oriented to informed and committed action. Unlike technical knowledge, the end towards which action is directed is not pre-defined. We need technical knowledge; for example, in order to make something, since we know in advance what we are going to produce (for example, a pot). In other words, without a known and given end, the notion of technical 'know-how' would be incoherent. At the same time, even though we might make different pots on different occasions, the technical 'know-how' required to make them will remain the same. None of this is the case with practical knowledge; not only is there no definable end-state or end-product, there is no particular kind of 'know-how' which can be known in advance. As Bernstein puts it 'the end itself is only concretely specified in deliberating about the means appropriate to this particular situation' (Bernstein, 1986:100). Ends and means, therefore, are shaped by the nature of the situation.

Third, practical knowledge has a necessary ethical dimension. Technical knowledge is essentially instrumental - when I use technical 'know-how' to make a pot I do not have to take ethical questions into account, my concern is solely with questions of efficiency and effectiveness. Practical knowledge, since it is concerned with appropriate action in the world, must consider the rightness of the action. Again this is a function of situatedness; since others are part of the situation then their welfare must be taken into account. The choice of means as instruments yields to decisions about means, which inevitably involve values. These are always inherent in ends, and decide the appropriateness of means. Means, therefore, are constituted by the values inherent in ends and, since these are situationally dependent, the particular kind of practical 'know-how' cannot be known in advance and outside of the circumstances of particular situations. Ends and means are therefore co-implicated and co-determined within a framework of values.

Both technical and practical knowledge are developed in and through practice - a 'doing' in and changing of the world. But the relationship of each to situatedness is very different. Earlier we noted that practical knowledge was about praxis - informed and committed action. However, we have to ask, what is it that informs and to what is the action committed? As far as the former is concerned, at one level action is informed by some 'universal' (a law formulated in a formal theory or some general ethical principle). The point is that the universal is never applied <u>as it is</u> but is always <u>mediated</u> in the light of a particular situation. As Warnke points out, practical knowledge involves understanding how a universal is given: 'concrete content - or what its meaning is ... with regard to a particular situation' (Warnke, 1987:93). With technical knowledge, however, the universal is applied in the sense that in telling us about the nature of the world it also suggests the most efficient and effective means to fulfil a given end.

The implication of this is that practical knowledge is reflexive; knowledge of the universal is itself changed as a result of its use in particular situations. Whilst the universal may allow us to understand our situation better and thus act appropriately within that situation, the use of that knowledge not only requires that the universal be modified but that the understanding generated through use may itself lead to further modification of the universal: 'maxims of action have to be applied to changing situations whereby the original knowledge is itself further developed' (Bleicher, 1980:127). There is, in other words, a constant interplay between the universal and the particular. The universal helps us to understand the particular and the particular helps us to understand the universal; in this interplay both may undergo change.

This co-implication of the universal and the particular parallels the co-implication of ends and means noted earlier. In both cases, the relationship is reciprocal and involves a mode of reasoning which is reflective: i.e. choosing how to act in the light of a particular situation, such that we 'cannot be spared the task of deliberation and decision by any learned or mastered technique' (Gadamer, 1981:92).

We are now also in a position to answer the other question (to what is the action committed?), since it is clear that the 'commitment' is both to an understanding of universals and to being attuned to the circumstances of particular situations (or, to put it another way, to situatedness).

At this point we need to remind ourselves of the analysis of hermeneutic understanding presented in Chapter 2, for we would now want to argue that the kind of understanding found in practical knowledge is essentially hermeneutic. Hermeneutic understanding involves the application of the universal to the particular in a mediated relationship. Equally, the kind of understanding found in practical knowledge consists of application as part of understanding, but where the nature of the application is such that the universal and the particular are co-implicated and co-determined.

We also argued in Chapter 2 that all understanding is hermeneutical. Hermeneutic understanding is not 'totally different from everyday human understanding (but) just one example of an everyday process through which persons make sense of their world' (Rowan and Reason, 1981:132). Every act of understanding is also an act of interpretation, in the sense that it always involves the conferring of meaning. For example, we always see something as something; in other words, the understanding and the conferring of meaning (interpretation) are in effect one and the same.

At the same time, we and our understanding are finitely situated in time, history, and culture; this is what we mean when we refer to situatedness. When we interpret, we place things within a context and connect them to other things. We can say, therefore, that we never understand without a context, or without our situatedness. The boundaries of interpretation, our frameworks, or paradigms as we have called them earlier, 'derive from our circumstances and experiences and these are always already informed by the history of the society and the culture to which we belong' (Warnke, 1987:168-9). One significant implication of this is that all forms of knowledge, including theoretical and technical knowledge, are themselves implicated within history and culture which, in their turn, are located within frameworks or paradigms and also have the characteristic of situatedness.

Another aspect of interpretation which we noted earlier was that it involved 'prejudices' or pre-judgements which are an essential part of our situatedness. We cannot stand outside our prejudices, although it is important to emphasize that these are not arbitrary or egotistical since they are always co-implicated with what Gadamer calls 'effective history' - interpretive traditions which transcend us and are given by history and culture. Far from being arbitrary expressions of personal preference, prejudices actually shape interpretation, in conjunction with 'traditions', in a way which brings together the 'subjective' and the 'objective'.

Application as well as interpretation is always involved in the moment of understanding. This again is a development of the argument that understanding is always situated. When we confer meaning we see something as something, but in so doing we <u>appropriate</u> (apply) it to ourselves. The meaning is a meaning for <u>me</u> in my particular situation. When I understand something I interpret it and apply it to myself; I assume that there is a 'truth' in the something, in the sense that it is trying to 'speak' to me, but I can only understand what it is trying to tell me within my situatedness, through the prejudices and traditions within the latter which define my questions and concerns.

At this point we are now in a position to relate the analysis to the specific concerns with which we started the chapter. Before doing so, however, the point can be made that the 'socio-practical', with its emphasis on solving problems (acting appropriately) and its concern for human welfare (acting rightly), is in the realm of practical knowledge and located in a mode of hermeneutic understanding.

The case we are seeking to make is that practitioners are always situated, so their way of making sense of their world of practice is always hermeneutic. This involves using practical knowledge in order to act rightly and appropriately within particular situations of practice. Therefore, although theoretical knowledge (knowledge of universals) may be used, the latter is always mediated in the light of the circumstances of the situation. Equally, although the knowledge used is a kind of 'know-how', it is not an instrumental or 'means-ends' know-how but is rather situational and ethical.

Understanding or 'making sense' is not a special kind of activity but is always present and always, as we have seen, involves interpretation and application (or, more accurately, appropriation). The latter, however, is not an 'applied science' or technical-rationality mode of application. Rather, one makes sense from one's own framework or paradigm, but this is itself part of a larger framework or paradigm located within situations and thus within practice.

If we theorize the 'practical' in this way, we end up with a very different picture to that projected by the technical-rationality model. The 'practical' need no longer be seen as a routine and habitual activity but as a realm of knowledge in its own right, such that other realms are presupposed by it. It is concerned with action of a particular kind and has its own appropriate modes of reasoning and understanding. However, the failure to recognize this is part of the 'tradition' of our positivistic culture which privileges the theoretical and the technical. Rather, what is being suggested here is that theoretical and technical knowledge and instrumental reasoning are actually special cases of practical knowledge and hermeneutic understanding.

RE-DEFINING THEORY IN ADULT EDUCATION

In earlier chapters, a distinction was drawn between 'formal' and 'informal' theory - where the former was theory in disciplines and the latter was located in practice. At this point it is worth pausing to unpack the notion of 'theory' further, and to try and relate it to our previous discussion of practical knowledge and hermeneutic understanding.

'Theory' can be conceptualized in terms of two dimensions. One is the 'formal-informal' dimension we have already discussed; the other, implied but not yet discussed as such, is a 'framework-products' dimension. The latter is a distinction between 'theory' (in the sense of a paradigm or framework of understandings, concepts, beliefs and values which characterize and underlie any activity be it theoretical or practical) and the particular theories which because they are rooted in these paradigms or frameworks can reasonably be called their products. It is clear also that it is through the process of research guided by the paradigms or frameworks that particular theories are evolved. In saying this, however, we are not assuming that this process is always positivistic or that it proceeds by always using associated canons of 'scientific method'.

In principle, the two dimensions yield four

permutations, each of which is a different form of theory: (a) formal theory as framework; (b) informal theory as framework; (c) formal theory as product; (d) informal theory as product. We have spoken of 'formal' theory extensively. A simple example of (a) would be behaviourism, and of (b) operant conditioning. For the moment, however, we will focus more on (c) and (d). Mee and Wiltshire (1978) provided examples of 'informal' theory when they referred to 'concepts' held by practising adult educators. These could be seen as part of a framework of principles, assumptions, values and beliefs, which structured the general approach to practice and influenced the kind of problem-solving action which might be taken in particular practice situations. An adult educator with a 'learning' framework might organize very different programmes to one with a 'community' framework, and would tackle problem-solving and decision-making in a very different way.

If 'theory as framework' is paradigmatic then 'theory as product' is perspective- or paradigm-dependent and generating it is an activity carried out by a community of workers who share the beliefs, values, assumptions, and conceptions of the paradigm. This is equally the case whether we are referring to formal or informal theory. 'Informal theory as product' which is situationally-dependent and action-oriented will be influenced by and draw upon paradigms located in practice.

An important point which emerges from this analysis is that framework and product, in all cases, are related in and through practice. Theory, both formal and informal, is produced through workers engaging in certain kinds of practice guided by a framework or paradigm or, to put it another way, the activity of research. Theorizing is therefore itself a practice. Furthermore, the relationship is not unidirectional. 'Theory as product' can affect practice and the latter can affect 'theory as framework'. This is an important way in which frameworks change over time - the process described by Kuhn (1970) as a 'paradigm shift'. Practice throws up so many problems or 'anomalies' that frameworks have to change to accommodate these - a process which involves fundamental changes with consequently different ways of interpreting practice and therefore different kinds of 'theory as product'.

The notion of informal theory, as we have argued in previous chapters, is a powerful one in helping us to recognize that practice is not simply 'mindless' activity. On the other hand, as we have also argued, particularly in Chapter 4, informal theory is problematic. Practice can be informed and committed action but it may also be routine and habitualized. Informal theory may not always be 'guiding' practice in the most productive way. That this should be the case, however, does have a very important implication. If informal theory is not always optimal then this presents the possibility for refining and improving it and thus provides both a justification and a means for educational intervention.

Carr and Kemmis (1986) point out that, within any educational practice, problems occur through a failure of informal theory. Because of its role in the structuring of practice, it generates expectations about the outcomes of particular acts of practice, of the kind: 'if I do X then Y should result'. Thus, action is both directed and justified: 'I did X because I expected Y to happen'. Now, if these expectations are not realized (if, in other words, the outcomes of practice are different from those expected so that what was supposed to happen does not actually happen), then practice no longer works and a problem exists. More significantly, it can be seen that informal theory (since it generated the expectations) is not working. An educational problem does not merely denote a failure of practice but also a failure in informal theory. Furthermore, this could be a failure in either informal theory as 'product' or as 'framework'. The adjustment of practice necessary may be more or less fundamental - if it is informal theory as 'framework' which is the source, then an entirely new way of understanding practice and a consequent major change in practice itself may be required.

This clearly has implications for the way we conceptualize educational theory in general and adult education theory in particular. By emphasizing the 'practical' there is a recognition of the centrality of context, and thus the focus is on educational practice seen as an activity informed by the informal theory of practitioners. This conception of the practitioner stresses the hermeneutic, interpretive dimension. The <u>framework</u> of adult education theory is 'defined' in practitioners and their activity within situated contexts. Practice is to be understood from practitioners' viewpoints, thus from the way they understand, interpret, and appropriate their contexts. The <u>content</u> of adult education theory is the problems arising from these contexts which enable situated understandings to be explored and systematized. The <u>purpose</u> of adult education theory is essentially pragmatic in helping practitioners to enhance and refine their understandings and hence their praxis.

If practitioners already possess a 'theory' which is common to a community of practitioners, then adult education 'theory' refers to this rather than the 'theory' in disciplines. Carr and Kemmis (1986) make the point that it is a mistake to suppose that a theory located outside educational practice could properly be educational theory. At the same time, however, they insist that characterizing educational theory simply as informal practitioner theory is not enough - a point which we would ourselves endorse.

It will be recalled that when we discussed the situatedness of practical knowledge and understanding we emphasized the influence of 'prejudices' and location in a 'tradition'. The difficulty lies in distinguishing between 'blind' and 'productive' prejudices and tradition, which can either limit or expand ones' horizons of understanding. As we have also noted, the most problematic feature is the part played by power and ideology in shaping knowledge and understanding. This raises two questions: first, to what extent are the practitioners' frameworks and informal theory genuinely their own?; second, what is their efficacy in dealing with problems implicated within the structural features of situations?

This is part of a wider problem which anyone who adopts an interpretive, hermeneutic framework must face. Its critique of the technical-rationality model and of positivistic frameworks generally is that there is a failure to take account of situatedness, that 'theory', for example, is seen as a universal which stands outside contexts. Yet it, too, has to recognize, but sometimes fails to do so, that practical knowledge in specific instances is itself situated in a context where practice can be distorted.

Informal theory may therefore be the starting point of an adult education theory but cannot constitute its <u>exclusive</u> content. A critical evaluation of the nature and adequacy of informal theory must also be included. If adult education as a field of study is not a field of knowledge in Hirst's (1974) sense, with a theory which integrates knowledge from appropriate disciplines, then the alternative of locating it in adult education as a field of practice must not only take account of the nature of the 'practical' but must also recognize its limitations.

IMPLICATIONS FOR CURRICULUM DESIGN AND TEACHING

A clear implication which has emerged so far is that a curriculum for adult education cannot be founded on disciplines, either separately or as an interdisciplinary composite. Any curriculum must appropriately reflect the location of the field of study in the practical and the critical. It further follows that adult education as a field of study must incorporate this in its own curricular practice so it, too, must be hermeneutical and critical. We can say that in adult education there is a 'double hermeneutic', since both the study and its object are located within paradigms, 'theoretical frameworks', or hermeneutic situations, from which they cannot be detached. The elucidations of these can only come about through dialogue between practitioners and between practitioners, teachers, and researchers. Hence the design of teaching and research must be such as to facilitate dialogue. As we saw in Chapter 6, however, dialogue must be critical, otherwise the factors which constrain and distort dialogue and understanding will never be acknowledged and assessed.

In what follows we will concentrate on the implications for curriculum design and teaching, leaving the question of research for later. In curricular terms, therefore, we would suggest that the starting point is not practice <u>per se</u> but practice problems. These need to be articulated, so that the frameworks of practice can be surfaced and analysed and the effects of discursive and structural constraints assessed. In effect, the process is one of examining the way in which practice is framed and constrained; this has been characterized as 'denormalizing' practice, since it results in practice no longer being seen as 'normal' or routinized (Usher, 1987). Practice, as we have seen, can be routine, habitual, and unproductive. The denormalizing of practice is, therefore, the beginnings of a critical, self-questioning approach to practice; the beginnings of a dialogue <u>with</u> and <u>about</u> practice which can lead to an appreciation of alternative possibilities but which always starts with and maintains a focus on particular practice problems.

However, this by itself is not enough. Adult education curricula which use experiential approaches do this, but then take things no further. Surfacing and questioning the frameworks of informal theory is an essential first step, but the frameworks themselves may be so constraining that they do not suggest the possibility of better options. It is at this point that 'formal' theory may play a part. This, as we have seen, takes the form of universals which aim to describe the world and by means of which the world can be explained, whereas informal theory is situated and concerned with action in the world. We have also seen that we cannot 'apply' formal theory to informal theory (in the sense that it cannot be directly 'mapped' onto informal theory), but it could probably help in perceiving the 'terrain' of the latter more clearly.

To understand clearly what we mean here we need to backtrack to a point made earlier, that formal theory as 'product' is generated through a practice informed by formal theory as 'framework'. The end to which the practice is directed in the case of formal theory is the generation of conceptual representations of an abstract kind that are designed to reflect and model the world. In this sense, the formal theorist is of the world but not in it; thus, the resulting theory is not ostensibly situated. De Castell and Freeman's notion of the 'theoretico-practical' as a mode of theorizing carried out 'as an end in itself' (de Castell and Freeman, 1978:20) and which treats contextual factors as invariant, nicely captures what we have in mind here.

Although the practice of generating formal theory as 'product' is an activity, it is not itself the activity of the practitioner. It is, in effect, one step removed from it, and the kinds of choices and decisions that are made reflect this. They are concerned with representation and explanation, whereas the informal theory of the practitioner is concerned with understanding, interpretation, and appropriation. How, therefore, can the representation and explanation of formal theory help? Formal theory (in the sense that it is 'outside' the immediate world of everyday practice) can help by facilitating the 're-presentation' of a practice problem, not through direct application but 'as a source of metaphor and sensitising concepts with which to view in a different way and to reformulate the problem' (Usher and Bryant, 1987:209).

The term 'review', given its connotation of 'looking back' and 'reconsidering', appropriately characterizes this process. As we saw in Chapter 4, 'review' suggests that formal theory is a kind of resource or 'sounding-board' for the development and refinement of informal theory - a way of bringing critical analysis to bear on the latter. Instead of formal theory being applied to practice, we have the notion of informal theory (and practice) 'reviewed' through formal theory. When we discussed disciplines as foundations in an earlier chapter, we criticized the whole notion of foundationalism and suggested instead a pragmatic approach. In the argument we are putting forward here, we can see formal theory not as foundational but more, following Rorty (1980), as an ingredient in a developing and edifying discourse which both helps us to cope with the world and to 'create' ourselves in the world. As Macdonald (1982) puts it, formal theory is not so much a body of knowledge but rather a 'bundle of illuminations'.

The biggest problem, however, is that formal and informal theory are always, in reality, found together. Again we discussed this in some detail in Chapter 4, so we will not reiterate the arguments here, but in terms of the analysis presented so far we can say that formal theory as 'product' (which is always present in the discursive and material practices of practitioners) clearly influences their informal theory as 'framework'. The curricular problem, therefore, is to surface the extent of this influence and examine its contribution, if any, to practice problems.

From a teaching point of view, dealing with formal theory as 'product' is difficult, since it is part of the 'taken for granted'. Formal theory as codified knowledge has a certain status and academic legitimacy, consequently practitioners when they become students tend to be overawed and reluctant to question it. At the same time, they feel that its concerns are not directly theirs, even though they cannot fully articulate their reasons for this. We have noted this problem earlier, and saw that it originated from the fact that formal and informal theory have different sites of origination but the same site of application in practice.

Given the relationship of formal theory as 'product' to formal theory as 'framework', it is more productive to start with the latter. When practitioners as students examine the underlying framework they can see, for example, how theories of learning take the particular form they do and how they are as much a construct and therefore amenable to problematization as their own informal theory. In a sense, one can see this as a process of putting formal theory as 'product' into a <u>context</u>, by examining the assumptions, concepts, values, and language of formal theory as 'framework'. Thus contextualized, it can be seen as explaining the world in a particular way and from a particular stand-point, and being more or less helpful in so doing - ultimately, therefore, a pragmatic test.

From this we can see that 'review' is a dialogical process, which mediates formal and informal theory and enables a process of counter-posing and mutual questioning. It is, in effect, a 'fusion of horizons' between formal and informal theory which deepens understanding and opens up the possibility of new experience and changes in practice. Informal theory can go beyond the 'taken for granted', practice can go beyond the routine, and habitual and formal theory can become pragmatic and edifying.

If adult education as a field of study is to be located in the practical, then the primary curriculum aim must be the enhancement and improvement of practice rather than the accumulation of formal knowledge. Such a curriculum should enable practitioners to develop a reflexive awareness of practice and facilitate their engagement in praxis.

The approach we are suggesting has a number of advantages. By focusing on practice and practice problems and by recognizing the existence of informal theory, the curriculum can thereby be made <u>relevant</u>. <u>Rigour</u> can be preserved. narrowness and anecdotage avoided, through starting with informal theory but allocating formal theory its proper pragmatic place. Through the use of processes such as 'denormalizing' and 'reviewing', teaching can be <u>congruent</u>. If the aim is to improve practice through enabling the development of reflexive awareness, then the teaching situation must provide the means for this to happen with teachers and trainers themselves engaging in praxis.

There are also a number of wider implications which need stressing. The first is that the distinction between 'theorists' and practitioners needs to be softened. Theorists and teachers, who in adult education tend to be one and the same, need to be both more aware and more knowledgeable about practice 'in the field'. Equally, practitioners need to become more aware of the place of 'theory' and theorizing in their work. Here, practitioner-based inquiry and research is a means of bringing about this awareness and we consider this below.

Another implication is that adult education, in adopting the 'practical', needs to reconceptualize its notion of 'theory' and thus its epistemology generally. Theory is not confined solely to the knowledge contained in disciplines; the knowledge contained in practice has to be recognized. Practitioners have to be seen not merely as actors but as informed and committed actors. The situatedness of practice needs to be recognized and 'theory' has to take on board the consequent social and moral dimensions.

A pragmatic orientation to theory and method is justified in terms of a commitment to the 'practical' but this justification is itself conditional on a commitment to the critical. Without this, theory becomes mere anecdotage and teaching becomes inspirational 'ego-boosting'. Adult education, by abandoning the traditional 'academic-disciplines' model can develop a critical theory and approach appropriate to its nature as a practical activity. Disciplines have a part to play but their role is to help ensure that horizons of understanding are as 'open' as possible. Locating adult education theory in practice and practice problems ensures its coherence as theory. At the same time, 'open' horizons of understanding ensure, by providing a context of relevance, that theorists (and curriculum designers) do not get 'lost' in disciplines (Vandenburg, 1974).

If the aim of adult education as a field of study is to develop the praxis which is always present (albeit in a distorted and incomplete form) in adult education as a field of practice, then practitioners as students need a mode of professional formation which brings that about. As we have seen, the emphasis has been on either transmitting formal theory, or 'working with experience', or an uneasy attempt to integrate the two through 'application'. We have also seen, however, that this has not worked very well, which is why we have argued for the need to locate adult education as a field of study in the 'practical'. It follows, therefore, that the knowledge, 'theory', and understanding distinctive of the 'practical' must inform the content of and approach to teaching. However, since praxis is about acting appropriately in concrete situations, and since within the latter power and ideology are always present, then the practical and the critical are co-implicated. Understanding and dialogue, the basis of praxis, can only function both in the world of practice and the world of the classroom through a recognition of the possibilities and limits of situatedness.

TEACHING AND EXPERIENCING RESEARCH

One of our purposes throughout this book has been to make explicit what is implicitly contained within foundational models of research practice, and to suggest ways of conducting research that are more consonant with the requirements of reflective practice. We take research <u>for</u> adult education to be concerned with enriching <u>our</u> understanding of a complex field of practice, and in that process contributing to a change in specific practice situations. By comparison, much of what passes for research <u>in</u> adult education does not do this.

Clearly, there is a sense in which research can be taught (for example, as a set of investigative techniques), that would allow the practitioner to do things that he/she could not do before. In this context, the teaching of research methods in order to increase the practitioner's technical competence and capabilities is obviously desirable. Nevertheless, a curriculum which equates research solely with the formal employment of specific methods in given circumstances will not serve the needs of the reflective practitioner, however many different methods are included. For a start, circumstances are never 'given' in practice such that an automatic choice of method would follow. Equally, a curriculum aimed at enhancing technique would not in itself assist the reflective practitioner, who is concerned with questioning the 'givenness' of practice. In so far as a curriculum which simply embodies different methodologies of research reduces the practice of inquiry to questions of method, it suggests that the improvement of practice follows from an appreciation of formal theory (methodology) and it ignores the informal theory that guides both practice and research.

An alternative way of teaching for research might be by way of a curriculum designed around examples of specific research practices. Here, the <u>actual doing</u>, and not just the formal 'necessities' of <u>research</u> as suggested by methodology, would be examined through case studies of particular investigations rather than via abstract procedures. In principle, there would be an opportunity to consider the ways in which research as a practice is itself guided by informal theory. This approach would potentially allow the practitioner as a student to examine critically the actual problems that confront researchers and the solutions adopted. Unfortunately, as we have already seen in Chapter 5, the way in which research is conventionally presented as 'sanitized text' rarely conveys the hunches, assumptions, false starts, informal theories, and inner reflections of the investigator. Students do not normally have a chance to 'surface' these reflections or to reveal the informal theories that guide inquiry in direct conversation with researchers, so that by their questioning they can expose their own informal theories to critical examination.

The above point does suggest a limitation on the use of distant exemplars in teaching about research. (Certainly, they should not be taught as paradigm cases for uncritical adoption.) However, it also implies that the teacher's own experience of doing research should itself be made available as a curricular component that is present and open to scrutiny. By 'making available' we mean the presentation of their own reflections in a teaching context in order to exemplify how the experienced academic researcher deals with the situatedness (which encompasses both the formal and informal theories) of his/her own practice. Adult educators as academics are expected to possess formal knowledge and to have an understanding of the value and limitations of formal theory. As 'mere' practitioners they will also have informal theories, for example those that guide their personal teaching and research routines. As reflective practitioners, however, they will embody an understanding of the relationships between formal and informal theory, and exemplify this in their teaching about research.

Teaching specific research methods, or teaching about research in more general and perhaps less formal terms, or even the exemplification of reflective practice, at best can only be a 'second-hand' by way of learning how to do research. None of these approaches directly engages with the informal theory of practitioners by obliging them to research their own practice. For that to happen, the practice of doing research has literally to be <u>experienced</u>. Here, we need to consider two things: first, what the experience of doing research is <u>like</u> for most practitioners; second, how that experience <u>might</u> be used in an edifying way to further reflective practice.

Graduate students of adult education in their professional formation and development as practitioners are normally required to attend courses in research methods in preparation for the submission of a thesis or dissertation, which in turn is likely to be an end-point of the process of certification for practice. In this context, the research is an exercise in the demonstration of competence. The research as a product is expected to satisfy certain academic specifications; for example with respect to its presentation form as text. These characteristics of graduate research are themselves aspects of the situatedness of academic practice and its valuation of 'proper' research.

In the foundation disciplines, which often have a teaching input into so-called 'adult education research' courses, the question of teaching about research is normally confined to matters of content and thesis supervision. Since the subsequent practices of psychology and sociology graduates cannot be known, the 'practical value' of the research can be conveniently ignored. In contrast, it is clear that the typical student of adult education <u>comes from and returns to practice</u>. Yet the paradigmatic and 'ideological' force of the foundation disciplines is such that the academic practice of teaching adult education students too often ignores the practice of these students, but without the justification for doing so that teachers of students in other disciplines rest on, however unjustifiably.

Certainly, we would accept that there is a place for 'conventional' academic research into adult education and for students of adult education to be taught about its procedures and findings. But this should not be at the cost of relegating or downgrading their own practice concerns. As experienced teachers of such students, we have considerable evidence suggesting a desire to address matters of practical relevance in the particular research topics that are chosen. Moreover, as we have already noted, this is invariably accompanied by a feeling that things are 'not quite right' in their own practice. In a sense, therefore, the motivation to engage in reflective practice already exists.

Although in principle the practitioner can learn about and have some experience of research in a 'protected' academic environment, the very situatedness of academic practice is a countervailing force. Academics need to recognize this and to 'open up' their own practices as a condition for opening up those of their students. For this to happen, however, it is not sufficient merely to act on recommendations for better research supervision. In their discussion of 'research as a personal process' Reason and Marshall argue for just such an enhancement of the research experience. Effective supervision is taken to be the considered use of a number of different intervention tactics as the research proceeds (Reason and Marshall, 1987:123-4). Their recommendations are derived from an analysis of the different purposes served by research, including the idea of research being 'for me' in relation to personal development, change and learning. However, their discussion of research as such is situated within 'a university's education process' (Reason and Marshall, 1987:112). It does not consider the implications of accepting the givenness of this process for personal research as a potential contribution to reflective practice.

We have previously argued that 'if we want practitioners to be reflective, critical and self-directing in the world of practice then we must create conditions, through teaching, for them to be reflective, critical and self-directing in the world of the classroom' (Usher and Bryant, 1987). For this to happen, however, it is necessary for teachers of research to do more than simply change their personal classroom or supervisory practices in line with current thinking. They must reflect-in-action on the situated practices of academic teaching and research generally if they are to commend and stimulate an equivalent process in their adult education students.

REFERENCES

Allman, P. (1983) 'The nature and process of adult development', in M. Tight (ed.), Adult Learning and Education, London: Croom Helm.

Bernstein, R.J. (1986) Philosophical Profiles, Oxford: Polity Press.

Bleicher, J. (1980) Contemporary Hermeneutics, London: Routledge & Kegan Paul.

Bright, B.P. (1985) 'The content-method relationship in the study of adult education' Studies in the Education of Adults, 17 (2), 168-83.

Carr, W. and Kemmis, S. (1986) Becoming Critical, Lewes: Falmer Press.

de Castell, S. and Freeman, H. (1978) 'Education as a socio-practical field: the theory-practice question reformulated', Journal of Philosophy of Education, 12, 12-28.

Chickering, A.W. et al. (1981) The Modern American College, San Francisco: Jossey-Bass.

Cross, K.P. (1982) Adults as Learners, San Francisco: Jossey-Bass.

Foucault, M. (1979) Discipline and Punish: The Birth of the Prison (trans. by A. Sheridan), New York: Vintage/Random House.

Gadamer, H.G. (1981) 'Hermeneutics as practical philosophy', in Reason in the Age of Science (trans. by F. Lawrence), Cambridge, Mass.: M.I.T. Press.

Griffin, C. (1983) Curriculum Theory in Adult and Lifelong Education, London: Croom Helm.

Hirst, P.H. (1974) Knowledge and the Curriculum, London: Routledge & Kegan Paul.

Knowles, M. (1978) The Adult Learner: A Neglected Species, Houston: Gulf Publishing.

Kuhn, T.S. (1970) The Structure of Scientific Revolutions, Chicago: University of Chicago Press.

Macdonald, J.B. (1982) 'How literal is curriculum theory?', Theory into Practice, 21 (1), 55-61.

Mee, G. and Wiltshire, H. (1978) Structure and Performance in Adult Education, London: Longman.

Nottingham Andragogy Group (1983) Towards a Developmental Theory of Andragogy, Nottingham: University of Nottingham.

Perry, W.G. (1970) Forms of Intellectual and Ethical Development in the College Years, New York: Holt, Rinehart & Winston.

Reason, P. and Marshall, J. (1987) 'Research as a personal process', in D. Boud, and V. Griffin, Appreciating Adults Learning, 112-26, London: Kogan Page.

Riegel, K.F. (1979) Foundations of Dialectical Psychology, New York: Academic Press.

Rorty, R. (1980) Philosophy and the Mirror of Nature, Oxford: Blackwell.

Rowan, J. and Reason, P. (1981) 'On making sense', in P. Reason and J. Rowan (eds.), Human Inquiry: A Sourcebook of New Paradigm Research, London: Wiley & Sons.

Squires, G. (1987) The Curriculum Beyond School, London: Hodder & Stoughton.

Usher, R. S. (1987) 'The place of theory in designing curricula for the continuing education of adult educators' Studies in the Education of Adults, 19(1), 26-36.

Usher, R.S. and Bryant, I. (1987) 'Re-examining the theory-practice relationship in continuing professional education', Studies in Higher Education, 12 (2), 201-12.

Vandenberg, D. (1974) 'Phenomenology and educational research', in D. Denton (ed.), Existentialism and Phenomenology in Education, New York: Teacher's College Press.

Warnke, G. (1987) *Gadamer: Hermeneutics, Tradition and Reason*, Oxford: Polity Press.
Welton, M.R. (1987) 'Vivisecting the nightingale: reflections on adult education as an object of study', *Studies in the Education of Adults*, 19, 46-68.

BIBLIOGRAPHY

Akroyd, S. and Hughes, J.A. (1981) Data Collection in Context, London: Longman.
Allman, P. (1983) 'The nature and process of adult development', in M. Tight (ed.) Adult Learning and Education, London: Croom Helm.
Anderson, R.J., Hughes, J.A. and Sharrock, W.W. (1986) Philosophy and the Social Sciences, London: Croom Helm.
Anyon, J. (1982) 'Adequate social science, curriculum investigations and theory', Theory into Practice, 21 (1), 34-7.
Argyris, C. (1982) Reasoning, Learning and Action, San Francisco: Jossey-Bass.
Argyris, C. and Schon, D.A. (1974) Theory in Practice, San Francisco, Jossey-Bass.
Ashcroft, R. and Jackson, K. (1974) 'Adult education and social action', in D. Jones and M. Mayo (eds) Community Work One, 44-65, London: Routledge & Kegan Paul.
Baldamus, W. (1977) 'The category of pragmatic knowledge in sociological analysis', in M. Bulmer (ed.) Sociological Research Methods, 283-300, London: Macmillan.
Bannister, D. (1981) 'Personal construct theory and research method', in P. Reason and J. Rowan (eds) Human Inquiry: A Sourcebook of New Paradigm Research, London: Wiley.
Bernstein, R.J. (1985) Beyond Objectivism and Relativism, Oxford: Blackwell.
---- (1986) Philosophical Profiles, Oxford: Polity Press.
Bleicher, J. (1980) Contemporary Hermeneutics, London:

Bibliography

Routledge & Kegan Paul.
Blumer, H. (1969) Symbolic Interactionism, New Jersey: Prentice-Hall.
Bohme, G. (1983) 'Knowledge and higher education', Studies in Higher Education, 2, Stockholm: NBUC.
Boxer, P. (1985) 'Judging the quality of development', in D. Boud, R. Keogh, and D. Walker (eds), Reflection: Turning Experience into Learning, London: Kogan Page.
Bright, B.P. (1985) 'The content-method relationship in the study of adult education', Studies in the Education of Adults, 17 (2), 168-83.
Brookfield, S.D. (1987) Developing Critical Thinkers, Milton Keynes: Open University Press.
Carr, W. (1980) 'The gap between theory and practice', Journal of Further and Higher Education, 4 (1), 60-9.
---- (1982) 'Treating the symptoms, neglecting the cause: diagnosing the problem of theory and practice', Journal of Further and Higher Education, 6 (2), 19-29.
---- (1986) 'Theories of theory and practice', Journal of Philosophy of Education, 20 (2), 177-86.
Carr, W. and Kemmis, S. (1986) Becoming Critical, Lewes: Falmer Press.
Chickering, A.W. et al. (1981) The Modern American College, San Francisco: Jossey-Bass.
Clark, C. (1976) 'Education is not an academic discipline', Educational Studies, 2 (1), 11-19.
Clark, P.A. (1972) Action Research and Organisational Change, London: Harper & Row.
Cohen, L. and Manion, L. (1985) Research Methods in Education (2nd edn), London: Croom Helm.
Cross, K.P. (1982) Adults as Learners, San Francisco: Jossey-Bass.
de Castell, S. and Freeman, H. (1978) 'Education as socio-practical field: the theory-practice question reformulated', Journal of Philosophy of Education, 12, 12-28.
Denzin, N.K. (1970) The Research Act in Sociology, London: Butterworth.
Derrida, J. (1978) Writing and Difference (tr. by Alan Bass), Chicago: University of Chicago Press.
Dreyfus, H.L. and Rabinow, P. (1982) Michel Foucault: Beyond Structuralism and Hermeneutics, Brighton, Sussex: Harvester Press.
Ebbutt, D. (1985) 'Educational action research: some general concerns and specific quibbles', in R.G. Burgess (ed.)

Bibliography

Issues in Educational Research: Qualitative Methods, Lewes: Falmer Press.
Egan, K. (1984) Education and Psychology, London: Methuen.
Elsey, B. (1986) Social Theory Perspectives on Adult Education, Nottingham.
Emler, N.P. and Heather, N. (1980) 'Intelligence: an ideological bias of conventional psychology', in P. Salmon (ed.) Coming to Know, London: Routledge & Kegan Paul.
Eraut, M. (1985) 'Knowledge creation and knowledge use in professional contexts', Studies in Higher Education, 10 (1), 117-37.
Fay, B. (1987) Critical Social Science, Oxford: Polity Press.
Finch, J. (1986) Research and Policy, Lewes: Falmer Press.
Foucault, M. (1979) Discipline and Punish: The Birth of the Prison (tr. by A. Sheridan), New York: Vintage/Random House.
Gadamer, H.G. (1975) Truth and Method, London: Sheed & Ward.
---- (1981) 'Hermeneutics as practical philosophy', in Reason in the Age of Science (tr. by F. Lawrence), Cambridge, Mass.: M.I.T. Press.
Geertz, C. (1975) 'On the nature of anthropological understanding', American Scientist, 63, 47-53.
Giddens, A. (1976) New Rules of Sociological Method, London: Hutchinson.
Glaser, B.G. and Strauss, A.L. (1967) The Discovery of Grounded Theory, New York: Aldine.
Goffman, E. (1974) Frame Analysis, Harmondsworth: Penguin.
Gouldner, A.W. (1957) 'Theoretical requirements of the applied social sciences', American Sociological Review, 92-102.
Griffin, C. (1983) Curriculum Theory in Adult and Lifelong Education, London: Croom Helm.
Habermas, J. (1972) Knowledge and Human Interests (tr. by J.J. Shapiro), London: Heinemann.
---- (1974) Theory and Practice (tr. by J. Viertel) London: Heinemann.
Hacking, I. (1983) Representing and Intervening, Cambridge: Cambridge University Press.
Hanson, N.R. (1958) Patterns of Discovery, Cambridge: Cambridge University Press.
Harre, R. (1980) 'Man as rhetorician', in A.J. Chapman and

Bibliography

D.M. Jones (eds) Models of Man, Leicester: British Psychological Society.
---- (1985) 'The language game of self-ascription: a note', in K.J. Gergen and K.E. Davis (eds) The Social Construction of the Person, New York: Springer-Verlag.
Harris, K. (1979) Education and Knowledge, London: Routledge & Kegan Paul.
Hartnett, M. and Naish. A. (1975) 'What theory cannot do for teachers', Education for Teaching, 96 (1), 12-19.
---- (1976) Theory and the Practice of Education, London: Heinemann.
Heaton, J.M. (1979) 'Theory in psychotherapy', in N. Bolton (ed.) Philosophical Problems in Psychology, London: Methuen.
Henriques, J. et al. (1984) Changing the Subject, London: Methuen.
Hirst, P.H. (1974) Knowledge and the Curriculum, London: Routledge & Kegan Paul.
Homans, G.C. (1964) 'Bringing men back in', American Sociological Review, 5, 808-18.
Hughes, J. (1980) The Philosophy of Social Research, London: Longman.
Jarvis, P. (1985) The Sociology of Adult and Continuing Education, London: Croom Helm.
Kelly, A. (1985) 'Action research: what is it and what can it do?', in R.G. Burgess (ed.) Issues in Educational Research: Qualitative Methods, Lewes: Falmer Press.
Kelly, G.A. (1963) A Theory of Personality: The Psychology of Personal Constructs, New York: Norton.
---- (1969) Clinical Psychology and Personality: the Selected Papers of George Kelly, New York: Wiley.
Kemmis, S. (1985) 'Action research and the politics of reflection', in D. Boud et al. (eds) Reflection: Turning Experience into Learning, 139-63, London: Kogan Page.
Kerlinger, F.N. (1970) Foundations of Behavioural Research, New York: Holt, Rinehart & Winston.
Knowles, M. (1978) The Adult Learner: A Neglected Species, Houston: Gulf Publishing.
Kockelmans, J. (1975) 'Towards an interpretive or hermeneutic social science', Graduate Faculty Philosophy Journal, 5 (1), 73-96.
Kuhn, T.S. (1970) The Structure of Scientific Revolutions (2nd edn), Chicago: University of Chicago Press.
Lewin, K. (1947) 'Frontiers in group dynamics: channels of group life: social planning and action research', Human

Relations, 1 (2), 143-53.
Louch, A.R. (1966) Explanation and Human Action, Oxford: Blackwell.
Lovett, T. et al. (1983) Adult Education and Community Action, London: Croom Helm.
Macdonald, J.B. (1982) 'How literal is curriculum theory?' Theory into Practice, 21 (1). 55-61.
Mead, G.H. (1962) Mind, Self and Society, Chicago: University of Chicago Press.
Mee, G. and Wiltshire, H. (1978) Structure and Performance in Adult Education, London: Longman.
Mills, C.W. (1959) The Sociological Imagination, New York: Oxford University Press.
Mittler, P.J. (1982) 'Applying developmental psychology', Educational Psychology, 2 (1), 1-5.
Moore, P. (1981) 'Relations between theory and practice: a critique of Wilfred Carr's views', Journal of Further and Higher Education, 5 (2), 44-56.
Morgan, G. (ed.) (1983) Beyond Method: Strategies for Social Research, London: Sage Books.
Nottingham Andragogy Group (1983) Towards a Developmental Theory of Andragogy, Nottingham: University of Nottingham.
Ottman, H. (1982) 'Cognitive interests and self-reflection', in J.B. Thompson and D. Held (eds) Habermas: Critical Debates 79-97, London: Macmillan.
Perry, W.G. (1970) Forms of Intellectual and Ethical Development in the College Years, New York: Holt, Rinehart & Winston.
Phillips, D.C. (1987) Philosophy, Science and Social Inquiry, Oxford: Pergamon.
Phillipson, M. (1981) 'Sociological practice and language', in P. Abrams et al., Practice and Progress: British Sociology 1950-1980, London: Allen & Unwin.
Polanyi, M. (1958) Personal Knowledge: Towards a Post-critical Philosophy, London: Routledge & Kegan Paul.
Popkewitz, T.S. (1984) Paradigm and Ideology in Educational Research, Lewes, Sussex: Falmer Press.
Potter, J. and Wetherell, M. (1987) Discourse and Social Psychology, London: Sage Books.
Pring, R. (1970) 'Philosophy of education and educational practice', Proceedings of the Philosophy of Education Society, 4, 61-75.
---- (1977) 'Common-sense and education', Proceedings of the Philosophy of Education Society, 11. 57-77.

Bibliography

Rapoport, R.N. (1970) 'Three dilemmas of action research', Human Relations, 23, 499-513.
Reason, P. and Marshall, J. (1987) 'Research as a personal process', in D. Boud and V. Griffin, Appreciating Adults Learning, 112-26, London: Kogan Page.
Reason, P. and Rowan, J. (eds) (1981) Human Inquiry: A Sourcebook of New Paradigm Research, London: Wiley.
Richardson, J.T.E. et al. (1987) Student Learning, Milton Keynes: Open University Press.
Rickman, H.P. (ed.) (1976) Dilthey, Selected Writings, Cambridge: Cambridge University Press.
Riegel, K.F. (1979) Foundations of Dialectical Psychology, New York: Academic Press.
Rogers, C.R. (1961) On Becoming a Person, Boston: Houghton Mifflin.
---- (1969) Freedom to Learn, Columbus, Ohio: Merrill.
Rorty, R. (1980) Philosophy and the Mirror of Nature, Oxford: Blackwell.
---- (1982) The Consequences of Pragmatism, Brighton: Harvester.
Rowan, J. and Reason, P. (1981) 'On making sense', in P. Reason and J. Rowan (eds) Human Inquiry: A Sourcebook of New Paradigm Research, London: Wiley & Sons.
Ruddock, R. (1972) Sociological Perspectives on Adult Education, Manchester, Monograph 2.
Rybash, J.M., Hoyer, W.J., and Roodin, P.A. (1984) Adult Cognition and Aging, Oxford: Pergamon.
Saljo, R. (1987) 'The educational construction of learning', in J.T.E. Richardson et al. (eds) Student Learning, Milton Keynes: Open University Press.
Salmon, P. (ed.) (1980) Coming to Know, London: Routledge & Kegan Paul.
---- (1985) 'Educational psychology and stances towards schooling', in G. Claxton et al., Psychology and Schooling: What's the Matter?, London: Institute of Education, University of London.
Sanford, N. (1981) 'A model for action research', in P. Reason and J. Rowan, Human Inquiry: A Sourcebook of New Paradigm Research, 173-81, London: Wiley.
Scheffler, I. (1986) Four Pragmatists: A Critical Introduction to Pierce, James, Mead and Dewey, London: Routledge & Kegan Paul.
Schon, D.A. (1983) The Reflective Practitioner: How Professionals Think in Action, London: Temple Smith.

Sjoberg, G. and Nett, R. (1968) A Methodology for Social Research, New York: Harper & Row.
Smail, D. (1980) 'Learning in Psychotherapy', in P. Salmon (ed.) Coming to Know, London: Routledge & Kegan Paul.
Solomon, R.C. (1988) Continental Philosophy Since 1750, Oxford: Oxford University Press.
Squires, G. (1982) The Analysis of Teaching, University of Hull, Department of Adult Education.
---- (1987) The Curriculum Beyond School, London: Hodder & Stoughton.
Stevens, R. (1983) Freud and Psychoanalysis, Milton Keynes: Open University Press.
Susman, G.I. (1983) 'Action research: a socio-technical systems perspective', in G. Morgan (ed.) Beyond Method: Strategies for Social Research, London: Sage Books.
Susman, G.I. and Evered, R. (1978) 'An assessment of the scientific merits of action research', Administrative Science Quarterly, 23, 582-603.
Swann, W. (1985) 'Psychological science and the practice of special education', in G. Claxton et al., Psychology and Schooling: What's the Matter?, London: Institute of Education, University of London.
Torbert, W.R. (1981) 'Why educational research has been so uneducational', in P. Reason and J. Rowan (eds) Human Inquiry: A Sourcebook of New Paradigm Research, 141-51, London: Wiley.
Usher, R.S. (1985) 'Beyond the anecdotal: adult learning and the use of experience', Studies in the Education of Adults, 17 (1), 59-74.
---- (1987) 'The place of theory in designing curricula for the continuing education of adult educators', Studies in the Education of Adults, 19 (1), 26-36.
Usher, R.S. and Bryant, I. (1987) 'Re-examining the theory-practice relationship in continuing professional education', Studies in Higher Education. 12 (2), 201-12.
Vallance, E. (1982) 'Practical uses of curriculum theory', Theory into Practice. 21 (1). 4-10.
Vandenberg, D. (1974) 'Phenomenology and educational research', in D. Denton (ed.) Existentialism and Phenomenology in Education, New York: Teacher's College Press.
Wain, K. (1987) Philosophy of Lifelong Education, London: Croom Helm.

Bibliography

Walkerdine, V. (1984) 'Developmental psychology and child-centred pedagogy', in J. Henriques et al., Changing the Subject, London: Methuen.
---- (1985) 'Psychological knowledge and educational practice: producing the truth about schools', in Claxton, G. et al., Psychology and Schooling: What's the Matter?, London: Institute of Education, University of London.
Walsh, D. (1978) 'Sociology and the social world', in P. Worsley (ed.), Modern Sociology (2nd edn), Harmondsworth: Penguin.
Warnke, G. (1987) Gadamer: Hermeneutics, Tradition and Reason, Oxford: Polity Press.
Weil, S.W. (1986) 'Non-traditional learners within traditional higher education institutions: discovery and disappointment', Studies in Higher Education, 11 (3), 219-35.
Welton, M.R. (1987) 'Vivisecting the nightingale: reflections on adult education as an object of study', Studies in the Education of Adults, 19, 46-68.
Woodley, A. et al. (1987) Choosing to Learn: Adults in Education, Oxford: Oxford University Press/SRHE.

INDEX

abstracted individualism 49
academic
  legitimacy 190
  practice 195
  work 111
action 21, 24, 75
  communicative 130
  reasoning 74
adult development 172
agency, research 149
agreement
  consensual 43
  intersubjective 36
analysis 3, 4
andragogy 95, 172
  discourse, models 52, 118
anomalies 15
applicability thesis,
  paradigm 51, 60, 119
application 4, 35, 42, 50-1
applied science research 43, 120
arena, research 150
assessment 52
attribution 24
authenticity 53, 131

behaviourism 185
being prudent, strategic 139
beliefs 67

bias 32
biography 46, 53
bounded rationality 74

categories 18, 19, 102
causal explanation 25, 28,
  44, 133, 138, 162, 166
change agency 119
circle, hermeneutic 9, 32-9
claims 24, 28, 165
  contested 154
  knowledge 65, 67, 129, 154, 159
  relevance 116
  truth 43
  validity 132
cognitive psychology 45
collaborative research 120, 127, 129, 131
commitment, value 27
common sense 26, 51, 54, 84, 114, 123
  knowledge 51, 92
communication 25, 27
  distorted 7, 134
  rational 20
community development 141
community research 143
concepts 13, 44, 48, 100
  contested 77

Index

everyday 123
conflict
  paradigm 48
  role 8
consensus 25, 36, 43
constructs 50-1, 54
construing-and-intending 162
contested claims, concepts 77, 154
contexts, contextualism 20, 45, 53, 61-2, 74, 124, 175
  organizational 123
  socio-cultural 46, 49
contingency 20, 45, 62, 65, 145
contract research 165
control 21, 24
  predictive 12
conventional research 161
conventional understanding 4, 5, 25, 34, 43, 65, 98, 165
correspondence theory 11, 17
creativity cycles 164
critical analysis, reflection, theory 1, 3-7, 47, 131-3, 138, 157, 192
critique, post-empiricist 14, 18
curriculum 8, 141, 169, 172, 188

data collection 23
decision-making 47, 73, 141
deconstruction 5-6, 28, 38, 118
deductive-nomological method 11-12, 25
denormalizing practice 188, 191
description 43, 45
determinism 52
development, adult 172
developmental psychology 52
dialectic 33, 36, 173
dialogue 5, 7, 9, 22, 25, 32-6, 65-6, 84, 94, 134, 138, 173, 188
disciplines 15, 41-4, 116, 130, 146, 187, 192, 195
discourse 7, 37-8, 53, 74, 94, 104, 113-23, 130-1, 135, 154, 173
distorted communication 7, 134
double hermeneutic 38-9, 54, 188
double-loop learning 87

eclecticism 145, 171
ecological validity 44, 77
edification 65, 68, 135, 159, 194
empirical validation 11-13, 17, 34
empiricism 23, 53, 103
engagement 94, 123, 134, 140, 148-9, 157
engineering 41, 73, 77, 169
epistemology 17, 61, 64, 104, 129
ethics, educational 180
  framework 122
  research 153
evaluation research 120
everyday conceptions, language 123, 155-6
evidence 15, 19, 25, 51
experience 12, 17, 25, 31, 36, 42-4, 56, 63, 108-9, 121, 145, 176, 188
experiment 19, 24, 44, 99
expertise 130
explanation, causal 28, 43, 133

facts 19, 31, 38, 52, 103, 161

Index

field of knowledge, study, practice 1-8, 41-2, 90, 169, 187
formal knowledge, research, theory 3, 6-8, 27, 29, 50, 57-9, 117, 120-3, 170, 176
formation, professional 8, 59, 72
foundation disciplines 4, 41-2, 54, 195
  metaphor 60, 116, 192
frameworks, framing 14-24, 47, 57, 61, 77, 83, 87, 121-2, 158, 181, 184
fusion of horizons 9, 35-6, 66, 85, 134-5, 189

grounded theory 7, 80, 109, 127, 149

hermeneutic understanding 6, 9, 28-39, 48, 54, 64, 67, 75, 82, 85, 92, 117, 135, 163, 182, 188
horizons, fusion of 9, 35-6, 66, 85, 134-5, 189
humanistic paradigm 173, 176
  psychology 46, 50, 155, 161
hypotheses 11, 13
hypothetico-deductive method 11, 23, 106, 127, 149

ideographic method 26, 48
ideology 8, 18, 22-7, 31, 62, 133, 146, 178, 192
inductive research 99
informal theory 7, 61, 79-82, 111, 130, 184
inquiry, hermeneutical 117
  logic of 162
  reflective 16
institutional language 7, 101
interaction, interactionism 8, 24, 26, 122, 152, 162
interests 131-2
interpretive paradigm 6, 8, 22-8, 32, 61, 64, 82-3, 122, 139

judgement, practical 22, 74-5
value 170
justification, rational, pragmatic 20, 117

knowledge, knowledge-claims 6-8, 13-17, 51, 65, 68, 75-9, 82, 92, 112, 121-31, 154, 159, 163, 178-81

language 7, 24, 100-2, 123, 177
law, laws 10-13, 44
learners, learner identity 45, 89, 110, 146
learning 45, 47, 87, 110, 140, 169, 174, 190
legitimacy 22, 190
linguistic practices 155
logic of inquiry 18, 34, 42, 57, 100, 162, 166

maturational theory 52-3
mature learners, students 109, 146
meanings 2, 23-9, 54, 109, 128
  negotiation of 153, 162
medicine 41, 73, 77
metaphor 4-5, 60-3, 189
meta-theory 105
methods
  research, scientific 11, 15, 17, 23, 25, 43-4, 98, 120, 184, 193
models of practice, persons, research 1, 6, 14-15, 23, 37, 44, 50, 71-3, 100, 118-

209

Index

27, 134, 149, 154, 192
motivation 105

natural science paradigm 6, 10-14, 21-2, 27-8, 38, 44
negotiation of meaning 24, 26, 153, 162
new paradigm research 150, 160
normal science 15-16

objective knowledge 13, 17-18, 25, 46
observation 17-18
participant 99, 102

paradigms 1, 4, 8, 10-16, 20-8, 39, 43-4, 48, 52, 71, 73, 82-3, 119, 122, 173, 176, 194
participant observation 99, 102
participation, research into 8, 51, 55, 57, 104-5, 113
participatory research 125, 131, 144
performance, performative knowledge 24, 121, 150
personal constructs 164
experience 42, 56, 152-4
research 113
positivism 23, 38, 44, 73, 119, 130
post-empiricist critique 14, 18, 20, 64
post-formal thinking 53, 90, 172
practical knowledge 79, 82, 179
reasoning 21-5
understanding 30
practice, critical, reflective 6-7, 116-17, 130, 193
linguistic 53, 101, 155
therapeutic 48

practitioners 2, 15, 27, 91
pragmatic knowledge, pragmatism 4-5, 8, 22, 37, 38, 65, 112, 117, 124, 137, 170, 178, 190
praxis 171, 179, 187
prediction 12, 48
prejudices 30-3, 38, 47, 68, 183
problems, problem-solving 15, 31, 71, 73, 81, 104, 120-2, 126-8, 141, 149, 151, 156, 172, 185
professional formation 8, 59, 71-2, 140, 166, 177, 192-4
psychoanalytic model 48, 134
psychology
cognitive 45
developmental 52
humanistic 46, 50, 155, 161
psychotherapy 44

qualitative research 26, 106
quantitative research 12, 26, 44

rationality 18-21, 26, 66, 73-4
reasoning, practical 21-2, 25
reflection, reflective practice 7, 16, 27, 80, 85-6, 109, 116-17, 125, 130, 181, 191
regulative idea 133, 138
relativism 18, 20, 34-5, 51, 67, 159
relevance, instantial situational 62-3, 116
research, methods and models 2, 7-8, 15, 53, 98-102, 106, 113-18, 120-2, 130-1, 143-4, 149-50, 160-1, 165, 193
issues and subjects 46,

Index

152-3, 165
research arena 150
review, process of 93-5, 113, 189, 191
roles 2, 8, 87, 148, 155
rules
  practitioner, social 21-4, 45

science, normal 15-16
scripts 150
self in discourse, research 8, 13, 36, 114, 146-9
self-criticism 157
sense-making 8, 155, 159, 162
single-loop learning 87, 140
situatedness of knowledge, practice, understanding 2, 5, 8-9, 28-30, 35-7, 57, 62-4, 75, 98, 100, 118, 121, 125, 129, 135, 144, 154, 180-2, 187, 192, 195
skill 75
  technical 152
social practice 16-17
  rules 23-5
social science, critical 133, 138
socio-practical 90, 170
sponsors of research 121, 153, 165
style of research 118, 152, 158
subjective meanings, processes, understanding 24-6, 34-5, 46, 138, 152, 159, 163
supervisory practices 195
survey research 100, 106-8
symbolic interaction 24, 38, 122

tacit knowledge 76
teaching 8, 42, 47, 128, 188, 194

technical knowledge, rationality, skills 72-3, 126, 152, 181
testing theories 13, 18-19, 53
text, reading practice and research as 4, 8, 29, 54, 193
theoretico-practical 189
theory, critical 7
  formal 8, 59, 117, 120, 170, 176
  grounded 80, 109, 149
  informal 59, 79-80, 130, 184
  practitioner 7, 91
theory-construction 57
theory-in-use 121
thesis, applicability 51, 60
thinking, dialectical 173
  post-formal 53, 172
tradition 30-2, 38, 64, 68, 133-5, 183
transmission models 149
truth, truth claims 16, 43, 49, 85, 128

understanding
  common-sense 26
  conventional 5
  hermeneutic 6, 28-30, 33, 36, 75, 182
  horizons of 121, 133

universal laws 11, 13, 44

validity 14, 16-18, 25, 44, 57, 65, 121, 125, 132
  ecological 44, 77
  experiential 145
value judgements 170
value-neutrality 14, 16, 18-19, 28, 49
values 16, 18, 27, 50, 77, 83, 126

Index

  contested 54
variables 13, 24
verification, empirical 34
verstehen 140
vocabularies, disciplinary 56

warrant, rational 19